MUG
BOOKIES

David Watts
and
Johnny Winall

Copyright © 3P Publishing
First published in 2022 in the UK

3P Publishing, C E C, London Road
Corby NN17 5EU

A catalogue number for this book is available
from the British Library

ISBN: 978-1-913740-51-1

Cover design: James Mossop

Illustrations: Liza Radley

We would like to thank all sources, customers and colleagues, who have made this book possible

Contents

Introduction

This is a true account written by David Watts and Johnny Winall, who combine over thirty years' experience as high street and on course bookmakers. The story is told from Johnny's perspective, portraying the vulnerability behind the scenes of a small independent bookmaker. With an entertaining blend of sporting anecdotes and gambling, the book also covers more serious social issues and poses the question: can you beat the bookies?

The details are remembered to the best of their ability and some names and places have been changed to preserve anonymity.

Chapter 1
Heads or Tails

On 24th September 1980, 29-year-old Texan William Lee Bergstorm, referred to as the Suitcase Man, walked into Binion's Horseshoe Casino in Las Vegas, placing the biggest wager in casino history at the time. With a plan to commit suicide if he lost the mostly borrowed money, he placed a single wager of $777,000. The craps dice rolled in his favour, doubling his money. William then packed his winnings into a suitcase and spent several years travelling the world.

Gambling can be fun, though it may become addictive or even destructive. My life has been intrinsically linked to gambling and sport; these two passions are like soul mates, as I navigate a hazardous journey in search of that elusive winning formula.

My name is Johnny Winall. I was nine years old when I placed my first bet on the 1967 Grand National. After writing my selection on a tatty piece of paper, I skipped the short path to my uncle's house and placed the wager - sixpence each way Castle Falls. Forty-four runners went to post and Castle Falls was leading when two loose horses veered to the right at the twenty-third fence, causing one of the most dramatic pile ups in racing history. Many of the contenders were brought to a standstill, catapulting their jockeys over the obstacle, while others ran in different directions. The blinkered Foinavon was 100 yards adrift, before emerging as the only horse to jump one of Aintree's lowest fences at the first attempt. Forging clear, he won the race by fifteen lengths at odds of 100/1. The owners considered Foinavon had no chance of winning and didn't bother to attend. On this occasion, luck favoured Foinavon and jockey John Buckingham, or was it their destiny?

On Sunday evenings, my dad, uncles and elder cousins would gather to play cards around the kitchen table. I was fixated by the gambling and by the time I was eleven I was allowed to join in. The usual game was pontoon (also known as blackjack or 21). I raided Mr Plod, my money box, in order to gamble with pennies, thruppences and sixpences. I noticed my elders preferred not to take the banker's role as they believed it was too risky; however, I identified the banker as the player most likely to win, holding the bank at every opportunity. The odds seemed to be stacked in the banker's favour and I saw a comparison with a bookmaker. I wondered whether anyone could become a bookmaker. Do they need much money starting out, and how much money do they make?

Twenty years later, I accompanied my friend David Watts to The Honeypot public house, where deviant landlord Don Dingle was to challenge us at Heads or Tails. Don supplied us with a drink on the house and proceeded to unleash a cunning plan to relieve us of cash. His younger girlfriend Sasha also joined in. This was our first introduction to a game whereby players take turns to act as banker, shuffling and stacking nine 10p coins. The other participants then bet in turn on whether the next coin is heads or tails. Very little money changed hands as Sasha and I dropped out, leaving Don to pit his wits against David.

In a bid to ensure fair play, I offered my services to shuffle the coins before stacking them. With David acting as banker, Don sank a shot of whisky declaring his first stake as £5 heads. David removed the top coin revealing a tail. Don shouted £10 heads for his second wager and David uncovered another tail. He stuck with heads for the next four calls, doubling his stakes and each time David revealed a tail. Another losing call of heads on the seventh coin, took his loss to £320. On breaking into a cold sweat, Don's cheeky grin disappeared along with another shot.

The atmosphere intensified as amused locals homed in relishing their landlord's plight. Don paused to consider the likelihood of eight tails in a row. Maybe something inside his head was convincing him that the law of averages would prevail. Besides, the odds for such a sequence are 128/1. Don stuck with heads, making his last shout of, '£320 double or quits.' Astonishingly, it was another tale of woe, as he duly signed David a cheque for £640.

The whisky may have played its part – or did Don simply get carried away with something known as the gambler's fallacy? This is an assumption that something happening more often than average in any given period will happen less frequently in the future. Like many gamblers, Don believed the frequency of tails meant that sooner or later it would be heads. Rather than seeing himself on a losing streak, he felt the balance would correct itself; all the same, Lady Luck had deserted him. In 1913, a Monte Carlo casino hosting a roulette table experienced twenty-six consecutive spins revealing a black number, where players reputedly lost fortunes. The chance of such an occurrence is sixty-six million to one.

Gambling or betting is the staking of money or an item of value on an event with an unknown outcome to gain a monetary or supplementary advantage. It dates back to ancient China. The earliest six-sided dice games were being played in Mesopotamia in 3000BCE. Card-playing emanated from China in the 9th century and poker can be traced back to a Persian game called As-Nas. The first known casino was the Ridotto, established in 1638 in Venice.

One mindset behind the psychology of betting suggests that many gamblers are drawn by the chance to win something for nothing. I once dreamt I had the winning lottery numbers, before waking in a cold sweat. I hurriedly wrote the numbers down and played in the next draw, but I didn't win. This was the only time I've played the lottery, as the odds are stacked too much against you. There is no scientific evidence to back up precognition, whereby individuals think they have a psychic power to foresee future events. Some may use this to their advantage, and whether they are psychic or merely benefiting from a coincidence, they believe in its existence. Twelve months prior to Leicester City winning the Premier League, David Watts had a vivid dream of their players appearing as major celebrities in a London nightclub. We can all be wise after the event. Nevertheless, had David realised any superstitious link, he may have taken odds of 5,000/1 at the start of the season.

Football was my main passion; I was inspired sat on my dad's knee watching England win the World Cup in 1966. My favourite player was Bobby Charlton. One Christmas, I told everyone I wanted footballs for presents and I ended up with eight new balls. They didn't last long, as the right-hand side of the lawn was surrounded by thorn bushes. To the left was my dad's big greenhouse, his pride and joy. My cousin Harry, who'd previously been on Bristol City's books, taught me to head the ball and when crosses went astray the ball would smash straight through the glass house.

My long-suffering dad gave one final warning: 'Any more broken glass and there's no more football in the garden.'

Within a few days it happened again and we decided to take desperate measures, stealing a pane of glass from a neighbour's shed window. I was on

6

lookout, while my two cousins and a mate set about removing the glass. In spite of my pathetic attempts at whistling the alarm, we were caught red-handed by the neighbour, who called the police. The local bobby let us off with a caution, followed by a clip around the ear from our parents.

Our only option was to play football on the tarmac pub car park whenever the pub was closed. In those days, public houses were generally restricted to opening during lunchtime and between 6 pm and 11 pm. There was a vicious Alsatian named Tosha living on the pub premises. In the house at the bottom of our shared drive lived another Alsatian, a man-eating beast called Nicky. On occasions, both Tosha and Nicky had been known to leap their respective fences. This left my sisters and I feeling very vulnerable on our daily walk to the bus stop. Somehow, I knew it was only a matter of time before I felt a set of sharp gnashers sinking into my flesh.

Like many other kids, I had aspirations to become a professional footballer. My cousin started driving me in his bright red Mini to watch third-division Bristol Rovers, who shared the Eastville Stadium until 1986 with greyhound racing. During a pre-season friendly, Birmingham City were the visitors and police had separated brawling fans in the area known as the Tote End, with patrolling Alsatians, by now known as German Shepherds. My cousin and I sat in the stands enjoying the game away from the bovver boys. At half time, I went down to purchase a couple of Cokes, waiting until the second half was about to kick off in order to avoid the disruptive crowd. My plan seemed to be working, as I quietly made my way from behind the stands with our drinks.

The roar of the crowd indicated the start of the second half. Suddenly, I heard people shouting, 'The dogs are loose,' followed by a stampeding horde heading in my direction. Soon a mass of hooligans appeared, barging past, soaking me in Coke. As I stood drenched and bewildered, the so-called fans quickly disappeared into a side entrance of the Tote End. Within seconds, a ferocious German Shepherd appeared without a handler, sinking its teeth straight through my denims into my buttocks.

For what seemed like an eternity, the dog dragged me backwards as I tried in vain to release its grip. Eventually a policeman caught up with the savage brute, and while struggling to free me from its jaws he told me to scarper in the most impolite terms. I was in tears on returning to my seat, where my cousin seemed to find my encounter rather amusing, asking 'Where's my Coke?'

I started losing interest in going to football and devoted more time to playing my pigskin Broadway drumkit, which my parents bought me on my sixth birthday. A couple of boys moved in nearby; guitarist Marvin, and Gerry, who played piano. We then formed a band with a couple of girl singers. Aged twelve, I was the youngest member of The New Diversion, playing our first gig in a Bristol social club. Our ten-song repertoire included cover versions of 'Nobody's Child', 'Eight Days A Week' and 'Ob-La-Di Ob-La-Da'. We were well received, although we had to play our short set three times over.

Mum's elder brother Unk and his family lived two doors down. He was born during the First World War, a real down-to-earth type with an unconventional approach to life and a wicked sense of humour, a creature of habit from a bygone era. He was thick skinned, and believed that clothes were something you didn't need to buy, as long as there were some hand-me-downs on offer. His disregard for social norms included not throwing both shoes away if only one was worn out. He'd then ask around to see if anyone had one similar in order to match it up. His wedding suit became a suit for all occasions, lasting him a lifetime. That said, he strictly adhered to a dress code of jacket shirt and tie, whilst appearing to have made no effort whatsoever.

He was a country boy at heart and enjoyed the simple things in life, holding good conversation with a pronounced Somerset accent. He tended to address males as Young Un and females as My Maid. On greeting me, he'd usually say 'How bist thee, Young Un?' or 'How bist getting?'

Unk spent his early working life down the pit, where he learnt first aid and later became a volunteer for St John Ambulance.

He was once quoted en route to a funeral saying, 'No good they trying to cremate I, there's so much coal dust inside of I, I'd burn forever.'

After progressing from the coal mine, he worked in a local factory and cycled to work every day. During family parties he'd perform his favourite tricks: breaking a raw egg over his head and catching his hair on fire. His main passion was horseracing, or as he would say, the hosses.

He became well known as a bookie's runner, taking bets from colleagues at the factory, before cycling home at lunchtime. He'd gather more bets on the way, while some punters came to the front door or telephoned. On his way back, he'd drop the bets off at the bookies. When it came to moneys owed, Unk was as sharp as a razor. He gleefully stashed punters losses in a malodourous cash bag made from an old trouser leg, which was also used for paying out. He liked to keep a close eye on it, therefore the bag travelled literally everywhere with him. This caused its fair share of chaos over the years, as he had a habit of leaving it in odd places.

Bookmakers provided runners with a bookie's clock, which was part of the modus operandi between the 1920s and the early 1970s. The device enabled runners to pass bets to the bookmaker once racing had commenced. It comprised of a stopwatch and a canvas bag within a steel case. As soon as the final bets were placed in the bag it was snapped shut, starting the stopwatch. The bookie had the only key and was able to check that bets were placed in the bag before the race. Runners earned their title literally running the bets between customer and bookie. A commission of approximately 10% was paid, though runners were often tempted to lay some bets themselves.

Bookmaker Burt Brazil would appear at Unk's house on Saturday evenings in order to exchange the weekly cash. Burt drove a blue Mercedes and was always elegantly dressed in a tailored suit, while puffing on a large Cuban cigar. On Sundays, Unk would do the rounds, visiting various punters in pubs and clubs, as well as their homes, in order to settle up the weekly credit.

Bookmakers' runners came into operation in 1853, after betting activities in so-called list shops were closed down by an Act of Parliament. Prior to this there were around 400 list shops in London alone. These were shops such as butchers or bakers laying bets as a sideline; however, the industry became tainted with an increasing number of rogues. Mr Dwyer, who ran a city cigar shop in St Martin's Lane, infamously disappeared overnight owing punters £25,000, after Nancy won the 1851 Tradesmen's Plate, now known as the Chester Cup.

Unk's dad enjoyed betting in thrupences. He would write out a long list of horses, posting the bets through Unk's letterbox during the afternoon. Unk would stand these bets, as they were small potential pay-outs; however, grandad's winnings were very much on the increase. Tensions grew when he bet a 33/1 winner and Unk became suspicious, accusing his dad of knowing the results:

'Theece bin slipping 'em through the box a'ter time.'

Grandad replied, 'Yeah I did hear the results, but I already writ 'em down.'

Aunt and Unk enjoyed daytrips to the seaside and occasionally caught a train to Weston-super-Mare, with hosses never far from Unk's mind. On one occasion just before departure, he jumped out of the carriage to fetch a *Sporting Life*. Seconds later, the train was about to pull out and aunt became anxious that he wouldn't make it back in time. Aunt jumped off at the same moment Unk was boarding a few carriages along. A little later, the forlorn figure of Unk arrived at the seaside, with an ice-cream and a copy of the *Sporting Life*.

In the early years, runners would usually visit punters in their homes, because it was unlawful to pass bets anywhere else. It was common to see runners outside various establishments or on street corners while hotly pursued by police. Local residents would sometimes give them an escape route by leaving their doors open.

Having been established in 1886, a credit bookmaker became known as Ladbrokes in 1902, named after the Warwickshire village where it was founded. Ladbrokes was initially only interested in serving the aristocracy of the time. Up until just after the First World War bookmakers were all male. During the 1920s, a well-connected Helen Vernet passed the Fit and Proper Character test and began working for Ladbrokes.

My thoughts of becoming a professional footballer were diminishing fast after 1 got dropped from the team before the inter-schools' cup final. I left school at the first opportunity without any qualifications, having been advised by my tutor that I would never get a job, unless I was employed as a comedian.

By coincidence, I attended my first job interview with a local timber supplier on the last day of school. I was interviewed by branch manager Mr Dixon, who told me off for not wearing a tie. I already knew him, as I played football with his son. He offered me a job as warehouse office clerk, and it certainly wasn't because of what I knew! I found the job to be tedious and hoped that there would be more to life.

I joined a three-piece band with a couple of older guys. Bob was our tittering front man on guitar and vocals. He had a front tooth missing and walked like a naughty schoolboy. The bass guitarist was Colin, who is best described as a little rough around the edges. Colin took over the bookings and our fee suddenly rose from £30 per night to £150. He was booking us out as a five-piece band, supposedly fronted by a girl singer. This was all very well until our agent turned up at a gig asking why there were only three of us on stage.

I've always shared an affinity with my fellow musos, in spite of the joke that 'a drummer is just someone who hangs out with musicians'. I was fortunate to play with some talented performers, who taught me much about stage presence, polish and professionalism. This begins from the moment of introduction and lasts for the whole duration. Having said that, I started keeping a diary with comments and a mark out of ten for every live gig. I was striving for perfection and never satisfied with my own or the other band members' standards. I continually scored our performances with low marks, which didn't go down too well with my elders. Meanwhile, I dreamed of jacking my job in and becoming a professional musician.

Chapter 2
The Unscrupulous Runner

Unk wasn't much of a drinker, though he enjoyed half a shandy. He had a reputation as a sore loser and captained the village pub darts team. He became notorious for distracting opponents at a critical stage, by dousing his hair and putting a match to it. One evening during a practice session, a stranger sat watching and Unk couldn't resist challenging him to play for a shilling. The stranger agreed to a game of 501 and enquired as to the rules.

Unk explained the requirement to finish on a double: 'If theece left with a finish of twenty, theece need to hit double ten.'

The stranger stepped forward for a practice throw and said, 'What, like this?', hitting three straight double tens.

Unbeknown to Unk he'd challenged the current *News of the World* Darts Champion. Rather than face the inevitable, he handed over a shilling without throwing a single dart.

Betting on sport is recognised as part of the UK leisure industry, an entertainment enjoyed by many for generations. Experts who study betting consider that on the whole women enjoy games of chance, while men tend to favour betting with skill, although ego and pride can inhibit their performance. For some it's fun, enhancing their enjoyment of a given sporting event. Others take a calculated approach, with the profit motive being the main driver. Mood can affect gambling and researchers have found that a positive mood can lead to a higher level of risk taking. Some people stake more than they can afford and addiction is waiting to entrap the less disciplined.

One Saturday afternoon, I was at a loose end and turned on the TV. There were only three TV channels at the time and both BBC 1 (*Grandstand*) and ITV (*World of Sport*) were broadcasting horseracing. The third channel (BBC 2) was offering something less appealing and I chose racing. Listening to the hype, the BBC presenter heightened my interest by talking up the 4/5 favourite, Grundy, a recent English and Irish Derby winner. Little did I realise I was about to witness a race which has since been described as the race of the century. Four-year-old Bustino was considered the chief threat among a very talented field of runners. I dashed around to Unk's, placing 50p to win on the three-year-old Grundy.

Ascot hosts the annual running of the prestigious King George VI and Queen Elizabeth Stakes in July, a one mile and a half flat race open to horses aged three years or older. The 1975 race was run at a blistering pace, as 4/1 shot Bustino ridden by Joe Mercer took up the running half a mile from home. Grundy, partnered by Pat Eddery, began closing in on the leader at the two-furlong pole. One furlong from home, the pair were eyeballing each other as they battled stride for stride. Grundy went ahead in the final half-furlong to prevail by half a length, breaking the course record by two and a half seconds. This was the moment I became hooked on horseracing.

The *Horse and Hound* article that followed read: 'For a moment two horses and two men came to near perfection, as any of the great ones around whom the history of the turf is built.'

Remarkably, neither Grundy or Bustino were to ever win again.

Flat races are run over a distance between five furlongs and two miles five and a half furlongs.

Furlongs are still used in horseracing: a furlong is measured as 220 yards, with eight furlongs equalling a mile. Anglo Saxons first measured farmland in furlongs, with one furlong being the length of a furrow in a one-acre field.

Flat racing runs throughout the calendar year, pausing only at Christmas for the customary four days. Traditionally, the flat season starts with the Lincoln at Doncaster around the end of March, and ends at the same venue with the November Handicap. The Jockeys Championship officially starts on 2,000 Guineas Day at Newmarket during early May, and finishes in mid-October on Champions Day at Ascot. The Trainers Championship runs from 1st January to 31st December.

I joined a four-piece professional band called Brandy and packed my job in. I remember my Uncle Bill asking what qualifications we had as so-called professionals. I guess it boils down to how much money you make and in our case the answer was very little. We spent most of the time gigging in the north-east of England, staying in cheap digs and performing in social clubs where the main attraction was bingo. In order to increase our earnings, we would often double up. This involved packing up our equipment in a social club around 11 pm, before dashing to a nightclub to perform another show, playing second fiddle to the disco. We also made regular Sunday lunchtime, 'men only' social club appearances, as a support act to the stripper.

In spite of any untapped talent, Brandy never made it into the big time. Like many other musical groups, we lacked vision and a business leader, relying instead on an agent who was unable to deliver his promise of lots of well-paid work. After about six months I decided to call it a day and signed on the dole, much to the amusement of Uncle Bill.

Shortly after this fiasco, I was headhunted by a professional five-piece cabaret pop group MG & The Headlights. Local musician Maurice Glastonbury and his band were looking to replace their drummer. Maurice was multi-talented, playing keyboards and trumpet at the same time. He also took a share of the lead vocals, and sang a haunting rendition of 'Smile', a song musically composed by Charlie Chaplin. Maurice was a well-built man, with a calm and trusty nature. He was also the band's manager, with a reputation for having plenty of contacts. This came as a pleasant surprise, as creative people sometimes lack business skills. Deep down, I knew if I really wanted to make it into the big time I needed to move to London and hang out with trendy ambitious bands, who were more likely to secure a record deal. After much consideration, I chose the easier route and joined MG & The Headlights.

Following a few weeks of rehearsals, we cut our first and only album at Mushroom Studios, Bristol. The eleven-track stereo recording was completed on a shoestring budget within four days, an insufficient timescale to produce anything of quality. The result was dire, though we did manage to sell five hundred vinyl copies for a fiver a piece at gigs.

We spent the next few years touring the UK, often hanging around in digs watching horseracing on TV. I encouraged the band members to bet and regularly played the role of bookie, with an aim to relieve them of cash. By the age of nineteen, I was spending more time in the betting shop, often losing a whole week's wages. I would also telephone Unk, who was ready and willing to take my bets, as my credit was good until the end of the week. Nevertheless, on one occasion I owed £40 and didn't have enough money to pay him. I felt very embarrassed and kept a low profile until I raised the cash.

Horseracing took place with chariot and mounted racing as far back as Roman times. The Romans are also said to have raced Arabian horses at Wetherby, Yorkshire, back in 200AD. Reports suggest that English riders didn't saddle their horses until 631AD. During the reign of Richard the Lionheart, 1189 to 1199, a racing purse of £40 was offered for a three-mile race where the riders were knights. In the 16th century, Henry VIII imported racehorses from Italy and Spain.

The world's longest surviving horse race is the Kiplingcotes Derby, first run in 1519. It's held in East Riding, Yorkshire, on the third Thursday of March annually. The traditional race is run over four miles across country, where first past the post receives £50. These days, second place takes home more prize money than the winner, as the fund is made up from participants' entry fees. If the race doesn't take place, the rules state it can never be run again. In the harsh winter of 1947, a farmer walked his horse over the course in order to preserve the race. In 2001, after the outbreak of Foot and Mouth, one horse and rider completed the course. In 2018 the course was waterlogged, and a single horse was led around. In 2020 and 2021, a few equestrians hacked around the course because of the coronavirus.

Unk was invited to join the Freemasons at Pingford, cycling the two-mile trip. On dismounting the pushbike, he noticed the line of posh motors on display. He knocked three times on the large oak door and was announced into the chamber. Thirty minutes later he was back home having a cup of tea.

On casting his eye around the room, he'd decided: 'From the twenty members in the room, nineteen needed help and none of 'em would make the good credit list.'

Through the decades, Unk dealt with many different types, categorising them as either 'He ent no good' or 'He's as straight as a gun barrel.'

Following the Masonic Lodge encounter, Unk was inspired to upgrade his mode of transport to an Austin A30. Obtaining a full driver's licence would usually be a straightforward transition; however, passing his driving test became a major obstacle. Having taken well over one hundred lessons, he'd failed eleven tests. Unk was advised by a local bookmaker that his cousin, a test examiner, would definitely pass him next time. Things didn't go to plan and when the examiner asked him to turn right, he drove around the traffic island in the wrong direction. He passed his driving test on the thirteenth attempt.

My passion for horseracing has mainly revolved around jump racing. My first visit to a racecourse was Wincanton in the late 1970s, where I remember backing the David Gandolfo-trained Trio J to win at fixed odds of 7/2. This pleasant experience sparked a mission, whereby I'd visit all of the racecourses in the UK; however, I hadn't bargained on the amount of time this feat would take.

On-course bookmakers give fixed odds at the moment a bet is placed. Starting price is the price appertaining to a horse or greyhound at the commencement of a race. Race recorders will take an average of the prices from a predetermined number of prominent bookmakers to obtain a fair reflection. The starting price is applied to winning bets, where off-course punters have not taken fixed odds beforehand. The first recorded bookmaker was Harry Ogden, who offered fixed odds on every horse in a race at Newmarket in 1795. Prior to this, the only option was to bet on one horse against the field. This was generally the favourite at even money. With only two possible outcomes, individuals betting between themselves were either for or against the favourite.

Off-course punters have the option of taking a fixed price or starting price. In this scenario, punters may use their own judgement as to whether the price may shorten in order to find the best value. This may present a dilemma for punters, although some bookmakers guarantee prices by offering fixed odds or starting price, whichever is the bigger. However, a high percentage of these concessions are not so readily available.

In the late 1970s, MG & The Headlights were offered a slot on ITV's *New Faces*, a popular talent show. This was our chance to break into the big time and secure the long-awaited record deal. This type of TV exposure offers a once in a lifetime chance of fame. Opportunities such as this should be grasped. The other band members, who were a few years older than me, were insisting on covering an old Stephen Stills classic in our own particular style. While I argued that we should perform one of our own compositions, because when pursuing a record deal, you need to sound and look original. Unfortunately, I was outvoted, as our singer knocked up some tailor-made trousers and waistcoats on her Singer sewing machine.

Nervous tension filled the air as we opened the show with our interpretation of 'Love The One You're With'. The first of four judges, Danny La Rue, was very complimentary about the performance. Nevertheless, he was quick to point out that our expensive crocodile-skin shoes were hidden under the home-made fifteen-inch flares. A couple of the other judges gave us top marks and next in line was Mickie Most. Mr Most, one of the world's top record producers, scored us well below average.

He said, 'You're not today's look and should have performed a song that was more original.'

Second to perform was a very talented lady jazz singer, scoring the highest marks to date in the show's four-year history, effectively ending the contest in round two. On viewing the remaining acts, the judges merely went through the motions, scoring all of them higher than us, including a dancing muscle man.

During the interval, Mickie Most spotted us sitting dejectedly in a corner and took the time to come over. He advised us to send him a recording of something more original and he'd have a listen.

Band leader Maurice told him, 'You don't know what the hell you're talking about.'

Mr Most took it well, shrugged his shoulders, smiled and walked away. It was a demoralising journey home, as I began pondering the evening's events. The percentage chances of making it in showbiz are slim, and on entering the spotlight we failed to get the edge and take advantage. Maurice had to be culpable for this tomfoolery, though I had learned one lesson: don't argue with one of the world's most successful people.

I stayed with the band for a couple more years and decided to quit after a five-month stint in the Middle East. We were playing for five hours a night, seven days a week in a five-star hotel. It was often quiet and monotonous, leaving me to feel less passionate about drumming. One big benefit to come out of this: I'd stopped gambling for five months, returning home with £2,000 in savings. Meanwhile, I turned down an opportunity with a band who went on to have chart success in Europe, opting to work for my dad on the building site.

My yellow Renault 10 with its engine positioned in the boot went rusty and conked out while I was abroad. I was gutted when I only got £15 for it at the scrapyard. On the bright side, I would no longer need to travel with a hundredweight bag of cement under the bonnet in a bid to keep the front wheels grounded. I bought myself a replacement, in the form of a second-hand Hillman Avenger, leaving me £1,100. Gambling was in my blood and I was aware that the last thing I should be doing was to squander my savings.

Unk continued his association with fire, after he left the cooker switched on prior to going on the annual two-week holiday to Bournemouth. On another occasion, he was expecting a visit from HM Customs and Excise and stupidly set light to a pile of old betting slips in a walk-in cupboard. The fire began escalating out of control, with black smoke billowing out of the windows. Luckily his daughter was on hand, as the pair frantically ran in and out fetching pails of water.

Saturday was Unk's busiest day. Like clockwork, you'd find him in the lounge, sitting in front of the window answering the telephone to credit punters. He was obsessed with taking bets and, although it was lawful, he was paranoid about the legalities of his role as a bookie's runner. For this reason, he always kept a sharp eye on the front door.

One Saturday I disguised myself as a tax inspector, wearing a trilby, white mackintosh, false moustache and glasses, while clutching a briefcase. As I strolled past the window, he leapt out of his seat, gathering the day's betting transactions in one sweeping motion. He looked completely petrified when he opened the door. I flashed a false identity and began questioning him on the legalities of taking bets. He was floundering while trying to justify his position as a legal operator. It was only after I threatened to fine him, that he twigged it was me, slamming the door in my face, cursing.

Unk was close to retirement and frequently spotted driving around with his tatty cash bag left on the roof of his car. He was also going through a phase where he wouldn't drive across the road whenever he needed to turn right. This meant he always turned left, driving for miles in the wrong direction to the next roundabout.

I started having a few occasional bets and I noticed some National Hunt horses winning unchallenged; this led me to devise a new betting strategy. The intention was to bet a series of winners and mug the bookies. Making profit through betting appealed to me, especially as I'd previously been more than generous in lining bookmakers' pockets. The system revolved around one large wager; thereafter I would

23

gamble with the bookies' money. I decided to risk all of my savings in one reckless hit and if the selection won, I'd return all of my initial outlay to the building society.

My strategy was to invest all of the accumulated winnings on disciplined horse wagers, which I believed couldn't lose, until I reached a profit of £100,000.

There are two types of National Hunt jump racing, steeplechases and hurdles, run at various distances starting at two miles, up to four and a half miles. There are also National Hunt flat races (bumpers), running at distances between thirteen and twenty furlongs. The term under rules is defined as any professional race. Point-to-point racing is steeplechasing for hunting horses and amateur jockeys. Many pointers move on to compete under rules.

The majority of National Hunt horses are geldings and usually much cheaper, because they have no breeding value. Steeplechases are run over fences, originating in the 18th century where horses raced from one church steeple to another. The first steeplechase was recorded in 1752, the consequence of a wager between Cornelius O'Callaghan and Edmund Blake, over four miles of countryside in County Cork. The first hurdle race took place in 1821 on Durdham Down near Bristol.

National Hunt racing steps up in earnest during the autumn, with the reappearance of classier horses who have been rested during the summer. Late April officially marks the end of the jumping season on finals day at Sandown Park. The new season restarts around five days later. Many jump horses are released from training during this time, and put out to field for the summer. In my opinion, National Hunt form becomes less reliable in late spring, offering a good opportunity to take a break from betting. That said, I do find summer jumping very dependable. There is usually a twelve-day National Hunt break in early August, and a further four-day break at Christmas.

I concede that there are many factors that can affect a horse's performance, such as poor hormone levels, pollen allergy and undetected respiratory problems, or it may simply be a bad traveller. During the race, a whole host of other issues may arise.

Having identified easy winners, my aim was to bet them next time out, with a disciplined approach of having no other bets in between. At this time I wasn't a big form studier, though I watched racing whenever possible, looking to spot a horse winning without being extended. In 1981, I found the perfect candidate in Little Owl, after he demonstrated a superb display of jumping at speed. Little Owl was the horse I would bet all of my savings on.

I withdrew £1,100 in cash on the eve of the race. The horse was due to run at Haydock in the Peter Marsh Chase on 24th January. I went to Coral bookmakers on Saturday morning and placed the wager: £1,000 to win on Little Owl, plus 10% tax, total stake £1,100. This was all the money I had in the world and I don't mind admitting I was a tad nervous. I settled into the armchair with my eyes glued to the TV, as the runners gathered down at the start. Unusually, I poured myself a large scotch, eagerly awaiting the action. Little Owl was a serious racehorse, traveling strongly throughout the race, and pulled clear of the other horses. As expected, he won under owner/rider Jim Wilson, by an easy fifteen lengths at odds of 8/13, netting me a profit after tax of £515.

The following Saturday, I decided to disregard my stake plan. Instead of betting the £515 win, I staked another £1,000 on Little Owl, who was reappearing just seven days later at Cheltenham. This time he won by six lengths at odds of 8/11. I'd won another £627, giving me a running total of £1,142.

Next in line was the Josh Gifford-trained Eddie, who had recently run well in defeat at Ascot. With my £1,100 safely back in my account, I put my faith in Eddie and jockey Bob Champion at Leicester on 3rd February. I was still labouring for Dad earning £60 per week. Dad didn't bet and told me I was crazy, as I parked up the wheelbarrow and headed for the bookies. I was carrying £1,142, with every intention of wagering the lot on Eddie.

Eddie was up against it, in the form of odds-on favourite Crimson Embers, whom top trainer Faulk Walwyn held in high regard. I admit I had another sweat on, particularly as this time my selection was not the favourite, and I was questioning my rationale as he hadn't won last time out. At the last minute, I changed my mind and reduced my stake to £200. It was a hard-fought finish with Eddie prevailing at 9/2, giving me a profit of £880.

After changing my carefully devised stake plan, my profit from three bets was £2,022. I waited for nearly three weeks for my next wager, betting on Eddie for a second time at Fontwell Park. Having no regard for the stake plan I bet £400 on Eddie, who won the race at 5/2. This gave me a profit of £960 and a running total of £2,982.

Four days later, I backed £1,000 to win on Spartan Missile, a horse who'd impressed me earlier in the month at Sandown. This high-class jumper was being described as one of the best hunter chasers ever. Unusually, the horse had been bred, owned and trained by his amateur jockey, John Thorne. There was an air of confidence at Kempton Park, where Spartan Missile won at odds of 8/13. I was now five winners from five races, with an overall profit of £3,497.

The day of 14th March stands out as one to remember. It was a bright sunny afternoon, marred only by another staking dilemma. I fancied two horses running on the same day, within a short space of time at different tracks, Spartan Missile, and Justafancy, who had caught my eye as a real battler in a race at Newcastle.

I considered splitting my winnings in half and betting approximately £1,750 on each horse. This way of thinking was more in line with the original staking. However, I couldn't bring myself to place the larger bets and bottled it, betting £200 on each horse and a £200 win double. Spartan Missile won easily at Sandown at 2/5, while up at Ayr Justafancy outbattled the favourite by a short head, winning at 4/1. My bets showed a profit of £2,020 and a running total of £5,517.

After an amazing sequence of winning bets, I recognised that luck played a big part. During a seven-week period, I bet on seven horses, backing seven winners. I was bound to do the maths. All the same, I knew I'd missed a golden opportunity, as I could have won £143,662. Within a few days I was at the Cheltenham Festival, where both Little Owl and Spartan Missile were due to line up in the Gold Cup. I was quietly thinking I would have a good size bet on Little Owl.

Lack of discipline got the better of me and my Steady Eddie approach went straight out of the window. Suddenly, every horse I backed was defeated. As the week dragged on, I couldn't seem to find a winner and come Gold Cup day, I deserted Little Owl, backing the Michael Dickinson-trained Silver Buck. Little Owl deserved far more loyalty from the likes of me, winning the race at 6/1. Winning jockey Jim

Wilson was the first amateur to win the race since 1947.

Sixteen days after finishing fourth to Little Owl in the Cheltenham Gold Cup, Spartan Missile and his game fifty-four-year-old jockey John Thorne finished second to Aldaniti, partnered by the inspirational Bob Champion in the Grand National. All the same, many a good judge was of the opinion that Spartan Missile would have won the race if he'd been ridden by professional jockey John Francome, who offered to take the ride. I have to admit to hearing about this, and on this basis, I bet £100 to win on Spartan Missile, at ante post odds of 8/1. Sadly, John Thorne tragically died the following year, after a fall at Bicester point-to-point.

British Horseracing Authority Rule J (1.1.3) permits owners to pay professional jockeys more than the standard rates as an incentive to win a race. During the 1980s, an acquaintance of mine called Vernon owned a successful National Hunt racehorse. Like many owners, Vernon enjoyed a gamble, and was well aware that his horse followed a pattern, reaching peak fitness at a particular time of the season. Once a year he would rely on maestro trainer Oliver Sherwood to get the chaser fit and ready to win. Having pulled off previous victories, the stable was hoping for a repeat performance. Regrettably, Vernon had fallen upon hard times and was becoming desperate to land the gamble.

Clive Cox was the conditional jockey attached to the Sherwood stable, and first in line to get the leg-up. Nevertheless, Vernon was taking no chances and decided to approach champion jockey Richard Dunwoody, a supreme professional of the highest order. Vernon was advised that the jockey would be asking for the usual fee, plus half of the prize money. The impoverished owner was having none of it and opted to run with Clive, an outstanding young claiming jockey, who would claim a weight allowance.

Vernon's charge went off at 9/2, and Clive found his mount in a tight tussle with the favourite, as the pair of handicappers fought out a head-bobbing finish. A photo was announced, leaving Vernon to pace the paddock, resembling a cat on a hot tin roof. The result went against the luckless owner, whose horse was beaten a short head. To rub salt into the wound, none other than Richard Dunwoody was aboard the winner. Clive Cox has since become a highly successful flat trainer.

Many punters agree that top jockeys are worth their weight in gold, especially when it comes to a tight finish. In contrast, during a steeplechase in 1923 at Belmont Park, New York, twenty-two-year-old jockey Frank Hayes suffered a fatal heart attack and died in the later part of a race while aboard 20/1 shot Sweet Kiss. Remarkably, he remained in the saddle and passed the winning post in first place. The official winning margin was a head. History records Frank Hayes as 'the first and only jockey, known to have won a race after death'.

A disastrous three days at the festival cost me a few thousand pounds. Back at the high-street betting shop I continued chasing my losses. This included an even £400 on another Michael Dickinson-trained horse, which was pulling clear of the field when unseating jockey Tommy Carmody. The staff cheered when Tommy hit the deck, maybe because of my previous successes. Nevertheless, he had time to remount before losing in a photo finish. Sadly, my luck was running out and I was back to square one.

I agonised over these seven bets for many years. I was determined, that in time, I would bet seven consecutive winners without losing my bottle.

Chapter 3
The Ignoramus

The lifting and wheeling of heavy barrows started taking its toll on my slender frame and I was soon to undergo a hernia operation. The doctor advised me to get a desk job and I approached a Bath bookmaker who was setting up as an independent. I told the likable owner that if he were to take a chance on me, I would be a big asset as I had a good eye for winners. Regrettably, he had other ideas.

I turned my attention to sales, securing a job as a Kirby vacuum cleaner salesman. The company had a bizarre motivational technique, whereby we were all expected to attend daily sales meetings, singing songs such as 'She'll Be Vacuuming Round the Mountain When She Comes'. In America, this gimmicky approach is supposed to psyche you up, but it wasn't going down too well in deepest Somerset and I refused to sing. My manager friend Gary Darkfoot, who always wore one light shoe and one dark shoe, told me the main boss was going to sack me the following day if I chose not to sing. I refused and was promptly dismissed on the grounds of non-musical versatility!

I left home aged twenty-two and shacked up with my girlfriend. Meanwhile, I dusted myself off and found another job in direct sales, as a self-employed double-glazing salesman. Gary Darkfoot and I were still the best of friends and we had a good laugh over my sacking. Gary was quite a gambler and sometimes accompanied me to the bookies. We also played backgammon, usually for £1 a point. I was disappointed when he said he was returning home to settle in Zimbabwe.

A couple of days before he was due to fly home, Gary and his partner came around for a last supper. While the ladies chatted late into the evening, he and I decided to play backgammon, our final game, for increased stakes of £10 per point. This meant if the six-sided gambling dice (2, 4, 8, 16, 32, 64) should be turned to 64, one of us would lose £640. I raced into a clear lead, turning the gambling dice to 64, and Gary accepted the risk. Towards the end of the game, I literally needed to roll my two dice to land the spoils. Before this Gary had one final shake, requiring a double six to snatch victory. After an extended shake and a good luck blow on the dice, he tumbled out the lucky double six. As it turned out, this changed my life forever.

On saying goodbye to Gary I was feeling down in the dumps, as I might never see my good friend again, and because of my lousy job prospects. Maybe my insecurities had got the better of me, because minutes later I made what turned out to be one of my biggest howlers. Without much thought I made a proposal of marriage to my girlfriend, and she accepted. Before I had a chance to reflect on my impulsive action, the register office was booked, and we were married within a couple of weeks.

I was now selling for a national double-glazing company on a commission-only basis. I won a prize of a cricket bat, autographed by the England team. I never saw the signed willow, and I realised later that my boss, Dennis Cane, was a keen cricket fan. Dennis was a straight-talking man who ruled with fear; he didn't suffer fools and either loved or hated you. He was a middle-aged man, lean and tall with a long beard and thick-rimmed glasses, which he removed before pinning salesman against the wall, when they rubbed him up the wrong way. He always sounded gruff, as though he was speaking from his deep throat. Fortunately, he took a shine to me and we shared a passion for horseracing and betting.

Dennis drove a black Porsche Turbo and used to clock himself driving to and from work, as he enjoyed the challenge of breaking his own speed record. When visiting clients, he'd park the Porsche down the road or take the wife's Vauxhall, as he didn't wish to appear too successful. He was always immaculately turned out in white collar and tie, and wore a large gold sovereign on the ring finger of his right hand. He believed that the ring held people's attention during a sales pitch.

What Dennis didn't know about direct sales techniques was probably not worth knowing. He demanded high standards from his salesman, such as: 'Know and believe in your product. On arrival, make sure the car radio is not playing at high volume. Park sensibly as the prospective buyer maybe watching you. Don't take a short cut by walking across the lawn, stay on the footpath. Ring the front doorbell and take a step back, never stand too close and invade someone's personal space. Don't lean against a wall, stand straight and remain polite. Most people enjoy talking about themselves, so show interest in their home and family using empathy.

'Ears are a salesman's most vital tool; listen to what the buyer wants. Eyes are second on the list; be observant and note their body language. Mouth is of least importance, once you have established the buyer's exact needs, sell it to him. Remember, every word you articulate could possibly gain or lose a potential sale. Show enthusiasm while creating desire and need, then sell the benefits. Don't be afraid to ask for the order. Objections are merely sign posts en route to the sale. Overcome all objections and if needs be, ask for the order repeatedly, then close the sale. When the buyer stops showing interest or their body language tells you that's enough, it may be time to quit. Arrange to call the buyer on a specific day at a specific time for a final decision. Remain professional for the whole duration.'

Interestingly, whenever I pitched to a musician, I always made a sale. I put this down to empathy. I find the role of a musician's stage performance comparable to that of a sales presentation. The show starts from the moment you come into view. Act professionally for the whole presentation, show enthusiasm, smile, concentrate on every note/word and always leave them wanting more.

Having made the decision to land myself a good job with a company car, I bought a new suit and met the MD of a corrugated paper company, dressed to impress. Sadly, I was kicked out of the interview halfway through for not showing enthusiasm. Within a week I was to be grilled by both the regional and national sales managers of a transport parcel company.

Armed with enthusiasm and empathy, I knew that I'd nailed the job when the straight-talking northern sales manager turned to his counter partner and said, 'Johnny reminds me of me.'

After a couple of months I received a warning, as I wasn't delivering on my interview promise, and it took a while to find my feet. Eventually, I got my act together, becoming one of the company's most consistent performers. While out cold calling, I inadvertently gate-crashed an IT sales seminar, where I was presented with a Sinclair Pocket TV. To this day I don't know who they thought I was, but I was grateful and made a quick exit. The TV came in very handy during afternoons in the sales office, as I was able to watch the televised racing. However, my thoughts kept drifting back to a missed opportunity with my lucky seven.

Gradually, I developed a burning desire to become a bookie with a new way of thinking: if you can't beat them, be them. I was trying to gauge my chances of success and I needed to acquire as much knowledge as possible. I looked for encouragement from an independent bookmaker who told me that I would never survive, because of my inexperience and the many risks attached. Nevertheless, he took the time to explain about the compiling of odds, and making a book. In betting terms, the chances of a selection winning any particular event is expressed in odds. For example, evens is a 50% chance, 2/1 is a 33% chance, and 3/1 is a 25% chance, 6/4 is a 40% chance (4 divided by (6+4) x 100), and 4/1 is a 20% chance (1 divided by (4+1) x 100). A punter placing a winning bet of £10 on a selection at odds of 5/1, returns winnings of £50 plus the initial stake of £10, giving a total return of £60. Bookmakers who are pricing an event build in a percentage profit, known as the overround. All of the percentages of individual selections are added together and the amount over 100 is the theoretical profit.

To demonstrate, using the starting prices from the 1988 Cheltenham Queen Mother Champion Chase:

	Starting price	Percentage
1. Pearlyman	15/8	34.8
2. Dessert Orchid	9/1	10.0
3. Very Promising	4/1	20.0
4. Midnight Count	25/1	3.8
5. Panto Prince	20/1	4.8
6. Weather the Storm	10/3	23.1
7. Long Engagement	9/1	10.0
8. Super Furrow	25/1	3.8
TOTAL		110.3

Using these figures, the bookmaker's profit equals 10.3 % of total moneys staked, based on proportional amounts bet on each horse.

On one occasion, unbeknown to my employers, I decided to cram four days' worth of appointments into one day. This would allow me to take three days off to watch the Cheltenham Racing Festival on TV. I set out bright and early on a Monday morning working flat out. I was exhausted by the end of the day and I was due to attend a company meeting at 7 pm. En route, I drove into a bend too fast and mounted the pavement bordering a village green, turning the car on its side and coming to rest on top of a hedgerow. Luckily, I was still in one piece, and, courtesy of a breakdown recovery driver, I made it to the meeting where I was presented with a replacement company car. Despite this minor setback I spent the next three days in front of the TV.

The Cheltenham Gold Cup started life as a flat race over three miles on nearby Cleeve Hill, in 1819. In 1829, Cheltenham Parish Priest Reverend Francis Close preached the evils of horseracing, believing the resulting entourage of prostitutes, drunks and pickpockets was detrimental to the clean-living of the town. The outburst aroused strong opposition amongst the congregation, who threw bottles and rocks at both jockeys and horses. In 1830, ringleader Close raised the ante and organised the grandstand to be razed to the ground. In order to overcome this violent conduct, the racecourse was moved the following year by approximately seven furlongs, to the tranquil setting of Prestbury Park.

It was first run as a jump race in 1924 and won by a 5/1 shot, Red Splash. The owner received a generous prize of £685. Golden Miller won the race five times between 1932 and 1936. In the 1960s, Arkle, trained by Tom Dreaper, won the cup three times in succession, and went off at the short price of 1/10 for his third victory in 1966. As a yearling, Arkle spotted some mares passing his paddock, and sustained serious injury while attempting to jump a barbed wire fence. Before administering forty stitches, the vet advised that the horse should be put down. However, he was reportedly nursed back to good health by the trainer's wife. Many a good judge believe Arkle's future outstanding jumping was the result of his painful encounter with barbed wire.

Since 1959, the race has been run on the new course over three miles two and a half furlongs, taking in twenty-two fences. Best Mate also won the race three times in a row between 2002 and 2004. In 2009, Kauto Star became the first horse to regain the Gold Cup, having first won the race in 2007. The best ever training feat was that of Michael Dickinson who saddled the first five home in 1983: Bregawn, Captain John, Wayward Lad, Silver Buck and Ashley House. To date, Dawn Run is the only horse to win both the Champion Hurdle (1984) and the Gold Cup (1986).

My life was changed in 1986 by the birth of my daughter. I was now a man with responsibilities and suddenly found myself wanting to climb the corporate ladder. My strategy was simple: keep the customer satisfied. I started demanding higher standards, though I was fighting a losing battle. I've often been disappointed by substandard business ethics, such as lack of pride, poor performance and resistance to positive change. It's also abundantly clear that well-trained, courteous staff are key factors in successful business.

Common sense suggests that leaving a business in the wrong hands will lead to a decline in trade, and without undue concern I wrote to the Managing Director advising him of the disarray in our region. It was therefore a great surprise when I was promoted to

Business Development Manager, a new position created to look after existing accounts.

My new role took me to Berkshire to visit one of our current accounts, a compilation album/record company, where I met despatch manager Dick Rowe. He introduced himself as the man who famously turned down the Beatles in 1962 while working for Decca, declaring: 'Guitar groups are on the way out.'

This phenomenon has since been described as the biggest blunder in the history of show business. Being a big Beatles fan, I have to admit to being mesmerised by his every word and I couldn't resist asking Dick questions about the Fab Four. We must have spent a good two hours discussing how different his life would have been if only he'd recognised their true potential. For many years I told the story of my exhilarating 1988 encounter. Twenty-eight years later I realised that I had been duped, when it came to my attention that the real Dick Rowe had passed away in 1986!

I was promptly promoted to Area Sales Manager, a position that I knew I would struggle in. I was branded a troublemaker for demanding high levels of service and change, making lots of enemies in the process. I decided to take the job, but I really wanted to run my own betting shop. I knew that I wouldn't enjoy my new position and it would in fact become the catalyst to start my own business as a high-street bookmaker. All the same, the switch would prove difficult to process, as I was earning good money with many perks.

I didn't realise how tough my role would become under new boss Ronnie Rowell. Ron was based in the Midlands, describing himself as a former frontman with a '60s pop group, who had major chart success after he left to pursue a solo career. Ron was a larger-than-life character, with a style of management that can only be described as all mouth and trousers, while resembling a bull in a china shop. For whatever reasons, Rocking Ron didn't like me and he made that clear from the start. He showed an interest in horseracing and gave me lots of losing tips, which he described as 'privileged information from a well-known member racing club'.

As a young man, I read the *Western Daily Press*, which was delivered daily to the family home. Captain Wessex and Bob Watts were the horseracing tipsters and I often bet their selections, though I never made a profit. I didn't know who they were, or anything about them for that matter. Tipsters' comments and prognostications on a horse's winning chances can be helpful. However, it's not something to fully rely upon, and shouldn't cloud your judgement. All the same, it's a useful way to gather information, as there might be something you've missed. Comments revealing a horse's latest outing, such as won easily, not extended, led on bit or effortlessly pulled clear, are often strong pointers when it comes to predicting a horse's current form and wellbeing.

Throughout time, lots of tips circulate through word of mouth. Punters often keep an ear to the ground in the hope of gleaning some inside information. Tips on racehorses often originate from stables, which are communicated through connections such as stable staff or farriers. Some owners get too close to horses and get carried away with their winning chances. The local pub sometimes aids the dissemination of tips: however, information can be vague as to its source, resulting in few winners.

Unk was a proper businessman, a man with his ear to the ground and forever asking punters, 'Ast got any today?' He was referring to tips and never asked where the information was sourced.

In the next breath he'd answer the phone to unsuspecting punters who were placing their daily bets and say, 'I got one for thee today,' proceeding to pass the information on. This was a shrewd move on Unk's behalf, as punters would then invest a further fiver or tenner on the day's good thing, which usually lost.

The industry has played host to a whole chain of tipping scams. I once parted with £100 for ten tips. My stake plan was set at £50 per race and I proceeded to back ten losers on the trot. More recently, a company reportedly working for bookmakers were accused of offering losing tips in nearly every UK horse race. This in turn costs punters monumental losses, while the tipsters themselves earn high commissions. It's also noted that their true success rate remains hidden from public scrutiny. Many gamblers use this information and do the opposite in order to avoid backing losing horses.

I was stressed to the eyeballs, as Ronnie ran me ragged at every opportunity. He phoned early one morning instructing me to be in the Essex office by lunchtime.

I drove for over three hours, and on arrival he said, 'It doesn't matter, yow can go back now.'

I've since learnt that this type of behaviour is a form of psychological deviancy. I decided that I'd had enough and it was the right time to kickstart my career as a bookmaker. I went to the doctor, who gave me two weeks on the sick for stress, and I wrote to Ronnie, giving one month's notice. My sicknote covered the first two weeks and I would take the latter two as holiday. Ronnie, not being one to miss an opportunity, demanded I return the company car immediately or he'd send the police over to confiscate it. He eventually confirmed that I had the right of use for the four-week duration, providing I report to him on the due date at 7 am sharp, just him and I in the sales office. This bought me some time to formulate a plan and raise some cash.

I arrived in the sales office bright and early as agreed, with Ronnie on hand to greet me. He began shouting and swearing, telling me I wouldn't survive in the outside world, and that I couldn't afford to leave such a well-paid job. He was in my face ranting and raving about how I'd let him down. When I finally lost my temper, I told him exactly what I thought of him and in no uncertain terms.

I was expecting a big reaction, but instead Ronnie said, 'I didn't know yow could get worked up like this. That's exactly what I want from my managers; we can work it out.'

I told him that I already had a ticket to ride and walked out. It appeared that Ronnie was impressed with my uncontrolled outburst and subsequently saw comparable traits to himself.

Chapter 4
Keep the Faith

Prior to the showdown with Ronnie, I came across an advert in *Sporting Life*: 'Betting Office for Sale, £8,500.' It was in a small town approximately fifteen miles north of where I lived. The term betting office refers to a business premises where members of the public can place bets on a variety of sporting and other events. Following the Betting and Gaming Act of 1960, betting offices became legal in 1961. Betting offices are also commonly known as betting shops, bookmakers, bookies or turf accountants.

I employed an accountant to accompany me on a mid-afternoon visit to the bookmakers, which had been up and running for over twenty years, albeit changing hands frequently. The current owner was a cockney, a personable skinny bloke named Mac Willis. On arrival, we were expecting to see a busy betting office. Instead there was a sign on the door that read, 'Gone for a cup of tea, back in ten minutes.' The betting shop was situated on the first floor, behind an Indian restaurant and adjacent to flats occupied by restaurant staff.

Mac turned up a few minutes later and showed us inside. We were shocked to see a tiny lock up, measuring approximately five metres by three metres with no toilet facilities. There was a small counter with a rusty bicycle leaning against it and no sign of any punters. Later I got to hear those locals referred to the building as The Chicken Coop. Mac told me he enjoyed a bet, and was approaching retirement when he purchased the bookmakers, assuming it would be fun. However, the worry over large bets gave him a stomach ulcer, leading him to bail out after just six months.

The accountant, whom I hadn't previously met, was unimpressed, and after a brief examination of the books came to the conclusion that the betting office was poorly positioned, too small and unprofitable. He nailed it. All the same, he was viewing the business as it was, while I was considering its potential as a stepping-stone to the future. I followed my instinct, paying him a one-off fee of £200, completely ignoring his advice. I was most likely paying over the odds. Nevertheless, I offered £8,000 for the good will of the business and the deal was done. There were no financial checks on bookmakers and no regulated training. In the meantime, I made an application to the Magistrates' Court in order to transfer the betting licence into my name; a simple transaction, providing the applicant has no previous convictions or bankruptcy.

I remortgaged the family home, raising enough money for the purchase, and a backup of £6,000 cash. This was a peculiar time, as I'd renamed the property Apple Tree Cottage, after an old apple tree in the front garden, expunging the previous name from antiquity - Faithful Cottage. The villagers were soon up in arms. I received a visit from the local vicar and a letter from the previous owner. They were expressing huge disappointment in me for changing the name, which was steeped in history and closely associated with the church. The loss of faith was a significant error on my part and something that I live to regret.

With limited space, the monthly shop rental was set at a modest £120. There was no running water, leaving staff and punters to use the public convenience across the road. Mac gave me a general rundown on how to use the settling machine, and advice on daily routines.

He told me, 'Big bets of £100 or more should be passed on, as it was not good business to stand such large wagers.'

He usually telephoned these bets to independent bookmaker Ron Bowen, who was based in another town. He also suggested that the maximum pay-out remain at £1,000 on any one bet per person; however, I decided to up this to £5,000. Pay-out limits are critical to all bookmakers, as large sums of money can accumulate rapidly.

On the eve of the grand opening, I started having concerns over my limited knowledge of the betting industry. I still didn't know much about the bookmaker's role, and I had to learn fast. There was only one man to turn to at such a critical stage, and that man was Unk.

UNK'S RULES

BETS TO AVOID:

forecast doubles, forecast trebles, tricast doubles, tricast trebles, any to come

RULES:

"accumulator bets" selections must be timed 15 minutes apart,

strict credit limits must be applied.

Reliable hedging facilities in place.

I asked, 'Can you give me a list of general rules so I don't go bust?'

He duly obliged, and these rules became the foundation of my business. In order to psyche myself up for the first day, I read Rudyard Kipling's famous quote: 'If you can meet success and disaster and treat those two imposters just the same.' In contrast, Unk inspired punters with his own words of wisdom: 'Put thee house on this un, young un. You'll win.'

My dad was shocked by my new business venture and couldn't hide his disappointment, warning: 'You'll end up losing everything.'

He was right to be wary, as I was entering a volatile industry that takes no prisoners. I had to start thinking like a bookmaker, and quickly. With the odds stacked in my favour, I would need to manage percentages to my advantage. I knew very little about the compiling of odds, though it wasn't critical because they were compiled by other firms and piped into betting shops via Extel and SIS. If I wanted to offer odds on sporting events outside of the norm, I would be able to find them in the racing papers or I could telephone one of the major bookmakers.

Being motivated by a combination of money and success, I was confident and never considered failure, even as a remote possibility. On 28th November 1988, I opened the doors to my new business, the Betting Coup. My cousin's wife Jane agreed to lend a hand while I found my feet. She knew about betting after assisting Unk on Saturdays. We chose a quiet Monday as our first day of trading, allowing time to get into the swing of things. While we were setting up shop, an irate Indian gentleman burst in. He was the owner of the restaurant and flats next door, accusing me of loitering in his bathroom, and demanding I get out. When he originally purchased the building next door, he believed he'd also acquired the adjoining bookies, which was only separated by a stud wall.

We opened the doors at 11 am during weekdays, and 10 am on Saturdays and Bank Holidays. We needed to be there thirty minutes before opening in order to get set up, though this was never my strongest point. First job was to display the runners, courtesy of *Sporting Life*, along with a complete copy of *Racing Post*. *Sporting Life* was first published in 1859. It ran until it merged with *Racing Post* in 1998, and is still available online. *Racing Post*, founded in 1986 by Mohammed Bin Rashid Al Maktoum, is currently the UK and Ireland's principal horseracing newspaper.

(A list of race card abbreviations and descriptions is detailed in Appendix i.)

At this time, betting offices were licensed to operate six days a week, and the doors had to be closed by 6 pm; evening bets had to be placed beforehand. This suited me, as I would be home during the evenings, and the sabbath was a day of rest. In the early days, betting offices were stigmatised as a smoke-filled, dark and dingy establishment, with a strict no-advertising policy, and blacked out or shuttered windows. Many punters didn't want to be seen going in or out, for fear their partners or neighbours might get to know about their gambling habits.

Rab Butler, the Home Secretary responsible for introducing the 1960 gambling legislation, would later write in his memoirs, 'The House of Commons was so intent on making betting shops as sad as possible, in order not to deprave the young, that they ended up more like undertakers' premises.'

In contrast, the Gambling Act of 2005 permitted advertising, and a bombardment of radio and TV adverts is deemed to have fuelled gambling addiction particularly among teenagers. No one under the age of eighteen is allowed to gamble. Underage gambling checks were introduced in 2013, whereby younger clientele entering betting shops and racecourses, should always be asked for proof of age. All the same, the real problem appears to lie at home, where easy access to online betting makes it easy to gamble.

Loss-leader business techniques, whereby advertisers seem to be giving something for nothing, are now banned in many countries, following concerns that anticompetitive practices eventually hurt consumers. During the year leading to March 2019, £14.4 billion was lost in UK betting. As a consequence, a reduction in maximum stakes on fixed odds betting terminals was introduced, from £100 down to £2, in an attempt to reduce the compulsive nature of gambling.

Another of the morning's tasks involved carefully crossing off the non-runners. Sometimes we'd accidently cross the wrong horse off, upsetting punters. Next, we advertised the day's special offers: for example, enhanced odds on specific races. The final job was to load the till with cash, before switching on the commentary for the early greyhound racing, and we were off.

As the clock struck eleven, a host of pleasant locals began to arrive, introducing themselves and placing bets. Among them was a quiet man known locally as the Singing Paintbrush. His unique attire comprised of red flannels, fluorescent orange polka dot shirt and a lime green cravat. An Irish gentleman named Alf also called in; he'd had a bad experience previously, accusing Mac of underpaying him a fiver. Without hesitation, I gave Alf a fiver as a good will gesture. This turned out to be a shrewd business move, because Alf spent the next couple of years recommending me as a genuine bookie.

The friendly clients would appear early morning, presenting winning tickets, thus allowing an opportunity to engage in conservation. Some punters would have the day's bets already written, while others studied form over a coffee, before writing out their selections. These bets were often multiple bets, such as Yankees, Patents and Lucky 15s. All slips would then be officially recorded and timed through the till. The top copy remained with the bookie, while punters received a duplicate. All bets were then filed, using a timed pigeonhole system.

(A list of popular bets is detailed in Appendix ii.)

It took a while to get used to things, and no two days were the same. However, the day would usually begin by checking the previous night's racing/sports bets. Sometimes, strangers would venture in looking for generous early odds. In winter, UK horseracing starts around midday, and in summertime around 2 pm. Before this we offered a limited fare of greyhound racing. The manager would usually work alone, until joined by a cashier just before the start of horseracing. During busy afternoons there was much banter amongst punters, creating a vibrant atmosphere. The manager would keep a close eye on all bets, in order to identify any dangerous pay-outs. We didn't utilise any computerised bet capture systems, relying instead on the skills of our settlers, who had the use of OTT settling machines (adapted calculators) for the purpose of working out single and multiple bets.

Prior to racing, a number of credit punters would telephone.

Mac had given me a list of clients who were good for credit and warned, 'Don't give credit to anyone whose name is not on the list.'

During racing, telephone bets continued sometimes hindering the manager's ability to keep on top of settling. At the end of business, the closing cash would be reconciled against the days take; pay-outs and a note of all uncollected winnings, referred to as holdovers, would be recorded in order to establish the day's profit or loss. The holdover figure was also used to organise the following day's opening cash float.

As the afternoon horseracing approached, regular customers, cousins Hank and Edmund Flook appeared. Hank was intent on testing me out, asking a series of awkward questions and quickly came to the conclusion that I was clueless.

I overheard him say, 'We've got another right un here.'

Hank an ex-policeman in his fifties, with rugged features and a mop of ginger hair was an angry individual with a persona that oozed pessimism. He regularly received duff racing tips and was constantly bemoaning his luck.

Next in was a local plumber, the Cousin. Cuz, as he was affectionately known, was a carefree type who loved his bet. He was a great advocate for the business, and if he wasn't in the bookies he could usually be found in the pub. Amid others to arrive was local restaurateur, Eddie, who'd always remark 'Easy money,' each time he collected winnings. The rest of the time he would shout obscenities whenever his horse looked beaten. Mack had previously advised me to hedge all of Eddie's wagers, as the stakes were usually between £100 and £200 singles. I also met ex-military man Graham Cordy for the first time. Another regular was Lawrence, a nice guy with a wicked sense of humour and a very laid-back persona. Lawrence had a habit of bringing his young son Clive in. With a strict policy of 'No Under Eighteens', I always asked Clive to wait outside.

During racing the phone rang and a Mr Cash wanted to place £30-worth of bets. I couldn't see his name on the credit list, but he assured me that, if he should lose, he'd come in and settle up. Foolishly, I agreed to lay the bet, which lost, and he never showed. For many weeks I remained suspicious that Mr Cash was lurking among regulars in the Coup. Given Mac's warning, I'd been incredibly naïve and paid the price. In those days all transactions were either cash or formal credit arrangements. As a routine, bookies would agree their clients credit limit in advance and send an invoice (or a cheque) fortnightly. Some punters would call in and settle up on an ad hoc basis.

On Mac's credit list was smooth sophisticated businessman Dan Lauda, who had a reputation as a big earner. Dan liked a bet on the horses and telephoned a £200 single wager every Saturday without fail. During the first couple of years, he failed to back a winner, and, to make matters even better, payment would arrive promptly. Dan was one of the unluckiest punters I ever met, becoming a reliable source of income.

The two Flooks were often armed with tips and system bets. Hank gained a reputation as a slammer. I coined this term for punters who slam their bet down on the counter, believing they're on to a good thing, or for slamming the door on the way out. He was also threatening to boycott the Betting Coup, as he believed the staff were a bad omen.

One time he came in with a hot tip, saying, 'I'll have you lot today', slamming £40 on the counter. Shortly after the off, his selection pulled up.

Hank was furious as he made his usual exit, shouting, 'You lot are poison. This has got to be the unluckiest **** place on the planet.'

For the first couple of weeks, I took Mac's advice and phoned all bets of £100 or more to Ron Bowen. We agreed that I would call on Ron every Monday to settle up the previous week's bill. By the end of the first week, I had placed a series of losing bets and paid

Ron dues of £500. It was a similar story in week two, as I paid Ron a further £600, courtesy of Easy Money Eddie and Dan Lauda. My idea of being in business was driven by the prospect of making profit, not giving it all away.

I began to hear rumours that Ron had a reputation for not wanting to pay out winnings to anyone receiving information on tipped horses. During week three, I placed three choice wagers with him, which all won. I arrived as usual on the Monday, but this time to collect winnings of £800. Ron was not happy and asked me if I had backed tipped horses.

He pointed out that he never usually had to pay Mac and said, 'If that's how it's going to be, I don't want your business.'

Ron had clearly overreacted, though I decided not to place any more bets with him.

Bets exchanged between bookmakers are referred to as hedge bets. These bets are placed when there is too much risk for a bookmaker to stand on any one wager, therefore the liability is spread. This is an integral part of the bookmaking industry, because bookies need to work within their financial limits. The consequence of losing too much money in one hit can be devastating, and may even threaten a business with closure. I soon changed Mac's poor strategy of hedging all of the bigger wagers, though I still needed to hedge some bets. I opted to use William Hill or Ladbrokes, as it was less hassle.

Soon after, I was approached by another independent bookmaker, Stuart Jenkins. He advised me that he was happy to take my hedge bets, though I became irritated by his constant advances. I also heard that he didn't have the best of reputations when it came to paying out. I didn't want any more encounters like the one with Ron and I refused to put any business his way. I was bemused by bookmakers with a poor attitude to paying out. In those days, high-street bookies would gross a profit of approximately 15p in the pound, leaving 85% to be paid out as winnings. Paying out with a smile is essential, because it's all part of building a strong, healthy business.

Eventually, I got to meet the infamous Mr Jenkins, a sophisticated gentleman in his fifties, with an imperious air and straggly, unkempt silver hair. He gave me a lift to a bookmaker meeting in London. At the meeting he introduced me to his specialist business advisor Phil Jellops, of whom he spoke very highly. Phil had saved his business a couple of years previously, when a national firm were trying to open a new site close by. This turned out to be a very influential introduction, as Phil Jellops would also become my business advisor.

Mr Jenkins and I played tennis together a few times at his upmarket club. I enjoyed tennis, although I was just a humble park-player, and despite the fact that he was always eager to beat me, he never managed it. During one meeting, I mentioned that my betting till was not functioning properly, and described the symptoms of my Anchor F7, which was an essential piece of equipment used to time bets. Mr Jenkins suggested that it would need a new solenoid valve and kindly offered to repair it. He came to the Betting Coup and proceeded to fit the solenoid. On completion, he switched the till on to a bright flash and a loud bang.

As the smoke, cleared he emerged from behind the till with a blackened face of thunder, announcing, 'I'm afraid that's all I can do for you today.'

Having grown up in a household where all visitors received a cup of tea on arrival, I extended this convivial approach to the Betting Coup, offering punters free coffee in paper cups whenever I had chance to put the kettle on, although I had to bring fresh water in a large container. In those days, bookies weren't generally offering free tea and coffee. At some point my generosity backfired; some new punters stopped coming in, as they believed that no one gives something for nothing.

While a percentage of credit clients paid like clockwork, I was wishing that I'd taken Mac's advice, after attracting too much bad credit. Little did I realise that credit debts would become the bane of my life. In this position, bookmakers would lose twice, with the unpaid debt and the loss of future cash trade, as these clients would avoid coming in. During this period, there was no legislation to enforce gambling debts and such transactions were regarded as a debt of honour.

Eddie was also a pain, because he started asking me to cash cheques of up to £200, and as a general rule I would oblige. All the same, he never wanted me to pay them into the bank. I would wait until he was on a winning streak before he claimed them back against the cash. One time I refused, because I already had too many cheques lying dormant in the desk drawer. Eddie wasn't impressed and picked up a stool, threatening to put it through the TV screen.

Local greyhound trainer Bill Cook owed £30 for some losing bets, but advised me that he had a greyhound running at Swindon that couldn't lose. He suggested that I have a good bet, and call it quits should his dog prevail. He advised that the greyhound had just come on heat, and had a prime draw from Trap 1. Brimming with confidence, he predicted that it would be first out of the traps, and wouldn't be caught.

I was convinced by his level of confidence and made the early evening trip. I was loaded with cash and noted the generous opening price of 7/2. I walked up to the bookie with £400 in crisp £20 notes.

Just as I was about to place my bet, Bill rushed up, saying, 'I'm not sure if my dog will win. I'm concerned about the favourite in Trap 5. It's up to you.'

This is a common trait among many gamblers, as race time approaches, confidence wavers. Maybe I should have known better. Nevertheless, these comments left me with no intention of backing his greyhound. Some five minutes later the race was underway Bill's dog flew out of the traps, went clear and won easily. He came over and asked if I'd backed it, to which I replied no.

He shrugged his shoulders and said, 'Oh well, we're quits now.'

Around this time many betting shops had no pictures or data. Boardmen operated by displaying prices obtained via audio transmission of price changes. This was accompanied by race-to-race commentaries, courtesy of Extel. In the Betting Coup, Jane and a couple of locals would take turns to mark up prices on the whiteboard during live racing. We also had a television allowing us to show live pictures whenever racing was on terrestrial TV. Satellite

Information Services (SIS) was incorporated in 1986. Live pictures of horse and greyhound racing launched to one hundred betting establishments in Bristol on 5th May 1987. The service eventually went live to 10,400 betting offices in the UK and the Republic of Ireland. With finances dictating, I was reluctant to introduce SIS coverage until 1990. Live pictures were shortly followed by data broadcasting live betting shows, signalling the end of board price displays. In the interim, Jane, who had been a real brick, landed herself a full-time job with Coral Bookmakers.

Chapter 5
Give Me Credit

For all of my positivity in business, I was also very naïve, assuming that everyone was honest. During my early bookmaking days I went to hospital for an ECG test. I was experiencing a new level of stress, mainly due to big liabilities and the vulnerability attached to the day-to-day bookmaking business. A new punter started coming in every lunchtime, betting on horses and greyhounds. He ran a business across the road, and made a habit of coming in with a mug of tea in one hand, keeping the other hand free to pull out a large wad of notes. One day he suggested that instead of paying for each wager up front we should settle up at the end of the lunch hour. I agreed, and from this moment his wagers increased substantially, as he ran up a bill for £2,000, and duly left without paying.

After this episode he stopped coming in, and I decided to call him regarding the debt. He was quick to tell me that there was nothing I could do, as gambling debts were unenforceable. He also said that, according to his memory, I owed him £2,000, and he would be in to collect it sometime. He never came in, and it was another big lesson. I often phoned to remind him of the debt, and threatened to send in the debt collectors. On the day he closed down his business, the Betting Coup link to live satellite also went down, due to the main supply cable being severed.

Shortly after, I was approached by a debt collecting agency, who said they had experience in collecting gambling debts. I agreed to use their service and bought a book of twelve £25 vouchers. The idea was to enter all contact details of the debtor on to each voucher, along with the outstanding sum. In return they would attempt to retrieve each debt within a set period of time. In the unlikely event of any failure, the used voucher would be replaced by a free one. I sent them a whole string of vouchers, though I never heard from them again.

With lots of new punters arriving, I was gaining a reputation as a bookmaker who'd lay a decent-sized bet. Outside of the cash trade, my commercial approach was simple: 'If the mountain will not come to Muhammad, then Muhammad must go to the mountain.' My sales background had given me the platform to build a strong telephone trade, which I used as a safety net for the cash business.

Having made big mistakes on the credit front, I wrote to all of the debtors, advising: 'After a successful year in business I am prepared to write off all debts as a gesture of good will.' While I was happy to honour my word, this was really a cunning ploy to regain their cash business, and, one by one, they started coming back. Outside of the good credit list, my new business model would offer credit to clients who lived beyond a five-mile radius. This way I wouldn't lose any local cash trade.

My first year at the Betting Coup had gone reasonably well, and I was recommended to an accountant called Eric. He worked for a firm of accountants in Cardiff, and spoke with an Eton plum in his mouth. He often didn't turn up for meetings, and if he did, he was usually a couple of hours late. Eric's first assignment was to submit my betting levy, which was based on turnover and needed to be submitted by a qualified accountant. After his professional computation, he informed me that I had to pay the Horse Betting Levy Board £3,500, which was due immediately. I queried this figure as it seemed excessive and a big burden on my finances, though Eric assured me it was correct.

Meanwhile, a mate introduced me to his work colleague, David Watts. David was a few years younger than me, a tall man, quietly spoken with a friendly attitude. On meeting him for the first time, I'd describe him as easy going. He enjoyed a bet, and was keen on various sports, including football, rugby and golf. He made his first appearance at a racecourse at Epsom on Derby day in 1988, during a drunken day out with rugby mates.

David's big interest in sports and betting appealed to me. In addition, he was enthusiastic, with a disciplined approach to gambling, and there was no doubting his integrity. Maybe his biggest appeal was thirteen years' experience in personnel, dealing with staffing issues and recruitment. I started pondering David Watts as a possible business partner. Nevertheless, I needed to know more about him.

David spent the early days of his life in the picturesque village of Redbook, nestled between England and Wales on the river Wye. A brook divided the two nations, and his first view of rural Welsh landscape came through the slats of a cot. As he peered westward through the coloured shadows, he couldn't possibly have known the anguish this passionate rugby nation would bestow on him in the years to follow. The family moved to Somerset during the harsh winter of 1962/63, which caused UK horseracing to be abandoned for three months. Their home was close to the Bread Rollers public house, a pub named after a tradition whereby people throw themselves down a steep hill in pursuit of an oversized bread roll.

By the age of seven, David was taking a keen interest in football and latched on to Leeds United who were doing well in the First Division. In fact, he became besotted with Leeds, shedding lots of tears after they lost against Chelsea in the 1970 FA Cup final replay. It was the same outcome in the 1973 final, where Sunderland goalkeeper Jimmy Montgomery made what was described by some as the best double save ever. David was very proud when he received the all-white Leeds kit for his ninth birthday. Sadly, he still recites the team line up: Sprake, Reaney, Cooper, Bremner (Captain), Charlton, Hunter, Lorimer, Clarke, Jones, Giles and Gray. Substitutes, Madeley and Yorath.

He was ultra-competitive, particularly when it came to younger brother Jeff. Football, tennis, cricket and Subbuteo were all part of everyday life. Their dad played rugby for a local team, and regularly took the scrawny urchins along to watch. However, they preferred watching football or just messing around, and once missed Dad scoring a classic try. David became hooked on rugby after watching a memorable match on *Grandstand*, when Gareth Edwards scored *that try*, the best ever, for the Barbarians against the All Blacks.

Cliff Morgan, commentating on the game, described the final passage: 'This is Gareth Edwards, a dramatic start, what a score. Oh, that fellow Edwards.' At the restart, he commented: 'If the greatest writer of the written word would have written that story, no one would have believed it. That really was something.'

David listened to the radio commentary of the British Lions v South Africa test matches in 1974. The Lions were unbeaten in the twenty-two-match tour, winning twenty-one games and drawing the fourth test 13-13. In this test, Lions flanker Fergus Slattery went over the line in the dying minutes, but the referee didn't see a grounding of the ball, denying the Lions a clean sweep. Many years later, David was present at a dinner where Lions captain Willie John McBride was guest speaker.

He asked, 'What was your opinion of the Fergus try in the last test in '74?'

Willie took a long puff on his pipe, blew out a cloud of smoke, and replied, 'Sonny, the referee didn't give it.'

He was a season ticket holder at Bath Rugby Club, and sometimes sneaked into the changing rooms to collect autographs. David was also a keen photographer, and on one occasion he stopped some England internationals, asking if he could take their photographs.

One of the star players stepped forward, saying, 'Son, you might want to remove the camera lens cover.'

In 1975 England beat Scotland 20-0 at Twickenham, and a graceful Scottish player took the time to take David's address and mail him all of the Scotland team autographs.

As a teenager in the mid '70s, he was all skin and bone. He enjoyed athletics and in particular running, though street runners were often ridiculed. He'd been inspired by his dad, who was also a long-distance runner. He represented the county at cross country and was given special dispensation to go running during school games. After being elected captain of the city Athletics cross country team, he didn't manage to compete because of a knee injury.

David and I began meeting up once a month to settle his account, and enjoyed chatting over a beer. We became great pals, and went on to challenge each other to a different sports game every month, with the loser buying the curry at the end of the evening. On one occasion, David challenged me to play football. His idea was that we play keep-ups, where you have to keep the ball off the ground for as long as possible. We agreed to have half a dozen goes each, with the winner having the highest aggregate total. Neither of us knew much about the other when it came to football skills. David went first and struggled to make five. During this gratifying moment, I was contemplating which gourmet curry I was going to order. On a good day I had been known to keep the ball in the air some five hundred times.

David drove an old rusty Ford Fiesta that had a habit of breaking down. He never seemed a natural behind the wheel, and I nicknamed him Reginald Molehusband, after a fictional character from the 1960s, who was depicted as the country's worst driver. On one of our customary meetings, he invited me to stay over at his place so I could indulge in a few beers. He made a plan to chauffer me after exchanging his Fiesta for a second-hand Cavalier a few hours earlier.

The brown 1.6 hatch was due for its first spin and raring to go. Disturbingly, he reversed off the drive straight into a parked car. During my feeble attempts to conceal my amusement, David got out to assess the damage. The Cavalier was still driveable, albeit with a smashed back end, and we made our way into town for a tranquil beer or two. Later, on leaving the curry house, we spotted a couple of thugs inside the mangled hatchback. Having broken the side window, they were in process of shorting the wires when we chased them off. In spite of a missing side window, a fragmented dashboard, exposed wiring and a buckled rear end, Reggie diligently drove home at snail's pace.

During work lunch breaks, David selected his daily bets before venturing into reception to use the payphones. Being careful not to be overheard, as the office was open plan, he developed a whisper. His first bet was £20 to win on Desert Orchid, who won by a head from Panto Prince with a memorable performance in the Victor Chandler Handicap Chase at Ascot. To begin with his bets were quite modest, though he was about to raise the stakes.

He bet £500 on First Division Coventry City at odds of 2/5, to beat Sutton United from the Conference League, in the 1989 third round of the FA Cup. While at home watching *Grandstand*, a latest score flashed up as Sutton 0-1 Coventry. David sat rubbing his hands in glee before the score was suddenly corrected, showing Sutton had taken the lead, not the Sky Blues. The non-league side went on to win the game 2-1, creating one of the biggest ever giant killing shocks in FA Cup history.

Coventry City FC also gained a reputation for their 1970s design of a universally detested football kit. The ill-famed chocolate brown away kit was reportedly made by a small firm in Leicestershire that made big pants for older ladies. The eyesore has since been described as a thing of beauty from a bygone age. It currently sells as a collector's item for around £500.

The 1989 Grand National signalled my first experience of the race as a bookmaker, yielding a massive cash turnover without profit. It was a lucky race for David, who bet a fiver on the winner Little Polvier at early odds of 66/1 after the horse caught his eye before falling in the big race twelve months earlier. David and I discussed the 1990 race in detail and I explained that I'd convinced myself that Durham Edition would win. I planned to hedge all of the win money I took for the horse who finished four-lengths runner up to Rhyme 'n' Reason in the 1988 National. If the scheme proved successful, I would retain a large sum of cash.

On the eve of the Grand National, Ron Bowen was guesting on a local radio show, describing a bookmaker's busiest day of the year. By this time, Ron's reputation for not wanting to pay out winnings on tipped horses was legendary, and at the end of the session the interviewer asked which horse he fancied to win the race. Hesitantly, he tipped Mr Frisk.

Coincidentally, Jane and her family backed the Kim Bailey-trained Mr Frisk, because they had a dog called Frisky. David also backed it to win at 16/1, together in a reverse forecast with Durham Edition, ridden by Chris Grant. The race leaders approached the final fence to the haunting sound of BBC commentator, Sir Peter O'Sullevan:

'There's not much in it. Mr Frisk leads from Durham Edition; is he going to win it for trainer Arthur Stephenson on his seventieth birthday?'

Mr Frisk prevailed by three quarters of a length in record time of 8 minutes 47.80 seconds, under amateur jockey Marcus Armitage. Consequently, I paid most of the takings out, as well as having to pay for my considerable hedging losses. I wasn't alone with this disheartening result. Word spread like wildfire after Ron's radio tip, as punters scurried from all sides of town to his betting shop, collecting winnings on Mr Frisk. In total, David took me for £800, and has since admitted that I turned his attention to second-placed Durham Edition.

David's luck continued during the 1990 World Cup final, where Argentina were playing Germany. He bet £20 on the German free kick taker, Andreas Brehme to score the first goal, at odds of 20/1, as well as a sizeable bet on Germany to win in 90 minutes. The game turned out to be the dullest final in world cup history, until Germany were awarded a penalty in the eighty-fifth minute. Much to everyone's surprise, Brehme was placing the ball on the penalty spot, because usual penalty taker Matthaus had been injured in the foul leading up to the penalty. Brehme proceeded to strike the football into the corner of the goal, netting David a further £800.

The tables were turned the following year in the 1991 World Cup final at Twickenham, where England were playing against Australia. David bet £10 on Australian prop forward Ewan Mackenzie to score the first try at odds of 100/1. He watched the game with a mate in a city boozer among a host of strangers. Early in the game Mackenzie was announced as the first try scorer, leaving David trying to conceal his joy. Despite Australia winning the match, David bought everyone a drink on account of his assumed £1,000 winnings. However, the try was awarded to fellow prop Tony Daly, after he wrestled the ball off Mackenzie under a pile of players.

Following a healthy increase of turnover during my second year's trading, the accounts also revealed a fall in profit, and I was dreading the sum I would have to pay the Levy Board, meanwhile I was learning to survive on a shoestring budget. Before releasing the forms to Eric, I decided to telephone the Levy Board in order to gain an understanding of the percentage paid against turnover. During the conversation, it transpired that this year's payment was going to be approximately £500, one seventh of the previous year's payment.

After more intense discussion, I was advised, 'There may have previously been an accounting error, though it's not our place to tell you.'

I telephoned Eric, as only he could claim a refund. He was adamant that he'd not made any errors, and that I'd misunderstood how levy payments were calculated. During the weeks that followed, Eric was unwilling to admit he had done anything wrong, and flatly refused to reclaim my £3,000. He ignored my phone messages, and instructed his receptionist not to put me through to any of his colleagues. One day I informed her that I was on my way to the office to complain about Eric in person. The one-hundred-and-twenty-mile round trip proved fruitful. On arrival Eric appeared in reception, apologising most profusely for his miscalculation, though without explanation. However, he assured me that he had written to the Levy Board reclaiming my overpayment. Having got a result with the levy refund, I dispensed with Eric's services.

The betting office environment hosts an interesting range of characters from different walks of life. One such person was a retired gentleman called Reg Kind, who phoned bets daily for both himself and neighbours. Reg was always in a hurry, and frequently complained that staff were too slow in writing his bets out, delaying himself further.

My first difficult encounter came when he rang asking to bet on the first goal scorer in a televised football match: £5 Harold Davis. After several minutes of incoherent blubbering, it turned out that he wanted to place his bet on the Argentinian Osvaldo Ardiles, who had just signed for Queens Park Rangers.

On another occasion, Reg phoned saying that he didn't want any time wasting: 'I'm in a desperate hurry and I don't want any messing around. I want to place an ante post bet on a horse race.'

Ante post bets are usually placed well before the event and punters can gain higher odds, while risking a loss if their selection doesn't make the starting line-up.

Johnny: 'When is the race?'

Reg: 'I'm not sure.'

Johnny: 'What is the name of the race?'

Reg: 'I can't remember, but you need to speed up, I'm in a hurry.'

Johnny: 'What is the name of the horse you wish to bet on?'

Reg: 'Oh, bugger I can't remember – um, what's the damn thing called?'

Johnny: 'What type of race is it?'

Reg: 'Come on, you should know what big races are coming up.'

Johnny: 'Who trains it?'

Reg: 'I can't remember the trainer's name. Thingamabob is the jockey. What the hell is his name?'

Johnny: 'I can't help you, Reg, unless you give me something.'

Reg: 'Come on. just give me a price. You're supposed to be a bloody bookie.'

Chapter 6
The Boondoggle

I was recommended to another accountant, Jeremy Norfolk. After submitting my annual accounts, Jeremy informed me that the Inland Revenue was intending to investigate my business. However, local tax inspector Mr Jones refused to enlighten me as to why. During the weeks that followed, Mr Jones regularly appeared unannounced, looking through boxes of betting transactions. He once took away a whole month's slips in order to examine them thoroughly. On one occasion he made a morning appointment to visit the Betting Coup before opening time. While awaiting his arrival, I became aware of someone watching me through the letterbox. On my shouting 'Come in,' Mr Jones made his entry wearing thick rimmed spectacles, trilby, and a turned-up anorak collar. I asked if he usually spied on people, but he evaded the question. I believed my submissions to be accurate; all the same, it would be a long wait while he continued his investigation.

Frank Black became a regular - an elderly gentleman who had just divorced for a second time. He was not in the greatest of health, and enjoyed a drink and a smoke, though his smoking habit had led to breathing problems. A Geordie through and through, he was a genuine character with a humorous nature. Frank and another regular, Alan Payne, became godfathers to my precious son. Alan also liked a drink and carried a permanent flask of whisky in his coat pocket. He bet on horses, though he couldn't bear to watch for fear of injury to the animals. He wore a paisley cravat, hiding a Second World War wound, following a bullet ricochet. Despite this, he often lowered his neckerchief in order to reveal the unsightly scar.

Frank and Alan knew lots of my clients had reneged on their credit bills, and being no-nonsense types, they insisted I got tougher with punters. There was one particular chap known as Warren Burrows who owed me £200. Frank knew Warren of old and disliked him, encouraging me to pay him a visit.

Warren, an elderly man, once told me that his wife, who was much younger, disapproved of gambling. This particular piece of information became very powerful when it came to chasing credit debts, which I referred to as the Achilles' heel. Many of my client's partners/wives didn't know they gambled, and I had no qualms using this to my advantage. Meanwhile, Frank knew Warren's address, and one evening we drove to his house to collect the debt. Frank waited in the car and was laughing his socks off as I knocked on the door. Warren's wife appeared in yellow marigolds and a pinny.

She asked abruptly, 'Who are you?'

I replied, 'I'm a friend of Warren,' and she signalled me to go through to the lounge.

I went in and discreetly closed the door to find Warren fast asleep. I coughed loudly and called Warren several times, but he was not stirring. After a few minutes, he jumped to his feet, wiping his eyes in disbelief. He sat down and told me he would come over the following day to settle the bill.

He said, 'Tell my wife you're here to view a painting. Don't mention you're a bookie.'

Suddenly his wife entered the room and Warren leapt to his feet for a second time. He began describing a random piece of art in detail, advising that he would sell at the right price.

He then showed me to the door, whispering, 'See you tomorrow.'

To his credit, Warren came in the next day carrying a painting under his arm. He paid the debt in full, and I hesitantly purchased the watercolour for £100. He stayed for a couple of hours only to lose it all on the horses. Warren muttered some expletives, slammed the door and was never seen again.

A few days later, Frank appeared in the Coup, still amused by the escapades with Warren. Frank was laden with a carrier bag of cash - £6,000 to be precise. He asked me if I would keep hold of it for personal reasons, as he knew he could trust me. I was quite flattered by this, and he went on to say that nobody knew about it apart from him and me.

He gave further instruction: 'If anything happens to me, give it to our Lisa.'

The last time I saw Frank he was in hospital. He was in agony with serious circulation problems and the morphine was no longer controlling his excruciating pain. He passed away later that day. This was not to be the last time I heard from Frank!

After the funeral, I phoned Lisa to tell her, 'I have £6,000 of your dad's money for you.'

She replied, 'Yes, I know, Johnny. He told me.'

Matt Richardson was another regular a nice chap, with a wicked sense of humour. He was in his late sixties when we first met. He lived alone, popping in most days for a bet, and we'd often share a laugh and a joke. He came from a wealthy family, was well read and demonstrated a passion for good food and fine wines. Over a period of time, Matt slowed down and started phoning his bets. He loved betting on sport, and in particular football and horseracing. However, his bets usually lost. As a rule, he remained approximately £300 in arrears. Nevertheless, like clockwork, he would appear every Friday and make a payment.

One day and out of the blue, Matt asked me what would happen if one of us died while owing the other money. I pointed out that we were not just business acquaintances, we were also good friends, so who cares about the money? Within a week, Matt passed away. He'd had cancer and hadn't told anyone. His sense of humour remained with him to the end, and I was filled with great sadness. All the same, our final business arrangement did draw a smile, leaving me £320 out of pocket.

After much to-ing and fro-ing, tax inspector Mr Jones invited me in to discuss matters at the local tax office. I advised Jeremy of our impending meeting, though he insisted it was nothing to do with him, and he didn't want to be involved. I was shocked, demanding that he should accompany me as my accountant.

On arrival, I couldn't resist asking the receptionist if Mr Jones was still spying on people through letterboxes.

She replied, 'Oh, they're all trained to do that, my love. It's part of their training.'

We sat down face to face with the tax inspector, and Jeremy made a point of moving his chair away from me. Mr Jones declared that the daily cash take didn't balance with the till roll. Without pause, I was able to explain that HM Customs & Excise insisted both cash and credit bets were recorded on the till roll, showing the day's business transactions as one total. Therefore, the till roll total and the final cash balance would never tally.

Mr Jones appeared bitterly disappointed, sinking his chin slowly into the palm of his left hand. I was very irritated, particularly as the daily cash/credit form was specifically designed as idiot proof, thus making the whole pantomime a complete waste of taxpayer's money. Eventually, a puzzled Mr Jones turned his attention to a £50 motor expense.

Pointing my finger at Jeremy, I responded, 'Ask him, that's his job,' while moving my chair further away from my unsupportive accountant.

The sorry twosome continued with a short dialogue and the investigation was over. As we were leaving Jeremy became overjoyed with the outcome. Nevertheless, I sacked him for the act of disloyalty.

Thirty-four-year-old bachelor Eddie originated from China. His life revolved around gambling and he remained a loyal supporter at the Betting Coup. It became obvious that he was a punter who just couldn't quit the habit, and quite frankly didn't want to. He was a bookie's dream, with his bets averaging between £100 and £200 singles. When he was winning large sums, you could almost guarantee he'd continue betting and lose most of it. Throughout losing streaks he'd reduce his wagers steadily down to £10, £5 and finally £1. He loved the thrill and appeared to get the same buzz from a £1 wager.

A problem gambler can be defined as someone who gambles continuously, despite negative consequences. They may be driven by boredom, to deflect problems or to solve monetary issues. In Eddie's case I believed it to be more about excitement. There is a biological explanation based on a lack of norepinephrine, which is secreted under stress. This theory claims that problem gamblers seek to make up for a deficiency by increasing excitement. Another explanation is based on psychological traits, such as a less sensitive approach to reward processing, risk seeking, impulsive behaviour, an illusion of control and unrealistic optimism.

Eddie worked hard in the restaurant six days a week. Wednesday was his customary day off and he'd head to the city bookmakers, followed by a visit to the casino. He'd always appear on Thursday, either loaded with cash laughing and joking, or quietly muttering swearwords, while staking a few £2 wagers. One day he hit a winning streak, increasing his initial £50 to £1,000. He continued with a succession of losing wagers, staking his last £2. Miraculously this selection won, starting another winning sequence and taking his profit back up to £800, claiming 'easy money'. As the afternoon progressed, Eddie's luck completely ran out, and he proceeded to blow his cash for a second time.

In jest I said, 'Easy come, easy go.'

He seemed to find this expression funny and kept repeating it. This was the day I launched Eddie's personal theme tune, reciting my version of the old Herman's Hermits song 'Years May Come, Years May Go'. To begin with he seemed slightly angry, even so when he was winning, he was the first to take the lead vocal with the modified lyrics:

Easy come, easy go,
Some go fast, some go slow,
Some are good, some are bad,
Some are happy, some are sad

Mr Jenkins continued pestering me and I succumbed, putting a few bets his way. During one busy Friday afternoon, two punters coincidentally bet on the same three Henry Cecil trained horses. Reg Kind backed a £1 Patent, while Yorkshireman Dick bet them in a £10 win treble. The first horse won at Ascot at 10/1, leaving me to assess the liability on the remaining two selections. The risk on the two bets combined totalled over £10,000. However, I had a maximum pay-out limit of £5,000 per wager, leaving me a total liability of £6,259. I then telephoned Mr Jenkins, placing a £70 win double on a 17/2 shot that won at Ascot, and a horse called Peter, running in the 8.10 at Ripon.

Out of courtesy, I telephoned Mr Jenkins pointing out that he had £665 running on to Peter, leaving him with a big liability should the horse win. He was quite rude, promptly assuring me that he was an experienced bookmaker who didn't need advice from a young upstart. Bookmakers have to equate sums quickly and think on their feet, particularly when races are closely timed. However, accumulative bets can usually be managed, providing you are disciplined with limits and have the appropriate hedging outlets.

As luck would have it, Peter won the race at odds of 8/1, leaving Mr Jenkins to cough up £5,985. In turn, I owed Dick £5,000 and Reg £1,259. This was a typical example of a hedge bet, where a bookmaker might cut his liability. Mr Jenkins had the opportunity to reduce his losses by betting on the last horse.

Hedging is an essential part of bookmaking, and something I found easy to adopt, where I set my limits and hedged bets accordingly. I didn't have a maximum pay-out sum ringfenced in a bank account. Nevertheless, I had the ability to raise funds through hedging, as well as three days' grace when paying punters by cheque, which was often very helpful.

First thing the following morning the phone rang; it was Mr Jenkins demanding to know whether the bet I had placed was a personal wager or a business hedge bet. He also enquired as to my maximum pay-out. I told him that was none of his business.

He then said, 'I suppose you want me to pay you,' advising me to call at his office later that afternoon. Russell, my old schoolmate, had agreed to become my Saturday assistant, and he accompanied me. He remained in the car as I entered the office, where there were still a couple of stragglers. Mr Jenkins then made a gesture to meet me outside. As I made my way back to the car, the embittered bookmaker bustled past, slamming a canvas bag full of notes on to my car bonnet, before scurrying back inside. Some of the notes blew on to the road, leaving me to dart around, frantically gathering them, as Russell looked on in astonishment. After this embarrassment, I refused to put any further business his way.

A few days later, I asked Dick why he'd bet Peter in the final leg of his treble, as the horse was the outsider of three Henry Cecil-trained entrants.

He replied, 'That's my grandson's name.'

I also asked if I could advertise his winning bet on the wall: at first, he was adamant that no one should know how much he'd won, so I suggested I would write the bet out again, strictly not telling anyone who it belonged to. The following Saturday, Cuz arrived in the Betting Coup along with the Singing Paintbrush, the two Flooks, and a jovial Lawrence. Dick came in, spotted the winning slip displayed on the shop wall and made a beeline for it.

He proceeded to point out in a strong accent, 'Someone's had a bit a luck then, ee bah gum. I wonder who the lucky winner is? I don't recognise the handwriting – some shrewdie, I suppose.'

He looked very disappointed when no one took any notice, though there were a few sniggers from Russell.

When Dick left, Lawrence seemed particularly amused, commenting, 'It was obviously his bet, then.'

Dick highlighted the fact that betting systems don't necessarily need to be complicated. His strategy was simply to follow a top trainer's horses. Other basic systems include following a particular tipster, top jockeys, trainers' birthdays, trainer debutants after a transfer from another stable and horses running for the first time in a handicap race. All of this information is available daily in *Racing Post*.

Sometimes I was too generous for my own good, particularly around Christmas time. This was highlighted when a local carpenter called Melvin kindly screwed a new open-closed sign to the shop door. As a rule he wasn't the luckiest of punters, and in return I told him to pick four horses and place his usual 10p Lucky 15 on the house. All four won and I lost £110.

A couple of days later I gave Melvin a free racing diary, which was customary at Christmas time. He commented that Ladbroke diaries had a £1 betting voucher attached, and cheekily asked if I would attach a free bet to his diary. Being a staunch advocate of customer relations, I wrote the words '£2 free bet' on a voucher. He was chuffed and returned the next day, placing a winning £2 accumulator, costing me £440.

I wasn't a soft touch when one of my regulars, known as Whiffer, started bringing in garlic sandwiches. He had a habit of leaving them on the side for hours before consumption. Meanwhile he'd place the odd 50p wager, while winding up other punters with a constant northern banter. Whiffer would be best described as a Selwyn Froggitt equivalent, an all-round public nuisance, from the 1970s hit TV series *Oh No It's Selwyn Froggitt*. Tempers reached boiling point when several punters complained about Whiffer's reeking sandwiches, while also threatening to boycott the Coup. I approached him on the subject, advising that his Hovis crust and garlic would no longer be tolerated.

He seemed a little put out and sharply replied, 'If the sandwiches go, I go.'

Being of a stiff-necked character, Whiffer would never again darken my door.

Come New Year's Day, Melvin returned grinning like the Cheshire Cat, and just couldn't resist complimenting me on my magnanimity. Melvin was becoming a nuisance, though technically I could only blame my own free hand generosity. On this occasion he placed £10 on a losing single bet. The following day he was back, advising me that he'd backed the wrong horse. He'd meant to back the winner, which won at 3/1. He then asked if I would be willing to honour the bet as it was a genuine error. On the spur of the moment, I made a decision to give him £40, as I believed he was telling the truth.

My colleague Ronald, who observed me, maintained, 'That's the most ridiculous thing I've ever witnessed, Winall.'

During one of our monthly meetings, David and I visited the Honeypot in Bath. I was always on the lookout to build my credit trade, and I had a habit of asking pub landlords if they enjoyed a bet. This was the day we first met enigmatic Geordie Don Dingle. Don had a cheeky face that reminded me of a naughty schoolboy. He was also very charming, extremely cunning and generally regarded as a likeable rogue. The landlord enjoyed a bet, and since I knew where to find him I confirmed the details of a credit account. In return, he claimed to know the jeweller responsible for engraving the Cheltenham Gold Cup, and invited David and me to join his regulars to view the bona fide cup on the eve of the big race. We were first to pose for a local photographer, who captured two unsuspecting mugs, holding a replica.

Don started to bet regularly on horseracing. However, in June 1991, he phoned to ask, 'What price a hole in one in the US Open golf tournament? I'm looking for 500/1.'

I phoned around to check if a price was available, though no firms were taking bets. I knew if the major bookmakers were not giving odds on any given event, it was usually dangerous not to follow suit. Within ten minutes Don called again.

'Have you got that price yet? Ladbroke's have already offered me 40/1, but these odds are too stingy. I'll accept 100/1.'

Having already spoken with Ladbrokes, I knew he was trying it on. Giving further thought to his request, I considered that it would be difficult to get a hole in one. All the same I could smell a rat, and guessed that the odds would be much lower. Before I had chance to conclude my deliberation he phoned again.

'Right, what price have you come up with? It's 100/1.'

I reluctantly agreed, accepting a maximum wager of £5, at odds of 100/1. He wasn't happy with this, and insisted I should take £100 or at the very least £50. I pointed out that I was accepting £5 as a good will gesture, limiting the damage to £500. The following day the hole in one story made national headlines and I realised the extent of the scam.

I learned there had been several holes in one during the first afternoon. The so-called Hole in One Gang had targeted independent bookmakers like me. The gang reputedly made £500,000 before bookmakers wised up to the correct odds. Not just this gang as it turned out: many other individuals also took advantage of overgenerous odds in various parts of the country.

Some bookmakers refused to pay, and upon arbitration were ordered to pay out on the basis that the odds given were not a palpable error, but an error of judgement. One bookmaker fled the scene, reputedly owing £43,000. As for me, I was intent on paying Don. I took the bait and laid the bet with a generous heart. At least I was likely to recoup my losses from his future horseracing bets.

At the time of laying Don's bet, there were a few pertinent points I was not aware of. First, the odds of any one named professional golfer achieving a hole in one at any given tournament are around 2,500/1. On average there are 120 competitors contesting professional tournaments, all of whom play the first two rounds, leaving 50% to contest the final two rounds. There will be approximately 1,440 realistic attempts at a hole in one on the par threes. The correct odds for a hole in one should be around 6/4. Furthermore, during the 1989 Oakhill US Open, four players made a hole in one within a two-hour spell. Each golfer used a seven iron on the 167-yard sixth hole.

I called Don advising him I was on my way to The Honeypot with his golf winnings. I arrived at the pub around six o'clock on Friday evening. Little did I realise it was another of Don's setups, as he'd shared the story with regulars. On entering the pub you could have heard a pin drop, while everyone stopped supping and stared at me. I gingerly made my way to the bar where I could see Don's smug face. Suddenly the locals erupted into uncontrollable laughter; in the fullness of time, I'd made centre stage.

David once teamed up with his Uncle Rad for a four-ball against a couple of mates, Badger and Igloo Pete. On the ninth tee, a 466-yard par 5, Rad took his usual three-quarter swing, drilling the ball up the fairway, striking the middle of a telegraph pole 130 yards ahead.

He placed another ball on the tee announcing, 'You're allowed to reload on this hole if you hit the telegraph pole.'

Igloo Pete offered him a tenner if he could hit the pole again. Rad struck the pole for a second time and was full of smiles as he tucked Igloo Pete's tenner into his trouser pocket. David pointed out that the odds for such a bet should be 40,000/1.

He elaborated: 'Uncle Rad hits the 50-yard-wide fairway nine times out of ten and the telegraph pole is approximately ten inches wide. 50 yards x 36 inches divided by 0.9 divided by 10 inches = 200: 200 x 200 equals 40,000.'

The odds of an amateur golfer achieving a hole in one are around 12,500/1, and for a non-golfer like myself infinitely bigger. I was invited by my bank manager friend Terry to make up a foursome, as one of his clients had let him down at the eleventh hour. I told him that I wasn't very good and hadn't played for fifteen years, though he was desperate the game should go ahead for business reasons. I was feeling apprehensive, and to make matters worse I was attending a top venue, St Pierre Country Club.

On the first tee my opening swing failed to connect with the ball, removing a massive divot. Shamefully, my second swing ended with the same result, and I received a warning from a club official:

'If you fail to hit the ball for a third time, sir, you'll be asked to leave the course.'

By now I also had Terry whispering in my ear, 'Just hit the bloody thing.'

I became very anxious, though this time I connected with the ball and it dribbled off the tee into the rough. A relieved Terry was very grateful to the official for letting me loose on the pristine course. After six hours of torture, Terry lamented that it was the slowest round he had ever played.

Following my humiliation on the golf course I got my own back on Terry. While we were consuming a platter of cheese and red wine over lunch I started bragging that I was a much better pool player. Terry, not renowned as the best of sports, was quick to take the bait, and we headed straight to the pool bar.

During the game I offered Terry a fiver if he could win the next frame, with me using a broom handle instead of a cue. Cockney barman Andy, who'd previously crossed swords with Terry, was delighted by my provocation and promptly produced a broom handle from the cupboard.

In the wake of my bullish challenge, an aggrieved Irish fellow called Pat stepped forward, keen to take me on. He took hold of the broom handle and offered it back to Andy, asking for the complete article. This time Andy divvied up a broom, and Pat handed me a cue. By now Terry was insisting he should play Pat, though I tried to convince Terry that Pat wanted to teach me a lesson. However, this only fell on deaf ears.

Terry, who often referred to me as Dude, took hold of the cue, cockily predicting, 'I'll take him, Dude.'

Eight minutes later it was all over. Terry had been swept off the table by a jubilant Irishman waving his triumphant broom. Meanwhile, a flustered Terry was moving at a rate of knots towards the exit, with Andy bellowing:

'You're a cretin Terry. You had everything to lose and nothing to gain, son.'

Chapter 7
It's a Knockout

In January 1992 I decided to expand the business, opening a second shop. Unk informed me that his local independent bookie was selling up, due to a lack of trade. It seemed a similar scenario to the Betting Coup and I believed I could turn this business around and make a go of it. I found myself a business partner in the form of Graham Cordy, who agreed to take a 50% share in the new venture. Graham was a regular at the Betting Coup who previously chalked up board prices. I'd warmed to his honest, laid-back personality; he was lean, tall, of similar age to myself and spoke in a quiet voice.

Graham managed the new shop, which was ideally situated next door to a pub, and aptly named Off the Rails, as it was close to a railway station. It was Graham who introduced me to businessman John Coyle, who became my well-ordered accountant. In the meantime, I carried on the good work at the Betting Coup. In spite of the new branding, Off the Rails was underperforming. We also got off to a poor start when relief manager Lance was followed into the office early one morning by a man allegedly concealing a gun under his coat. Lance flatly refused to hand over the cash, and the robber proceeded to lock him in the toilet. Foolishly, he hadn't realised that Lance had the day's £800 float on his person. He continued his search for the money and probably got jittery, before fleeing the scene empty handed.

Off the Rails had another thorn in its side, a well-informed punter backing more than his fair share of big-priced winners. He was a successful businessman who on one occasion asked me to step outside to view his brand-new Mercedes Sport soft top, while thanking me for my contribution. It's usual practice within the bookmaking industry to cut successful punters back. In this instance, I reduced his £100 wagers to £50. In addition, bookmakers might also prohibit them from taking early odds, allowing starting price only. Shrewd punters take early prices, because fancied horses often shorten in price. This was a practice that I had to adopt occasionally in order to keep a viable business.

Don Dingle introduced me to his mate Pete Hogan, another gambling publican in his fifties. Pete appeared well mannered, but nevertheless he had trouble written all over him. The first time I called at his pub to collect the month's losses he climbed the open plan staircase in full view of diners tucking into their evening meal, tied a hangman's noose, and threw it over an oak beam. The diners looked on in disbelief as he announced that the bookie had arrived to collect. He then moved towards the dangling rope and began placing his head in the noose.

There was a big gasp and much concern before he announced, 'Only joking.'

As the months passed, Pete continued to telephone his bets and I would make monthly visits to his pub to settle the account. Win or lose, I liked to get accounts settled within a set period of time, even if there wasn't much money owed. Credit betting has the potential to get out of hand, therefore credit limits and timescales were introduced to wipe the slate clean. However, some punters didn't respond well to being stopped once they'd reached their maximum limit.

During day two of the Aintree festival, Pete phoned in a drunken stupor, advising that he was being chauffeured to the Betting Coup. He arrived soon after with a carrier bag stuffed full of £20 notes.

On stumbling through the door, he slurred, 'Pick me one out in the next and help yourself to the cash, put as much as you like on.'

I was grateful his driver was sober, and although he didn't know anything about betting, I shifted the burden of selection to him. Pete proceeded to spend the next few hours arguing with his driver, as he wanted to place the whole bag of money on any random horse race. The driver was having none of it and continued to place a string of £200 bets. Surprisingly, by the time they left, all of the cash was back in the carrier bag.

Pete soon exceeded his credit limit, and was unimpressed when I stopped him placing further bets. One evening he tried it on by phoning my home while I was out, placing a succession of £1,000 single bets on the evening race card at Ascot. Fortunately they all lost, though I didn't take his losses seriously, as the bets were taken in error. Unbeknown to me, his bankruptcy was imminent, and Pete was desperately trying to stay afloat. Within a few days he announced that he was insolvent, and soon afterwards emigrated to Australia.

In 2020, a survey carried out at Oxford University revealed that of the people who gamble one third or more of their wages, 37% are likely to die within five years. Meanwhile, other research uncovered that casino games and slot machines are three times more addictive than sports betting, because it is a much faster way to gamble, and should be separated from sports betting.

Pete remained adamant that he wanted to honour his debt, and that one day he'd return to settle up. A couple of years later I heard he was settled in Australia and regrettably dying of cancer. Astonishingly, he came back the following year looking as right as rain.

He marched up to the counter and said, 'I've not forgotten my debt, I'm a man of my word.'

I was elated and just for a moment I believed in fairy tales.

Sadly, he continued, 'I'll be back to pay you one of these days.'

Monday was my day to manage Off the Rails, giving me a weekly opportunity to assess trade. On one occasion, I was watching a two-mile novice chase with only one punter for company. The race had just four runners and the even money favourite was clear with about half a mile to race. Suddenly, I noticed a £50 note on top of a betting slip. My instincts kicked in and I asked the punter if the bet was for this favourite. He became angry and told me it had been on the counter since the start of the race. I advised that if he was so desperate, I would honour the bet, and rang it through the till. The favourite looked home and hosed until falling two from home.

Another Off the Rails client was a burly Scottish fellow called Angus; he introduced himself as a munition's worker. He told me to be wary as he didn't like bookmakers. I'd heard about Angus through Mr Jenkins, whose betting office was close to Angus's home. Mr Jenkins once told me that the sturdy Scotsman had knocked him out, though he was oblivious as to why. On the day in question, as Mr Jenkins appeared from behind the betting counter, Angus delivered the knockout blow.

I asked Angus what the problem was, to which he replied, 'I don't like him.'

Mr Jenkins once called me out of the blue, accusing me of pinching one of his punters. He was insisting that the Judas under suspicion was gathering bets in a local pub and telephoning the transactions to me. I was shocked at such an accusation and asked what evidence he had to back up such a slur on my integrity. He claimed that he'd gone to the pub disguised in a gaberdine mackintosh and dark glasses, spying on the individual from across the bar. Furthermore, passing bets inside a public house was illegal, and he threatened to shop me to HM Customs and Excise, as lawfully the bets need to be passed on outside of the building. This episode enlightened me to the extreme level of Mr Jenkins irritating behaviour, and why someone like Angus might want to punch his lights out.

Unk put me in touch with his old mate Jack from the social club. He was an elderly man whom Unk described as: 'Straight as a bloody gun barrel, though a little bit deaf.' Unk enjoyed his chats with Jack, and one day, after a good natter in the car park, Unk pulled away with his grubby money bag sitting on the roof of the car. Jack desperately tried to get his attention to warn him, though Unk remained incognisant and continued the two-mile journey home. On arrival, Unk was surprised to see the bag perched on the car roof, trying frantically to recall the morning's transactions.

In August 1992, Sky broadcast the first live goal in Premier League history, when Teddy Sheringham scored for Nottingham Forest in a 1-0 victory over Liverpool. With Sunday closure still in effect, Unk asked if Jack could phone bets to my home. A few days later, Jack called after taking lots of single football bets from social club members for the afternoon televised match. I had been expecting a call from my mother, and I wasn't too bothered when my two-year-old son answered the phone talking gobbledygook.

After a couple of minutes I grabbed the phone only to hear Jack say, 'That's all of the bets for now, thanks very much, cheerio.'

This farcical state of affairs set me off on a ten-mile round trip to find Jack and retrieve the wagers. Jack was sat in his garden, and had absolutely no idea he'd been conversing with a two-year-old.

Liverpool striker John Barnes became a headache for me, scoring goals that resulted in many punters cashing in. Years later I was fortunate to be introduced to John over dinner. I told him that he cost me a few quid back in the day, to which he seemed rather amused. I asked him about the goal he scored for England, when The Three Lions won in Brazil on the first occasion. The goal was described as one of the most memorable of all time. Receiving a pass on the left wing, he glided past seven defenders before slotting the ball past the keeper.

John, very humbly played the goal down, suggesting, 'I was lucky; the ball just ran for me.'

During my early years at the Betting Coup, a local businessman who owned several high-calibre jump horses began generating a big following among local residents, who frequently turned out to place a wager at big odds. I often stood these bets for large sums, which might well have wiped out a big slice of my reserves, though I was fortunate and always seemed to get away with it. By contrast, they wouldn't bet when these horses won at short odds. There were also some nearby trainers whose horses were often tipped; however, results consistently worked in my favour. Unlike Ron Bowen, I was willing to take these bets on, and losing tips became a main source of income.

Unexpectedly, I received a call from musician Maurice Glastonbury, whom I hadn't had any contact with for thirteen years. I heard through the grapevine that he'd launched a new career with his own management company, promoting up-and-coming talented singers and bands. This came as somewhat of a surprise, as he had previously blown his own chances of stardom – and mine too, for that matter – after his rebuttal with record producer Mickie Most.

We arranged to meet and he enthusiastically told me about his latest prodigy from the USA, asking if I would like to invest in shares. His star performer was Elvis Junior, the so-called son of the late Elvis Presley, who was soon to make a debut performance in the UK. Maurice was eager to show me the contract revealing exclusive rights. He then produced DNA results, laying claim to Elvis Junior, as the King of Rock and Roll's legitimate son.

Maurice's track record was a big concern, and I was quietly thinking, if anyone was in the wrong business surely it must be Maurice. Despite this I decided to take a punt, and I invested £2,000. Elvis Junior arrived in the UK and Maurice whizzed him straight into the TV studios for a live 1 pm show. This turned into an out of key disaster. Shareholders were off to a quivering start, and furthermore, Elvis Juniors were springing up like wild mushroom all around the globe. With the many newfound sons of Elvis, it wasn't long before Maurice's exclusive version disappeared, along with my investment. All I got from the deal was a couple of free tickets to one of the shows.

Maurice admitted, 'The whole thing has been a disaster. All that remains is a shed full of CDs. You can have as many as you want.'

Soon after, I was crying into a beer, and David Watts was on hand to suffer my hard luck story. He recommended I buy some penny shares in a company he'd been researching, in order to recoup my losses. He persuaded me it was a sure thing and without hesitation I invested £1,000. However, the company was struck off within twenty-four hours of my investment for insider trading. Being a forgiving soul, I still looked forward to our monthly meetings. We had much in common, as we were both going through divorce and each had a daughter and son of similar ages.

Roderick was a new face in the Betting Coup. A well-rounded man, always smartly dressed in suit, collar and tie, he enjoyed a bet on the horses, usually wagers of £100 to win. He must have been earning well, because he would sometimes lose hundreds of pounds and not bat an eyelid. He was an estate agent, and I had his business card on file.

One time, he bet £100 on a horse and settled down to enjoy the action. As I handed him a cup of coffee, his selection wrapped the top of a fence and he jerked, throwing the scalding coffee all over his head. Miraculously, the race continued, with both horse and punter unscathed.

One day as the summer heat intensified, Roderick placed £100 to win on a 4/1 shot ridden by Willie Carson, and the selection obliged. As usual, I paid him his returns soon after the race. Technically, I should have waited for the official weigh in, which is announced about ten minutes after the race, although most bookies pay out before the weigh in, in order to keep the cash flowing.

After I paid him, there came an announcement: 'The Clerk of the Scales is objecting to the winner, on the grounds of weighing in with an incorrect weight.'

Some punters are quick to collect winnings, particularly if they believe the result might be the subject of a Stewards Enquiry. An enquiry is usually called after a jockey weighs in with an incorrect weight, after interference occurs between horses or when a horse may appear not to be trying. A panel of stewards then question the jockeys/trainers on the running of the race. They also study film from different angles, in order to observe any possible breach of racing rules that may have affected the result. The stewards usually call the enquiry, though sometimes objections are raised by the jockeys themselves. After reviewing the evidence, stewards may reverse the placings.

Roderick asked me what happens in such an event. I explained that the winner was likely to be disqualified, and while gambling debts remained unenforceable, all betting transactions are recognised as a debt of honour, and I would expect him to pay back the £500. This principle is known as a gentlemen's agreement and equal to both parties. There was no response from Roderick, and I continued to settle the afternoon's bets. A couple of minutes later, I glanced out of the window and saw his portly shape galloping down the street, with my five hundred quid tucked in his pocket. As the saying goes, honour dies where interest lies.

A couple of hours later I telephoned him at his office, explaining that I didn't want to lose his business. He was quick to point out that it was my fault for paying out winnings before the official weigh in. I suggested that he might make a token gesture, by paying some of the money back.

He asked, 'How much?'

I told him that it was his choice, and he offered to pay a tenner, to which I agreed. The likelihood was that I would have never seen Roderick again if I hadn't enticed him back. I always strived to keep valued custom, as it's key to survival, and sometimes requires taking extreme measures.

Roderick appeared the following week approaching the counter with a degree of trepidation, before handing over a tenner. I assured him that we had reached a gentlemen's agreement and we shook hands. I got the impression that he'd won a sum of cash elsewhere, as he was holding a substantial wad. I told him I would honour all winning bets in full, and I was grateful to keep his custom. That afternoon, much to my surprise, he placed a succession of losing wagers, totalling £2,000.

In future I would pay out on both the official result and first past the post. At least punters knew where they stood, leaving them to concentrate on the next betting event. I believed this to be a good concession and felt that the cost was worth it, particularly as the overturning of results was quite rare. At the racecourse a Klaxon signals a Stewards Enquiry, and pay-outs are suspended until the outcome is announced. The nature of on-course bookmaking leaves bookmakers to pay out on the official result only. However, a delay in the Klaxon sounding sometimes causes confusion.

In July 2012, stewards at Worcester racecourse called an enquiry into a race, after jockey Paul Moloney weighed in one and a half pounds below his assigned weight. Officials accepted his explanation of excessive sweat on a particularly hot day, and opted not to disqualify his winning mount, Green To Gold. This was believed to be the first case of its kind. Coincidentally, I was at the racecourse, and I thought I was on to a good thing when the enquiry was announced, having bet on the Twiston-Davies team runner-up, Papradon.

On leaving school, David secured a position as clerical trainee in the open plan offices at the Electricity Board. He was singled out as someone not known for his dress sense, as his trousers were divorced from his ankles, displaying white mod socks. This was the day he first laid eyes on Mal Davis (Flatulence Mal), a man with an insatiable appetite for scrumpy cider, and a flawless accounting brain. Mal introduced David to a vicious spiral of drinking and gambling, and such impulsive addiction ended his running dreams. David began spending a disproportionate amount of time gambling on three-card brag, poker and daily visits to the bookies.

A degree of affordable calculated risk can be advantageous in betting. However, gambling problems (also known as pathological gambling, compulsive gambling and gambling disorder) can arise, and are defined by being impulsive and life disruptive. Spending too much money and chasing losses can have serious consequences. Gambling can be regular or occasional, though it may be problematic in either circumstance. Addictive problems sometimes manifest in other underlying conditions, such as stress, depression and anxiety.

David was a strong company man with a planned career path; he found his position in personnel both interesting and rewarding. He felt a constant need to keep his paperwork up to date, but nevertheless, his desk was a shambles and the thought of anyone rifling through his papers was a matter of grave concern. For this reason, he stressed over impending holidays. He was once advised by his boss: 'The graveyard is full of indispensable people.'

The office environment offered an opportunity to consider ways in which to beat the bookie. In a bid to get the edge, he'd sometimes stay on and record the results from a full season's jump racing. After entering the data on to a computer, results showed that the most napped horses (tipsters selections) won on average: one out of two novice chases, one out of four novice hurdles, one out of four handicap chases and one out of eight handicap hurdles. He concluded that handicap hurdles are the most competitive of races and difficult to predict.

He began doing particularly well betting on rugby. So well in fact, that I told him to place his rugger wagers elsewhere, after he and Mal were successful with a bet on Bath to win the Courage League title in 1991/92. They utilised their winnings to fund a trip to Paris to watch France v Scotland. The uncultured pair may have appeared slightly out of place when locating themselves in a boutique hotel within the old Jewish Quarter, in Le Marais, on the right bank of the river Seine. The area is steeped in history and hosts numerous kosher restaurants, which are very popular among bourgeois bohemian Parisians. After some initial enquiries to the whereabouts of the world-famous Pompidou Centre, they had a change of heart and began seeking out local watering holes.

The pleasure-seekers entered Le Parc des Princes Stadium a little worse for wear. With absolutely no idea where their seats were located, they were left to view the entire game from the exit steps behind the posts. They looked a sad sight, wearing recently acquired French shirts while singing 'Flower of Scotland'. Back in the old Jewish Quarter, and without much to celebrate, dinner for two was served in an upmarket Chinese restaurant. Having quickly demolished the first deux courses of crispy duck and chicken chow mein, Flatulence suggested a repeat dose. While tucking in, David accidently spilled a bottle of rouge vin over a perturbed bourgeois diner.

Chapter 8
At the Crossroads

With trading conditions noticeably tough, high overheads were a constant worry. The cost of the SIS service was substantially higher than Extel commentaries, becoming quite a burden on independent betting shops. The monthly fees represented my biggest operating cost. Two of the big betting chains, William Hill and Ladbrokes, are both major shareholders, and as such still have a competitive advantage over the smaller operator. With small independents being squeezed, operating conditions of the early 1990s were tough.

In response, on 27th January 1993, a group of independent bookmakers established the British Betting Office Association. Racing Data plc was incorporated five months later to compete with the SIS information service. Live pictures were still the domain of SIS, though independent bookies now had an alternative supplier of data. I signed up for the Racing Data service at the Betting Coup with costs notably reduced. Racing Data was a viable alternative; however, the model depended on a level of subscription, and before too long the company ceased trading. The only alternative was to return to the monopoly provider, SIS.

SIS continued to monopolise the market place, with exclusive media rights for all UK horseracing. In 2007, The Racecourse Media Group (RMG) was looking to maximise revenues for its own product, and decided to offer a service, creating direct competition to SIS. This was something that bookmakers had been hoping would happen for a long time. Disappointingly, it only succeeded in splitting UK horse race broadcasts down the middle, driving costs higher. These days, RMG rights are vested with SIS, while the Arena Racing Group offers its own broadcasts via the Racing Partnership. This has led to a combined annual picture service, costing bookmakers close to £40,000 per shop.

(A list of Arena racecourses is listed in Appendix iii.)

I was becoming more ambitious and arranged a meeting with specialist business adviser Phil Jellops, who was an encyclopaedia of knowledge on betting legislation. I had an opportunity to move the Betting Coup to a larger unit across town, at the top of a hill. I then shook hands on a deal in advance of Phil's visit. I also wanted his input on an underperforming Off the Rails; furthermore I planned to show him a third site. We arranged to meet at a Little Chef, though there was no sign of Phil, and I couldn't get hold of him by phone. He eventually called telling me to meet him at a service station on the M5 some fifteen miles away.

In order to save time I decided to take the back roads, with a view to enter the service station via the rear entrance. I soon got lost, calling in on a small business unit. An employee telephoned Phil, giving him directions to meet me on a cattle grid on the nearby common. A few minutes later I found myself in the middle of nowhere, with cattle grids all around, no sign of Phil and no signal on the mobile. After a two-hour delay our paths crossed, and I received a rollicking for wasting his time.

First stop was the proposed new site, which Phil quickly dismissed, as the town wasn't big enough to support a second bookmaker. The day wasn't going to plan and I was apprehensive about the proposed move of the Betting Coup.

After viewing the location, Phil advised, 'You shouldn't position a business at the top of a hill. People don't like walking up hills.'

The site was clearly not viable, though the disgruntled owner accused me of welshing, and not being a man of my word. For the time being, the Betting Coup remained in situ. I learned some valid points on siting: for example, look to site a business on the sunny side of the street; the general public are also more likely to enter if they walk past the door, and don't have to cross the road.

Next stop was Off the Rails, where I was thinking things couldn't get any worse. Graham was enjoying a day off, leaving Lance to hold the fort. While Phil and I were chatting about the lack of business, Lance announced that racing had finished for the day, and locked the door. As he began cashing up someone tried the door handle. Before I realised what was happening, Phil said that there was still another race to be run.

He then smiled at me, saying, 'If you want to increase the number of punters coming in, I suggest you keep the door unlocked.'

Phil came to the conclusion that the shop was poorly positioned, and it wouldn't generate sufficient turnover unless we relocated to a busier part of the high street. I agreed with his findings, and discussed the possibilities of moving with Graham, who wasn't sharing my ambitions. Not long after, I sold my share to Graham, and although the business had not been a success I managed to break even.

Friends and family were often roped in to assist on Grand National day, and in 1993 this included David, who was by now fascinated with my bookmaking operation and gearing up to join the ranks. He arrived early on Saturday morning, and I explained that we never made much profit on the Grand National, and that it was more of a public relations exercise: taking lumps of cash, and paying most of it back out. David enjoyed the experience, assisting first time punters to understand the rudiments of win and each way betting.

Each way bets can sometimes confuse inexperienced punters, whereby £1 each way actually costs £2: £1 of the £2 being to win, and £1 to place. For example, in a twelve-to-fifteen-runner handicap with odds at 8/1, a wager of £1 each way on the winner returns £9 for the win and £3 for the place: a total return of £12. Where the horse is placed second or third, the return is paid at one quarter of the odds, i.e., £3. When there are sixteen runners or more in handicaps, such as the Grand National, a place includes fourth.

(A full list of place terms is detailed in Appendix iv.)

As customary, locals flocked into the Betting Coup, and we'd taken a substantial wedge of cash by the off. However, there was a big rumpus at Aintree, with fifteen animal rights protestors invading the course. Following their removal, the race was about to commence when the starting tape became wrapped around some of the jockeys. This led the starter to wave his red flag, declaring a false start to one of the world's most famous race's. Although some horses jumped off, they were recalled by another official 100 yards down the course, and summoned back for a restart.

During a second attempt to start the race, the tape caught around jockey Richard Dunwoody's neck. The starter waved his red flag once again, but on this occasion it didn't unfurl. This left thirty of the thirty-nine runners racing towards the first fence.

Meanwhile, race officials posted further down the course were unaware of the second false start. As we continued watching the bedlam unfold on live TV, one race official ran out waving a flag, in a last-ditch attempt to stop the race.

At this point, one of my staff leapt to his feet, calling out, 'That's our dad!'

The race continued, though many of the riders became aware that something was amiss and dropped their mounts out. Eventually, seven horses completed the race and were led home by Jenny Pitman's Esha Ness, ridden by amateur jockey, John White, at odds of 50/1. The seven oblivious jockeys had ignored race officials, particularly at the fence known as The Chair, assuming they were protestors attempting to disrupt the race. Esha Ness's time was the second fastest ever.

The mood changed in the Betting Coup, with customers crammed in like sardines, demanding their money back. Much confusion reigned and we were uncertain of the result. Eventually a stewards enquiry declared the race void. This created a mammoth task throughout the country, as distraught bookmakers paid back a total of £75 million. The 1993 National has since been referred to as The Race That Never Was.

In spite of the Grand National catastrophe, David enjoyed the experience, and began working for me on Saturdays, as well as covering the odd day off. He found it stressful working at the Betting Coup on his own, as he would fret about the lack of toilet facilities. This became a real problem for David, particularly during busy afternoons, when a quick dash to the public toilet was not a viable option.

Excited by the prospect of a career change, David was gearing himself up to become a bookmaker, and a voluntary redundancy payment of £30,000 was a decent incentive. He was already an experienced gambler with an aversion to risk. Sport was ingrained in him as a participant and a spectator, and a chance to enter an industry combining the two was very tempting indeed. As part of the Electricity Board's privatisation process, one overriding principle to support staff reductions was that managers couldn't refuse any voluntary redundancy requests. The company offered some excellent retraining packages, and he soon registered an interest.

After the consultation process, he was taken to one side for a poster he'd displayed in the office: 'DAVID'S TOP 10', including 'Should I Stay or Should I Go', 'We Gotta Get Out of This Place', 'I Want To Break Free' and 'Howzat'. Some colleagues were not viewing the impending privatisation with the same excitement, and he was asked to remove the flippant references.

Setting up a new venture offered the chance to use his previous training and business skills. The generous severance package of the electricity company included time off with pay, in order to develop an alternative career. Management were quick to respond and confirmed his termination.

Meanwhile, David was considering what I had to offer as a potential business partner.

His solicitor Zac Brown advised him that many business partners set out with similar objectives, but for various reasons they may not be aligned in the future.

David told Zac: 'Johnny wasn't offering a betting empire or even a flagship shop. On the contrary, he was operating from a dingy little hut that offered less facilities than the bus stop down the road. His marketing was more about what you couldn't bet on rather than what you could. His time keeping was not impeccable either. Johnny was nevertheless a very good front man, a personable fellow whose sales experience was being put to good use. He had a very good knowledge of National Hunt racing, though not much bookmaking experience.'

We decided it was time to thrash out a deal, which was quite straight forward: each to invest the same amount of cash and share the profits on a fifty-fifty basis. David was happy for me to retain the Betting Coup as he felt sure our venture would outperform the Coup by a country mile. All the same, to ensure a consistency of approach, he would buy in at a later stage.

The year 1993 saw a change in legislation, introducing evening opening into UK betting offices. It was a hectic time for me, having split the business partnership with Graham Cordy, I also divorced my wife. This was a costly time, where financially speaking I had to start again. On the positive side, I still had a business, and I set my self a goal to retire before I reached the age of fifty. David became my new business partner and we shared a vision to develop a chain of high-street betting shops, with a view to selling out to one of the national companies, securing our fortune.

I developed a good rapport with two of my clients, Robin and Danny. They were successful businessmen, who firmly believed that property investment was the best way to make money. Danny had built four detached houses on the edge of town overlooking the valley, all with stunning views. He'd sold three, and for some reason he was intent on selling me the final property. Each time he came in, usually accompanied by Robin, he would continue trying to persuade me. Finally, I gave in and agreed to a viewing just to keep him quiet, as I didn't want to live in the area, and I knew that I wouldn't be able to afford it.

On arrival, I took one look at the magnificent view and fell in love with the place. I told Danny that I really liked the house, but there was no way I could raise the money. On the spur of the moment, Danny came up with an idea for me to pay a deposit, and the balance on a pay-as-you-go basis. He suggested that he'd keep a note listing all payments, and charge me a low interest rate for the duration. He also planned to place credit bets, whereby if he lost, he'd knock the sum off the purchase price.

I looked into the chances of obtaining a mortgage, but I didn't have a big enough deposit. Danny was having none of it, insisting that his pay-as-you-go scheme would work. My gut instinct told me this was all wrong. That said, on the shake of a hand I went ahead and gave Danny a £3,000 cash deposit. In the interim, I moved all of my worldly possessions (a drum kit and a TV) into the garage of the property, awaiting completion of final decorations.

Soon after, the pay-as-you-go scheme was seriously bothering me, and I called Danny to say I felt uneasy. For some reason he wasn't listening, and assured me that all would be fine.

I was a little stunned when he announced, 'I have to go now, as I'm on my way to hospital for an operation. I'll be in for a couple of days, and we'll get things sorted when I'm out.'

Danny died the following day from deep vein thrombosis. After the initial shock, it dawned on me that my £3,000 had been lost into the bargain. With no proof of payment, I wasn't sure if Danny had told anyone. A couple of weeks later Robin advised me that he knew about the deposit. He suggested that he'd mention our arrangement to Celia, Danny's widow, when the time was right.

A few weeks later Robin set up a meeting. Celia invited me to take a seat on her sofa and tell my story. After I explained my predicament, she made reference to lots of people crawling out of the woodwork, claiming Danny owed them money.

On reaching for her chequebook, she said, 'You shouldn't have been hassling Danny on the day he went into hospital. And I never approved of his gambling.'

She then wrote a cheque for £1,000, before dropping it into my lap and sending me on my way.

David's enthusiasm was gaining momentum. With considerable knowledge of the local area, he was very good at spotting business opportunities, spending significant time evaluating potential betting shop sites. Having armed himself with as much data as possible, including population and demographics, he researched the social mix and clientele of public houses. Traditionally, bookmakers like to site betting offices close to sports bars and pubs, and in close proximity to council estates.

He identified a betting office on the outskirts of the city, which had recently closed. The proposed site offered the opportunity to purchase at a discounted rate. Initially, I quizzed him as to why we were considering investing in a business that had previously failed. Having assessed the area thoroughly, and taking into account a Coral shop situated next door to a pub approximately one mile away, he convinced me the catchment area was sufficient to support both bookmakers.

The shop displayed a notice on the door advising on the closure, and how clients may collect winnings. Gut instinct told us that previous bookmaker, Marco, was a man of honour. We met Marco, a bronzed middle-aged Greek Cypriot with chiselled contours, who was happy to release betting slips for analysis. After viewing some claims with a degree of scepticism, we warmed to Marco's character. He was genuinely trying to assist us and he proved very reliable.

Having procured the services of Mr Jellops, he confirmed the site was workable, and proceeded to represent us with an application to the Magistrates Court, to obtain a joint betting licence. There were some spurious objections, which Phil dealt with in a confident manner, and the licence was granted. After divvying up the agreed purchase price, the deal was sealed and we took over the leasehold.

Phil ran a five-day betting shop manager training course, which David decided to attend. Within a few weeks, the newly named Winallot Racing was ready to launch, with David at the helm. This left me to continue developing the Betting Coup, which for the time being I retained in my own right. Meanwhile, I upped the maximum pay-out to £10,000, in order to attract more business.

Winallot Racing opened without much of a do in October, introducing a maximum pay-out limit of

£25,000. To start with there was a steady trickle of customers, many of whom were previous regulars. David was a little apprehensive, and kept a close eye on the door. First in was local hardman Keith Fry, offering his services as a debt collector. Keith also owned the nearby chip shop, delivering daily portions of burgers and chips, which became David's staple diet. Business grew quite rapidly along with David's girth, as a continuous throng of punters gained confidence in Winallot. The new boss was grasping things quickly, and relished the challenge when less scrupulous punters tried to get one over.

One trick was to write a selection as half of one name and half of another: for example, with horses named Black Rain and Blue Sky, a punter might deliberately write Black Sky, and later claim they meant the winner, if either horse prevailed. Another trick was deliberately to under-stake complicated permed bets (splitting the stake for a bet between multiple combined selections to cover different possible outcomes), in the hope that the settler wouldn't notice. One punter began beating himself in every race, betting 80% of the runners in combination forecasts; not the shrewdest way to bet, because the continued cost of multiple staking makes it practically impossible to win.

In December 1993, England were looking to replace Graham Taylor, after they failed to gain qualification for the 1994 USA FIFA World Cup. One of David's pals, Smithy, came into Winallot and bet £100 on Terry Venables to become the next England football manager, at odds of 10/1. We assumed it would be easy money, after recent allegations that Tottenham Hotspur manager Venables was involved in underhand dealings over the signing of Teddy Sheringham from Nottingham Forest. Venables had previously managed Barcelona, where he was better known by the sobriquet of El Tel, winning La Liga in 1985. He was favourite to replace Bobby Robson as England manager back in 1990, though, because of probity issues, he never made the short list of three.

Venables was announced in charge of England in January 1994, albeit as Coach. This was good enough for Smithy to secure his bet, and winnings of £1,000. El Tel remained popular amongst players and punters, particularly during Euro 96, where we had liabilities of some £15,000 on England to win the tournament. I fancied Germany to beat England over ninety minutes in the semi-final, and tried to bet £500 with a major bookmaker. Fortunately I was knocked back, as they were supposedly laying a maximum £200 to the trade.

David nervously watched the match in a bar, while holidaying in Lyme Regis. Meanwhile, I was having a beer with my cousin Pete, a staunch England supporter, who picked up on the fact that I wasn't cheering England, accusing me of being unpatriotic and wanting Germany to win. It was always difficult during these moments, where David and I both admit to having divided loyalties. While our heart was with England, we wanted them out. With the score at 1-1 after ninety minutes, Germany went on to win 6-5 on penalties. Soon after, Venables stood down because of impending court cases, which may have become a distraction towards his team's 1998 World Cup qualifying campaign. His record in charge of England was eleven wins, eleven draws and one loss.

After warning David on the pitfalls of credit, I was disappointed when he allowed punters to run up large debts, and we began to lose custom. We didn't take up the offer from chip shop muscle Keith, writing the debts off as yet another learning process. We firmly believed that we had punters' best interest at heart. An example of this came when David, in his infinite wisdom, approached Donald, a reliable customer who was in the process of running up a bill of a few hundred pounds.

He discreetly told him, 'I don't want you to lose any more money,' and capped his betting on the spot. Donald became angry, saying he had no right to suggest how much money he could lose.

He warned, 'I'll be in tomorrow to pay, but that's the end of the road.' Donald settled his dues, and we never saw him again.

Customers were knowledgeable on the core betting of horse and greyhound racing, while sports betting represented a small proportion of turnover. Saturdays saw a steady stream of clientele from the moment the doors opened. This included Stan and Ashley who frequented Winallot most days before departing for work. Stan's favourite bet was a Flag, which consists of eight trebles in the form of a Union Jack. The Flag is often referred to as a mug's bet, because if the middle selection loses it wipes out half of the bet.

Another character was Bert, who whenever he lost would quip, 'There's always the river,' a phrase coined by bookmakers at Worcester racecourse, because of its close proximity to the river.

By eleven o' clock there was a throng of activity among punters, many of whom smoked cigarettes. As the morning fare of greyhounds commenced from Hackney and Crayford, a convivial smoky atmosphere would appear in a halo effect. Hackney was closed in 1997, to be replaced by Romford. Banter proliferated, and the rush of greyhound bets was only interrupted by wagers for the afternoon's horseracing and football.

The televised race meetings on BBC's *Grandstand* and *Channel Four Racing* attracted lots of betting interest. The feature races were very popular, and very much a focal point for debate and predictions. As the shop became busier the level of smoke intensified, and the air conditioning was cranked up. When horseracing started, a further array of punters would emerge for race-to-race action. Good humour and micky-taking would prevail, while some had frequented the pub and were noticeably jollier than others.

Chapter 9
Down on Your Luck

I was still in the process of buying a house when my old band friends Colin and Karen offered me a room in their pub. Karen would often telephone bets through to the Betting Coup, as some of the regulars enjoyed a wager. One of them was builder Kenny Gibbons, a bit of a rough diamond, with a good sense of humour. He enjoyed a pint or two, as well as a flutter on the gee-gees and visits to the casino.

Karen phoned one afternoon, saying Kenny didn't fancy betting on horseracing, and asked if I would gamble over the phone; £100 on the turn of a card - one cut each, and the highest card wins. I agreed, as I trusted Karen implicitly. She then shuffled the pack and cut my card first, declaring a 3. I could hear Kenny cheering in the background, as his cut revealed a 10.

This became a regular occurrence. Whenever Kenny was bored, Karen would call me for the usual £100 cut. Kenny had taken quite a shine to me, and wanted to relieve me of cash at every opportunity. He was often awaiting my return for a late-night cut of the deck, pouncing on me as I made my way through the bar area, back to my room. Sometimes, when I was exhausted, I'd try and sneak through the back entrance, provided the in-house Rottweiler, Jet Black, wasn't on patrol.

Kenny and I became good matcs, and we decided to have a night out at the casino. On the way in he told me he was carrying £2,000 in cash, and I told him I was holding £1,600. I had no office safe in those early days, and I would often carry the entire float in my pocket.

On arrival I went to hang my coat, while Kenny headed straight for the tables. In an instant, Kenny came over saying he'd lost £2,000 on one spin of the wheel. He asked if I would loan him a grand in cash, and headed back to the tables.

I'd just bought us a couple of beers, when Kenny came back, saying, 'Come on, let's go. I've lost again.'

Casino players are often seen fervently recording roulette numbers in order to establish emerging patterns. Some gamblers adopt all manners of systems to beat the house. One of the most common is perhaps the Martingale system, which originated in 18th-century France, the simplest of approach, whereby a doubling up of stakes will eventually win. However, a losing run often finds gamblers having to invest a disproportionate amount of money. The theory also relies on time, limitless funds and in-house limits not being imposed.

A stranger once appeared bright and early at Winallot. He'd come to bet on the morning greyhounds, proclaiming that his system couldn't possibly fail. This was the last thing we wanted him to be saying to our regular customers. He explained that since there are only six greyhounds in a race, by selecting a random number and sticking with it, you'll eventually win. He was talking about the Martingale system. He continued by saying his chosen number was four, and by doubling the stakes in successive races Trap 4 would eventually win. Nevertheless, he would only bet when the odds were above evens, stopping at a winner, and guaranteeing a profit.

After all the talk, his first wager was 20p, which lost. He then proceeded to bet a sequence of doubling up, and losing on the elusive Trap 4 (40p, 80p, £1.60,

£3.20, £6.40, £12.80, £25.60, £51.20 £102.40). At this point he signalled that he was going to the bank, as he'd run out of cash. There was no bank in close proximity, and I guessed he wouldn't make it back in time to continue the sequence. The next dog race set off, and he was nowhere to be seen. As luck would have it, Trap 4 won at 7/2. Had he stuck with the plan, his final stake would have been £204.80, showing an overall profit of £512.20.

My Saturday assistant, and former schoolboy draughts champion, Russell, was now a brilliant mathematician. Russell was astute, a proven statistician, who designed his own bet settler on a calculator. He was very careful with money and always erred towards the side of caution, especially when it came to placing bets. Russell's bets were usually small wagers at big odds. He had his own theory on value betting: for example, in a ten-runner field he would only bet when the odds were at least 9/1, and in a six-runner field 5/1.

I sponsored a local charity event by donating several prizes and, as luck would have it, Russell won a free bet. As the weeks passed, I found myself reminding him to use it. However, it became clear that he was waiting for the right opportunity, even though I pointed out, 'It's a free bet, so whatever happens you can't lose.'

On 9th October 1993, two men, dubbed as the best of enemies, Nigel Benn and Chris Eubank, clashed in a Super Middleweight Championship fight, remembered as Judgement Day. Russell decided to place his freebee on Eubank, at short odds of 2/5, and also bet some of his own cash on Benn at 9/4.

Russell was confident, stating that he would make a profit on whichever boxer won. Bearing in mind he was the statistician, he didn't seem bothered when I suggested he might have a small wager on the draw, at

14/1, just to cover all eventualities. He declined, as during the risk assessment, statistics revealed the draw as a very unlikely outcome. The fight ended in a stalemate, leaving me to quote Russell as 'One of the only men in history to lose money while placing a free bet.'

On another occasion my honest nature got the better of me, much to Russell's disapproval. Two mug punters walked in, each wanting to bet on the Oxford v Cambridge boat race. One wanted to bet a fiver on Oxford at odds of 5/6, and his mate wanted the same bet on Cambridge. In this scenario, had I taken both bets, I was guaranteed to make a profit of 83p. I proceeded to tell the pair that they'd be better off having an even fiver between themselves, this way one of them would win a fiver, instead of £4.17. While I was keen to promote my integrity and good will, a bewildered Russell considered my business ethics as commercial suicide.

Early one morning, I was in the process of setting up shop when in walked a fast-talking American character called Basil. He was short in stature, casually dressed and spoke with an American Irish accent. I was meeting him for the first time, after he'd recently moved from Ireland with his wife. He wasted no time in telling me that his wife's brother was a successful bookmaker over in Ireland, operating with just one golden rule: never give punters credit. He was contemplating opening his own store, and threatening to knock spots off local traders, by opening 24/7, 'just like they do in the States'. Basil was brash and full of himself, predicting that he would soon be successful, whatever line of work he chose.

He was expressing interest in becoming an independent bookmaker, though he was astounded when I told him that I offered credit. He deemed all betting transactions should be strictly cash only. His brother-in-law had warned him about the pitfalls of credit, which were still unenforceable through the courts, making this a definite no-no. During the weeks that followed he became a regular at the Betting Coup, first through the door every morning and last to leave. He never came in on a weekend, the reason being that his wife didn't approve of gambling. I twigged that she worked Monday to Friday, and was probably unaware that he was spending all day in the bookies.

Basil was becoming besotted with my setup, and became a pest because he didn't bet much, placing just a few 50p wagers during the course of a day. He spent the rest of the time asking questions about the bookmaking industry. When he wasn't asking me direct questions, he was wearing me down with verbal diarrhoea, and I devised a plan to stop him coming in. He mentioned that he fancied a particular horse in the big race on Saturday and was considering placing a bet. I was quick to put him to the Achilles' heel test, advising that he was welcome to phone a credit bet on the day. He'd most likely forgotten that he'd given me his home phone number, and I guessed that if he welshed on the bet he wouldn't want his wife to find out about his gambling.

Russell was sniggering as he answered the phone, scribbling down Basil's vastly increased stake of £30. Basil insisted that he would be in on Monday to square up, come what may. The horse lost and Monday came, but there was no show from Basil. I waited a couple of weeks and decided to phone him, with an amused Russell present. This was more for fun than anything else, as I didn't want him back in the Betting Coup, making a nuisance of himself. Basil was a good example of a tightwad. Tightwads are usually very careful with money, and likely to spend much more when paying by credit. They tend to enjoy the purchase without the pain of parting with cash, which often leads to increased spending.

Basil answered the phone, and I asked him if he was going to honour his debt. Holding on to his nose, he pretended to be a lady housekeeper, but there was no real disguise.

I played along and asked if I could speak to Basil's wife about the debt, to which he replied in a very high-pitched nasally voice, 'Both Mr and Mrs are away in London for the whole of the weekend.'

I then asked him to pass a message to Basil's wife: 'The local bookmaker is chasing Basil for an outstanding credit debt,' and he agreed to pass it on.

Within five minutes Basil telephoned to say he'd received a message from the housekeeper, and would be in first thing on Monday to pay. He also warned me never to phone his home again. On this occasion Basil was true to his word, and paid off the debt. This was the last time I saw him, and I never got to hear how his career panned out.

Six months after the Winallot launch, we learned that a betting shop in the nearby town of Badgeport was up for sale. David was particularly excited about this as he knew the town well, and the shop was the only one in the area. We expressed our interest to the vendors, who were retiring from the industry. They stipulated that they would sell the business to the highest bidder, and liked the fact that we were experienced bookmakers. The shop was well established, and after examining betting slips and general financial information, we made a bid for the shop. Unfortunately, our bid fell £2,000 short and despite an increased offer to match the higher bid, the vendors stuck by their principle.

David was getting quite nervy over some of the bigger bets. Marco was singing our praises to ex-client Stanley, a high roller, who placed some sizeable football bets. He usually selected four odds on shots in accumulators. Sometimes the liabilities were too big, and we would hedge part of the bet. We had a good run with Stanley. However, his latest bet of £2,000 on Tottenham Hotspur to be winning at both half time and full time against Southampton was a concern, because we decided to stand it. As we sat watching the match in a local pub, Jurgen Klinsmann scored in the sixth minute, and Stanley's bet was up and running. Spurs were leading 1-0 at half time, leaving us to sweat on a potential £3,250 loss. Southampton were awarded a penalty in the seventy-fifth minute, and Matt Le Tissier converted. As Tottenham pressed for a winner, Le Tissier finally eased our nerves with an eighty-ninth-minute winner.

Football betting had been restricted to a minimum of trebles, in order to avoid match fixing. In the 1978 World Cup, Argentina needed to beat Peru by four clear goals. It's claimed that the dictators of both countries agreed that the Argentinians would win by enough goals to qualify for the final, winning 6-0 at the expense of Brazil. This was in exchange for thirteen Peruvian political dissidents, who were sent to Argentina to procure falsely signed confessions. Argentina went on to beat Holland 3-1 in the final. In a 1982 World Cup group game in Gijon, Spain, West Germany and Austria would both qualify if West Germany won 1-0, or 2-0. West Germany scored after ten minutes and the rest of the game was played at pedestrian pace with very few chances. It's remembered as 'The disgrace of Gijon'.

In 1994, Liverpool goalkeeper Bruce Grobbelaar was claimed to have taken a bribe of £40,000 to throw a match against Newcastle back in November 1993, when Liverpool lost 3-0. Grobbelaar denied the charges and was acquitted. He also won a liable case against *The Sun* newspaper. All the same, his name was tainted. Single bets on football matches were permitted from 2002, enabling football betting to flourish with a whole new range of bets.

Winallot proved to be a good site, surpassing all expectations, and breaking even within a couple of months. After the disappointment of losing out on the Badgeport site, we still had plans to expand, and turned our attention to the city centre. David identified a potential opportunity, this time an empty shop backing on to the train station, smack in the heart of the city. We asked Phil Jellops for his views, and after assessing the area, he confirmed the location had great potential. The landlords opted for us to become the new tenants, subject to the granting of a betting licence. Each site needed to be individually licensed, as there was a requirement to demonstrate sufficient demand within any given area. Individuals or companies would often object to proposals, which required us to be thoroughly prepared.

The main objections came from a local estate agent who had joined forces with the manager of a photography shop two doors from the proposed site. The grounds of objection were:

a. lowering the tone of the area

b. not complementing the other businesses on the parade

c. too many betting shops within the city boundary

They had got their facts wrong, with no evidence to back their claims, including the number of bookmakers in the city. The magistrates found this unsettling after Mr Jellops produced photographic evidence. Film supplied by the photography shop showed one of the bookmaker's positioned outside of the city boundary, on a quiet residential street. Phil's trump card was more graphic film, capturing a city bookmaker located on a busy high street with a large crowd of people in shot. The chief magistrate lost patience with their petty objections, tossing the images on to the desk and granting the licence.

By now I had a new girlfriend and I wanted to make a good impression. I decided not to tell her I was a bookmaker. This was because some people view bookmakers with scepticism and I didn't want to risk any disapproval.

On our first date, we were having a bite to eat when she asked, 'So what do you do for a living?'

Bearing in mind I always try to tell the truth, I paused for a moment and said, 'I'm an accountant.'

She then asked, 'Chartered?'

I replied, 'No, turf.'

Chapter 10
Odds and Sods

We agreed I would manage the latest Winallot office, which became our Headquarters. David lived close by, kindly offering me a place to stay while I was awaiting completion of a new house build. I was apprehensive letting go of the reins at the Betting Coup, given the blood sweat and tears involved in building up trade. However, my new housemate was also my ace card in recruitment and soon found me a replacement manager.

Unlike our other shops, Headquarters was a new site presenting us with a golden opportunity within the city. The shop had considerable floor space, with front and rear double-fronted glass door entrances, creating a bright warm atmosphere. We employed a specialist company to carry out the refurbishment, spending a large sum of money on a pristine design in our familiar shade of blue. Upstairs we had toilets and more offices, which we used for meetings and storage.

David introduced me to our new handyman, Bunny, who was also one of his poker mates. Bunny could be best described as a forty-eight-year-old, weathered-faced, wiry, Liverpudlian scallywag. As a boy he was paid to catch rats on the Liverpool docklands, where the rodents were used for baiting and illegal betting purposes. David asked Bunny, who was usually on the shovel, to install some shelves. With the Saturday morning greyhounds in full flow, Bunny arrived to carry out works in the upstairs office. Bunny was rumbled, when he was spotted

115

wrestling with a tatty piece of ply which he'd rescued from the site skip. It materialised that it had been cut to the wrong measurement and some last-minute adjustment was required. The shelves were way out of line and without middle supports, causing our files to slide from one end to the other. I wasn't impressed and insisted that his services were no longer required.

We didn't quite know what to expect in the city, and guessed it would present us with a new level of difficulties. We organised an elaborate opening, giving ourselves the perfect opportunity to introduce ourselves to lots of punters, while promoting a new maximum pay-out of £50,000. We invited two jockeys to officially open the doors: Carl Lewellyn, who rode Party Politics to win the 1992 Grand National, and Rodney Farrant, who went on to win the 1995 Scottish Grand National aboard twelve-year-old Willsford.

I got to know a sports reporter who wrote columns for a local newspaper. He advised us to offer a back show in order to attract more punters. I discussed the pros and cons with David, and we agreed it would be a good way of attracting cash trade. The back show concession is where the price of a horse has moved, for example, from 10/1 to 9/1 and the bookmaker is still willing to offer the odds at 10/1.

While David continued to build trade in his branch, I became focused on Headquarters. During the rare occasions we were seen together, we'd often be referred to as Laurel and Hardy, usually by disgruntled punters. Most of them seemed to like us and the fact that we paid out with a smile. However, we were good at hiding our emotions. On reflection, we were offering generous odds and acting with the utmost integrity in an industry often renowned for covetous gain.

During November 1994, bookmakers were hit by a relaunch of the National Lottery. The first English lottery was launched by Queen Elizabeth I in 1567, in order to raise money to repair harbours and coastal defences. The latest sweepstake saw its popularity grow into the people's bet. Many were disappointed to see Richard Branson fail in his bid to run the lottery on a non-profit basis. Prior to this, football pools were the nation's popular wager. The pools were introduced in 1923, and fell outside of gambling laws because they were considered a game of skill.

The betting industry was now up in arms because turf accountants were not permitted to sell lottery tickets. We faced the prospect of losing custom, as small stake punters might be encouraged to play for the bigger jackpot. During the launch, David, a vehement objector to the lottery, appeared on the front of a local newspaper burning lottery tickets. He pointed to the fact that the unguaranteed £10 pay-out for three winning numbers should be closer to £100.

The traditional high-street bookmaker needed to adapt in order to survive. Fixed odds betting on the Irish lottery was introduced, as legislation permitted this on the Irish draw. In a bid to compensate for the missed opportunity, we were able to offer higher odds than those given on the English lottery. The industry was constantly thinking of new ways to generate business, introducing an in-house lottery style, 49 numbers draw, which was intended to cash in on the lottery craze. Our worst fears were realised when a study found that bookmakers profits were 35% down, following the introduction of the English lottery. Indeed, some four hundred betting shops closed by the end of 1995. We were also feeling the pinch and began questioning whether we could survive.

During the 1994 Football World Cup, Italy were playing Norway. David offered his eight-year-old son a pack of World Cup stickers provided he could name the first goal scorer, and he picked out Roberto Baggio. David was in the shop when Dino Baggio scored the first goal. Almost immediately the phone rang.

'Dad, you know I said Roberto Baggio to score the first goal? Well, I really meant Dino Baggio.'

The city centre had its fair share of scheming punters waiting to pounce at every opportunity, and we knew we were there to be shot at. The industry was vulnerable to an array of scams and dishonest practices. SIS would often broadcast the known whereabouts of notorious fraudsters. One individual, known as the Pencil Man because of his practice of using a pencil to write bets, was appearing regularly on text bulletins. After writing a bet out in pencil for a later race, the betting slip would be processed through the till recording the time of the transaction. As usual, the bookie would retain the top copy, and return the duplicate. Before the race was due off, the Pencil Man would approach the counter at a busy time, and somehow retrieve the bookie's copy. He would then erase his original selection, substituting it for a winning forecast (1st and 2nd) or tricast (1st, 2nd and 3rd) paying high dividends. Following this, he'd slide his bet surreptitiously over the counter. He made fortunes from his scam, eventually doing time in prison.

Another fraudster, from the Midlands, would write dog selections using the greyhound's name only, omitting the time of race and the venue. This was unusual, as greyhound bets would normally be written as trap numbers – for example, Trap 1. He would target independent shops that didn't use off slips or were slack in their use. Off slips would be entered into the till, recording an exact start time and signifying no more bets. His trick was to place his bet at a time when it was obvious that his selection was going to win. Unsuspecting cashiers would not realise there was any connection to the dog race that was about to finish, assuming it was a wager for a horse race. He'd then present his winning slip while causing a commotion and make a quick exit.

One afternoon, despite SIS warnings, Winallot Racing fell foul of the fraudster's trick, after the cashier accepted a £200 bet on a 5/2 winner. The friendless punter approached the counter to collect his winnings, just as David realised who he was. David sarcastically commented on the bet being placed late. Nevertheless, our cashier had failed to use an off slip, and David felt that he had no basis to challenge the deception.

Dog betting was sometimes subject to the slow count. This is where the punter hands over their betting slip for a greyhound race, immediately prior to the off. It was usually a large stake, for which they'd count the money out in a slow and deliberate manner as the race progressed. Keeping a close eye on the race, if it became apparent their selection wasn't going to win, they'd gather up the money and scarper.

Headquarters was proving quite a challenge, particularly as our premises were situated close to the train station. Despite what our objecting friend from the local photography shop had implied, the location was renowned for congregating delinquents, some of whom sneaked in to consume alcohol or smoke illegal substances. They were not exactly good for trade and sometimes became aggressive when we asked them to leave. David once looked up to see a young man with his head immersed in a paper bag, and naively thought nothing of it.

One afternoon a stranger walked in, moving a stool up against the counter. He then placed a series of £5 combination forecasts and tricasts on greyhounds. I began feeling uncomfortable, as I had an inkling that he was up to no good. He was losing about £700 when I noticed he had the shop copy of a bet slip in his hand, and proceeded to drop it over my side of the counter. I soon realised that he had changed the trap numbers from a previous race, in an attempt to con me. I don't mind admitting I saw red as I walked around the counter, and without any commotion I marched him to the door. Maybe I had witnessed the Pencil Man, or just a cheapskate version.

One regular known as Mr Connor, tried to cheat us by leaving his bet and stake money on the counter, before legging it upstairs to the toilet. Without hesitation, the cashier handed me the slip, revealing a winner from a race that had already run. On his return, he had the audacity to ask if we had processed his bet. I refused to pay, because he was clearly trying it on. He became very agitated and complained about the poor level of service, bringing our business dealings to an abrupt end.

David came up with an idea to consolidate our relationship with regular clients. We arranged to take punters from both Winallot shops to Chepstow races, for a boozy Saturday night out. The trip was organised on a first come first serve basis, and two forty-seat coaches departed mid-afternoon. This left both betting shops empty on our busiest day of the week: in hindsight, not the shrewdest of moves. The racing was fun, and afterwards we set off into town as planned. We made an arrangement with our respective coach drivers to return by midnight and make a prompt departure for home. Unfortunately, three punters were absent for the return journey, having been arrested during a bar brawl and locked up for the weekend.

Wednesday became my regular day off, leaving David to take charge at Headquarters, where the slip volume was increasing rapidly. The average bet size was also much bigger than in our other shops. He enjoyed the higher stake bets and emphasised the importance of monitoring weekly trade. The national bookmakers were also keeping an eye on our bet volume by sending their staff in to place bets. This was easily done, as a sequential number would automatically print on the bottom of each slip. Sometimes they would cheekily ask us to put bets through both tills.

David got a buzz working at Headquarters, as lots of the wagers were for £100 or more. One high-rolling Chinese businessman was betting up to £400 a race, on both horses and dogs, just before the off. During the mid '90s there was no in-running betting available. Therefore, large wagers taken on the off denied bookmakers the opportunity to hedge bets. This gave cause for concern, as we were wary that a lucky streak might wipe out the week's profit, leaving us with significant cashflow problems.

Anyone can pick a winner, but it's what you lose in the interim that's most damaging. With this thought in mind, we welcomed big punters in the hope they'd lose in the long run. It was common for this particular Chinese gentleman to break even after wagering as much as £5,000. This scenario would leave us with a tax liability of £337.50, because of a 6.75% tax payable on turnover. During this period, the industry was charging punters 9% tax on stakes if they paid in advance, or 9% on returns.

David appeared to tolerate the dropouts a little more than I ever did, maybe because he could drink profusely, though his favourite tipple was real ale! On one occasion, a character called Jimmy wandered in, clearly under the influence. Jimmy had long, knotted hair, a rosy complexion and a trench coat that looked like it had seen service during the First World War.

Jimmy placed some small bets to extend his stay, before disappearing upstairs to the toilet. Moments later there was a loud thud and Jimmy came tumbling down, landing in a heap at the foot of the counter, knocking himself unconscious. Our cashier had first aid training and quickly put him in the recovery position, while David phoned for an ambulance. The majority of diehard punters were not perturbed, and continued to place their bets with legs astride a bloodied Jimmy.

One day a bloke called Jeff sneaked in and fell asleep behind the coffee machine. Approaching closing time, a punter advised that Jeff was stretched out on the floor, with his German Shepherd lying next to him. Before I had chance to consider my options, the last of the customers had left, leaving me alone with one man and his dog. Fortunately, the counter separating me from the troublesome pair was quite high, with a locked door to the side. I yelled at Jeff in an attempt to wake him, but the only response came from his snarling best friend, who was creeping ever closer. I was petrified and had visions of the animal leaping over the counter. Luckily, the dog soon lost interest in me and returned to its unconscious owner. I quietly telephoned the police explaining my predicament, and within twenty minutes my nightmare was over, as police swiftly removed both Mutt and Jeff.

When it came to paying out large sums, some punters failed to understand the bookmaker's hedging procedures. A good example of this was regular punter, Mr Wong, who placed a £10-win Yankee on a busy Saturday. The first two horses went in at starting price odds of 6/1, and 5/4 respectively. This left a total liability close to £16,000, should the other two horses win. I made the decision to hedge a £350 win double, in a bid to cover the whole liability. With large-staking punters, we were comfortable doubling the risk along with our usual hedging stakes, because we were likely to recover losses quickly. After the third horse won at 15/2, the best possible result all round was for 9/2 shot Kamikaze to win the final leg. This was because my cover bet would return a sum of £16,362, including the £350 stake.

Kamikaze was clear of the field at Uttoxeter, in the Bet With Tote Novices Handicap Chase, but came to grief after somersaulting the last fence, unscathed. An unhappy Mr Wong said I was lucky, and refused to believe that I wanted Kamikaze to win. He was narked, warning other punters of my insincerity, and I failed to convince him otherwise. His bet was still showing a profit of £2,172, while a full house would have paid him £15,812. From a business point of view, Kamikaze's failure to jump the last exposed Winallot to an overall loss of £2,522. Had Kamikaze won, we would have been successful in covering the whole liability, plus a further £200 profit.

Chapter 11
Gone to the Dogs

The first Sunday racing on a British racecourse was held on a trial basis, at Doncaster on 26th July 1992. While no on-course betting was permitted, a crowd of twenty-three thousand turned out for the spectacle. The Sunday Trading Act of 1994 came into force on 26th August, after further trials at Cheltenham and Lingfield, confirming there was a demand for Sunday racing. The first Sunday meeting permitting both on and off-course betting was the 1,000 Guineas meeting at Newmarket on 7th May 1995. The advent of Sunday racing meant that betting shops were now open seven days a week. This put a strain on some independent chains because of the extra manpower required. Our days of unwinding on the sabbath were about to become a distant memory.

We introduced a free-entry Saturday Nap Competition at Headquarters, which was designed to encourage cash customers into the shop. The contest involved punters writing their name and chosen horse on a betting slip and dropping it into the nap box, which was positioned on the counter adjacent to the till. We were offering a generous £200 free bet to the winner, on a specified handicap hurdle race. We chose a competitive race, where it was difficult to predict the winner. I would keep a tally of winning selections over an eight-week period, and whoever acquired the highest accumulative odds won the prize.

David encouraged me to monitor our performance on a weekly basis, using spreadsheets. This included data showing the average spend per slip, number of slips, the monitoring of expenses and overall profitability. Monday evenings were reserved for business meetings, where David utilised his secretarial skills, providing formal agendas and succinct minutes. I often put forward agenda items for debate, matters of importance that needed to be discussed. Despite my endeavours, time and time again he blanked me, and the agenda would show no reference to these matters. Instead, there would be a lengthy list of more futile issues. David liked playing company secretary, and enjoyed pointing out that my matters couldn't be addressed as they weren't on the agenda. The last item for discussion fell under any other business, an opportunity to raise topics that were not known previous to the meeting. Much to my consternation, my issues were often consigned to the end of the evening, in the pub.

During week six of the nap competition, a disgruntled contender notified me that the leader was slipping his selection into the box after the horse had won. By now, there was only two weeks to go and I set out to catch him red handed, keeping my beady eye on him during the penultimate Saturday. Towards the end of play, the same punter advised that the cheat had done it again. I checked the box and to my horror there it was, another winner at big odds. With one day remaining, I left the box on the counter as usual, as I was determined to catch him in the act.

David continued to consider new ways of developing customer loyalty, and before long he came up with a hairbrained scheme to own a company greyhound. Henry, one of the Winallot faithful, was supposedly knowledgeable about dog racing, suggesting we should invest in a greyhound and form a punter syndicate. The idea was that the business would fork out £500 for the purchase, leaving

Winallot punters to pay for its training fees and general expenditure. David was completely sold on the idea, and in spite of my reluctance and the fact that I'd never met Henry, he set out to persuade me otherwise.

At our next meeting, he added the words greyhound purchase to the agenda. Part of his cunning plan was to name the dog after the business, bringing good marketing from live betting shop broadcasts. This was a definite no-no for me, because it had clear potential for disaster. Relying on punters to pay for the dog's keep was of major concern, as I was worried about losing future trade.

Soon after, I went on holiday and, upon my return, David announced that he'd purchased a greyhound and named it Winallot. I was disappointed and expressed my frustration with this unilateral action. The punter syndicate was up and running, at a cost of £5 per week. David's only response was 'Don't worry about it, pal.' He gained sufficient interest, uniting punters with a promise of nights out at Bristol Greyhound Stadium, the same venue where I'd suffered a bad dog experience some twenty-five years previous. He left the purchase to dog phenomenon Henry, who would liaise with trainer Ben Strate, and update syndicate members as to the greyhound's progress. Winallot was evidently a greyhound with ability, and David was predicting that our dog would nett us a few winning wagers.

The final day of the nap's contest arrived, and I checked the nap box every half hour, while keeping my eyes glued on the cheat. Come mid-afternoon I checked the box for a fourth time, even though he'd not been anywhere near it. Woefully there it was, another winning selection, assuring that he'd win the prize. I was gutted, concluding that I was no Sherlock Holmes. All the same, I realised he must have an accomplice, slipping in two selections at the same time.

Come the day of the free bet race, I was quietly fuming as the cheat came to the counter to place his £200, taking early odds of 9/2. His selection was backed into 2/1 favourite and was pulling clear on jumping the third last hurdle. He was looking likely to relieve us of £900, which we would much rather pay to a more deserving punter. As luck would have it, the favourite crashed out at the second last, proving that cheats don't always prosper. This was the only time the staff and I high-fived a punter's misfortune.

On the eve of Winallot's first race, dog syndicate members were eagerly asking David if Winallot would win.

David hesitated, becoming bemused when someone else asked, 'Well, is it trying tomorrow or is it being stopped?'

His considered reply was that Ben Strate had Winallot fit and ready, with every chance of winning his race. He also stated that we would not get involved in anything underhand. In the meantime, I telephoned David, adding to his irritation, as I had impatient punters demanding answers to the same question.

David's advice was to back it, as the opposition was mediocre. Several syndicate members travelled to Bristol for Winallot's debut, each armed with sufficient funds. Sadly, he ran poorly, finishing in fourth position. A few days later it transpired that the dog had obtained an injury and would now be side-lined for up to four weeks. This caused David to chase weekly payments from disgruntled syndicate members, who were complaining about paying for an injured greyhound.

One of our latest clients was on-course bookmaker Roger Bunco, a blunt Yorkshireman bordering on arrogant, with an accent that didn't conceal his origins. He had a humourless face and wispy hair, and was only just tall enough to see over the counter. Whatever the weather, he was known for wearing a long khaki raincoat that barely cleared the floor. Roger's authoritative disposition lulled you into taking his integrity at face value. He placed lots of cash wagers, and asked if he could telephone credit bets from the racecourse. He said he'd sometimes get overloaded with money for one horse, and might wish to use us as an outlet to hedge bets. Our generous back show was particularly appealing to Roger, as this meant he could lay a shorter price on course and bet it back at bigger odds. David and I discussed the matter, and although the offer was originally aimed at cash punters, we decided to accept his bets.

Winallot was soon back in training, and David was continually being asked if our greyhound would win his next contest. He reiterated that the trainer was bona fide, and the dog would be trying his best. Henry was now keeping a low profile, leaving David to answer the questions. Soon Henry got word that the dog had real prospects of winning his next race, and we all lumped on.

Winallot performed admirably, though he was again defeated. Within a couple of weeks, he was due to race again, and Henry advised that the trainer was confident of its winning chances. We waded in with some hefty bets, though Winallot lost for a third time, leaving us with no return on our investment.

We started having concerns that Roger may be another conman, after he began querying losses on several straightforward bets. The final straw came when Roger took himself to Worcester races. He phoned just before the 2.30, placing £500 to win on the favourite at inflated odds of 7/4. One of our reliable cashiers took the call and referred the bet to me. Within a few minutes the race was over, and the favourite failed to win. Roger phoned within seconds, insisting that he had said he would call back to confirm, if he wished to place the £500 wager. The cashier had no recall of him mentioning anything of the sort. It was a straightforward case of Roger the Dodger not being a man of honour.

The Jockey Club was formed in 1750, a high-society social club with responsibility for regulating horseracing and the prevention of dishonesty. The first meetings in England were held in the Star and Garter, a tavern in Pall Mall, London, before moving to its current home in Newmarket. The year 1758 brought the first resolution, that riders must weigh in after a race. The Jockey Club took its name in reference to the medieval word for horsemen, pronounced *yachey*, and by Royal Charter it ploughs all its income back into horseracing. In 1783, jockeys were instructed to wear the colours of the horse owners. Until this time they wore whatever they liked, which often caused confusion. There are now eighteen colours to choose from and each set of colours must be unique.

There was little talk about Winallot's next race, until Henry advised David of the trainer's comments, that 'he wouldn't win'. In turn, David told punters not to bet Winallot. I also advised customers in the other shops not to back it. The opening show came through at 9/2, before gradually shortening into 13/8 favourite. In the meanwhile, punters were asking what the hell was going on, and why it had been backed in to favourite. However, I could only reiterate David's instruction. Much to our embarrassment, Winallot romped home, and none of our punters had backed it, and neither had David or me. As it turned out, Winallot had run his final race due to another injury, bringing the curtain down on this whole sorry saga.

Cashflow was becoming very tight, and we invited Phil Jellops to give his opinion on our falling profit margin. He was quick to spot that the back show was cutting profits by 4%. I must admit this should have been obvious, and probably my biggest failing as a bookmaker. After a series of self-inflicted mishaps, matters reached boiling point when a weekend's bad results wiped out our entire float. Before leaving the house on Monday morning, I found myself scrimping around for a float to fill the till at Headquarters. I was desperate for cash, and shamefully emptied my seven-year-old son's moneybox, for the paltry sum of £8.50. This increased the day's opening float to a totally inadequate £36. Not good for a city-centre bookmaker! With a chequebook on hand, we scraped through Monday by the seat of our pants, after Mr Wong and a few other hefty punters had a bad day at the office. Consequently, I was able to replace the £8.50 with a clear conscience.

On setting out in business, an accountant warned me about the pitfalls of expansion; in particular, at the point of three or four shops, where cash is often tight after business acquisition and development costs. In addition, owners who have to man one of the units have a tendency to get caught up in day-to-day management, losing sight of performance levels at the other outlets. This is a critical stage until a business acquires sufficient outlets to support the employment of an area manager.

With falling tax revenues from betting, the government introduced the Deregulation (Gaming Machines and Betting Office Facilities) Order, 1996. This facilitated open shop fronts and marketing in all betting shop windows for the first time. In the early stages, we were nervous about the general public being able to see who was inside our establishments, and continued to leave our shop fronts blanked out. There were two other facets to the legislation: first, we were allowed to sell snacks and refreshments; second, we installed two Amusement with Prizes machines per shop (fruit machines/one-armed bandits), with a maximum pay-out of £10.

Given the industry was heavily regulated, the introduction of fruit machines was a small concession. However, you were still able to play these machines in social clubs and enjoy a maximum pay-out of £100. David was keen to engage with our customers as to which machines to install. We chose a particular model that was popular in pubs, yielding a good average profit. This was good for trade, though David had concerns over certain individuals becoming addicted to this form of gambling.

One particular young lady would play the fruit machine on a daily basis, and appeared to contribute highly to the day's profits. David felt uncomfortable with the level of her losses, though he chose not to intervene. On the whole, we tried to be fair and give customers value, but at the same time we were in business to make money. The 78% fruit machine pay-out was heavily stacked in favour of the operator, with no prospect of a life-changing jackpot for players. There were no formal gambling awareness initiatives at this time, causing the development of gaming machines to create major social issues.

High-street bookmakers were unable to claim back VAT, as we didn't sell any goods. Though, after the introduction of confectionery, tea and coffee sales in betting shops, a new loophole gave us the right to claim VAT. Being VAT registered was good for betting offices, because we began receiving a quarterly cheque from HMRC which compensated for the hefty monthly SIS payment.

David considered himself as a part-time accountant, and suggested that he should claim our VAT returns, instead of the accountant. I wasn't confident that he was up to this task, but he argued he was professionally qualified in accounting. I pointed out that we were paying our accountant an annual fee, which included all tax returns. He claimed that the quarterly return couldn't be simpler, and there was absolutely no point in sending off paperwork to our accountant. I reluctantly agreed, providing he didn't mess up. He concluded our exchange uttering the words 'Don't worry about it, pal.'

David was at the Winallot office when two suited individuals marched up to the counter, announcing themselves as HMRC officers. On entering the back office, they wanted to inspect our VAT returns for the substantial amounts claimed. It transpired that the threshold for the amount of VAT that could be claimed had been exceeded. David and I were then invited to attend an interrogation meeting. In his attempt to take on the accountant's role, David failed to realise there was a claim limit. To make matters worse, if you exceed the limit you lose all of the claim. We were subsequently left to pay £7,000 back to the revenue. This was a costly error that would severely stretch both our finances and business relationship.

Chapter 12
The Bookmakers' Bawl

After a solo period at Off the Rails, Graham stuck his neck out on an accumulator. It was a familiar tale of a bookmaker taking a risk on an accumulating bet. With one leg left to run, he took a chance on a 33/1 shot in a competitive handicap race. This was the end of the road for Graham, who breached his maximum pay-out limit of £10,000. He had to raise the money in order to honour the debt, and was distraught about the whole incident. On the verge of closing his shop, I persuaded him to stay put and try to find a buyer. In the interim, I would be responsible for the profit and loss, while paying him a manager's salary. We agreed this, and introduced a conventional hedging procedure.

I helped Graham on the basis that he would receive all of the sale proceeds, should we find a buyer. This is when I first met a middle-aged gentleman called Gordon Bennett and his eccentric business partner Ross Forsyth. They already owned one betting shop and were looking to expand their business. The unsuspecting pair took a look at the books and decided to take a chance with Off the Rails. Meanwhile, Graham was grateful for the sale, even though he hadn't recovered all that he'd forked out. I became mates with Gordon, who was soon complaining about the lack of punters at Off the Rails. Fortunately, he was blaming Graham for selling him a dummy, not my good self.

Unbeknown to me, David had started exchanging bets with his new mate Mr Jenkins. One day Mr Jenkins called me, advising that we owed him a couple of grand. I told him not to bother me, as the debt belonged to David.

He wasn't accepting my story and said, 'The debt is part of your business hedging, and I'm holding you jointly responsible.'

This wasn't the case and I confronted David, who was embarrassed by the matter. I was unhappy with this latest development, as we were already strapped for cash. I offered to assist in paying the debt, and between us we managed to find the cash. I agreed this on the basis that David would no longer place bets with Mr Jenkins and cut all ties.

A few weeks later, I received another call from Mr Jenkins, asking if he could come and see me. He said it was a matter of the utmost importance. He called at my home, telling me that David had run up another bill, this time for £3,000. Once again, he was holding me responsible, insisting that it was a joint business debt. Wearily, I argued that it was nothing to do with me, though I would make sure he got his money. I sarcastically thanked him for breaking up my business partnership with David a result of his persistence, and showed him to the door. So that was it: the straw that broke the camel's back. With grave concern that David might sink, and take me with him, I made a decision to end our business relationship.

I met with David soon after, confronting him on the debt, though he could not justify his actions. I announced that our trust had been compromised and I needed to cut loose. David who once described me as combative, kind and forgiving, was upset. He asked me to change my mind, but the damage was done. During the weeks that followed, I felt awkward about the split and questioned myself over my ruthless actions. After all, David was my friend. The situation had the potential to challenge our friendship, as we attempted to divide the assets. To his great credit, we were able to divide the business on an equitable basis, and to this day we remain the best of friends.

We called on Mr Jellops to value the two branches of Winallot Racing. I gave David first pick, and he decided to take the smaller branch, leaving me with Headquarters. I now had to find funds of £20,000 to buy him out. Predictably, I was struggling to raise the money, as the banks refused a loan facility. I decided to approach Robin from the Betting Coup, my wealthy business friend. He said he would assist in my hour of need, but for some reason changed his mind at the last minute. In the interim, David and I parted company. As fate would have it, there was an additional financial crisis looming.

On the morning of 26th September 1996, David's helping hand, Badger, walked into work, commenting on Frankie Dettori's good book of rides. He passed over his wife's Lucky 15 slip, comprising four of Frankie's mounts. Meanwhile, back at Headquarters, I had a similar conversation with one of my punters, advising him that I fancied Frankie's rides, and planned to back all seven in a Super Heinz. Frankie's selections were popular in shops all over the country, with many punters jumping on the bandwagon.

The first race was the Cumberland Lodge Stakes with Frankie riding Wall Street, which he had earlier announced as his most likely winner of the day. Frankie dominated on the 2/1 favourite, eventually prevailing by half a length.

There were twelve runners for the Diamond Stakes, with Frankie aboard an inconsistent 12/1 shot, Diffident. Diffident burst through very late, to win the race by a short head. Next came the Group One Queen Elizabeth II Stakes. Frankie's mount was a 100/30 shot, Mark of Esteem, renowned for his turn of foot, accelerating past Bosra Sham in the final furlong to win convincingly. By now, bookmakers and punters alike were caught up in the excitement, sensing that something extraordinary was happening.

In the interim, I'd forgot to place my own bet on Frankie's mounts. However, I was reassured when Russell advised me that we had no multiple bets riding on Frankie, and I rubbed my hands in relief, believing I'd got away with it.

The fourth race was the twenty-six runner Tote Festival Handicap. Frankie was on the 7/1 chance, Decorated Hero, which shortened from an opening show of 12/1. The horse was burdened with top weight of 9st 13lb. Nevertheless, Decorated Hero forged clear to win by three and a half lengths. Alarm bells began ringing with bookmakers all around the country, pondering liabilities and the chance of Frankie winning all seven.

At this moment I got the dreaded call from the manager in the Betting Coup, advising that we had two bets accumulating on Frankie's mounts. This was very disappointing, as my staff were experienced with the hedging rules and should have hedged the bets earlier. Staff were trained to stand bets up to a maximum of £1,000, and therefore any liabilities exceeding this figure had to be hedged with other bookmakers. With his mounts continuing to win, early morning odds tumbled, leaving me in a precarious position.

When it comes to large liabilities, a bookmaker may sink or swim. The combined liability of the two bets were £16,000. Therefore, I had to cover £15,000 on Frankie's final three selections. However, when it came to small staking punters, I tried to work within a maximum of £200 hedge stakes. I had the option to bet singles, doubles or a treble, in the eventuality that any combination may win. On the spur of the moment, I decided to place a single £800 on Frankie's fifth mount, Faithfully, the 7/4 favourite in an 18-runner handicap. Faithfully duly obliged, winning the Rosemary Stakes by half a length.

The problem with hedging so late in the day was that we'd laid much bigger early morning odds. Staff had authority to hedge bets without referral, and the correct time to cover liabilities was after race two. Having netted £1,400 on Faithfully, I decided to bet a further £1,500 double on Frankie's last two rides. This way, I knew if both selections should win, I would cover £10,000, leaving me £6,000 out of pocket. I could have chosen to bet a £2,500 double, covering the whole liability, though it was just a balancing act, given either one or both horses might lose.

The sixth race was the Blue Seal Stakes, a five-runner event, which Frankie also won aboard 5/4 favourite Loch Angel. By the time of the last race, the two-mile Gordon Carter Handicap, odds on Frankie's mount, Fujiyama Crest, trained by Michael Stoute, had tumbled from an early morning 12/1, to 2/1. With tensions rising, the BBC interrupted its scheduled coverage in order to show the last race. Frankie sent his horse off in front with an uncontested lead and quickened up in the home straight. He was challenged by Pat Eddery on Northern Fleet, who could only close the gap to within a neck, and history was made. Not only did Frankie win all seven races, but he also achieved this amazing feat during one of the most competitive days on the racing calendar. The starting price cumulative odds for the seven-timer, referred to as 'The Magnificent Seven' was 25,096/1. Shrewd punters who had taken early morning prices, secured approximately 236,000/1.

David paid Badger's wife £980 for her Lucky 15, and one other punter who won £3.50, after betting all seven winners in 10p singles at starting price. Nevertheless, she failed to add the 25,096/1 accumulator. Ironically, it was my ex-business partner Graham Cordy who backed one loser along with the Frankie seven, in a 5p each way Goliath, breaking my maximum £10,000 pay-out, the exact amount that he'd borrowed against the losing accumulator that forced him out of Off the Rails. Having taken early morning odds, his return totalled a staggering £41,447, for a stake of just £24.70. Graham was well aware of the Betting Coup's pay-out limit, which was always prominently advertised. All around the country bookmakers were licking their wounds. I personally lost £6,000 after covering £10,000 in hedge bets, while the industry coughed up a total of £40 million. I felt a little demoralised about my own experience, as this would prove to be my biggest financial hit during eighteen years of bookmaking.

In February 2008, fifty-nine-year-old Fred Craggs from Thirsk in North Yorkshire placed a 50p, eight-horse accumulator with William Hill. He hadn't checked the results, and called into the shop the following day, where staff advised him of a windfall. All eight horses won, at combined odds of 2.8 million to one. This was reportedly the first time a William Hill betting shop had paid out their maximum limit, of £1 million. The winning bet accumulated £1.4 million; however, the small print resulted in a reduced pay-out. Mr Cragg's final selection ran in the Wolverhampton 9.20. The aptly named A Dream Come True prevailed at odds of 2/1.

As a novice punter, I was well aware of bookmakers' maximum pay-out limits. For this reason, I would avoid putting accumulating bets on with independents, because their limits are usually much lower. Without a capped payment in mind, it's most likely that an unsuspecting Mr Craggs hadn't done any sums over his accumulative wager. Otherwise he may have staked a sum closer to 35p instead of 50p!

As well as finding the money to buy David out, Frankie's Ascot bonanza added to my financial woes, as I needed to find £26,000. In the end, my dear mother took a loan on my behalf for £12,000, while another £8,000 was generously offered up by an old band mate. I agreed to pay them both back with interest during a set period of time. As for the Graham Cordy pay-out, he said he would wait a while, which bought me more time. All the same, he was becoming a little impatient by the time I finally raised the money.

David and I made an agreement that I would pay him a sum to retain the Winallot brand. He chose to trade under the new name of Lostalot Racing. Six months later, I had to remind him that he still had the Winallot sign hanging in the window. This was a big adjustment period for both of us, out here on our own. With trade picking up and results turning in our favour, we were on the up. While David still had ambitions to create his own chain of shops, I resigned myself to the fact that my dreams of expansion had evaporated, along with David.

Come the autumn, with the National Hunt season swinging into full action, a sight for sore eyes appeared at Lostalot in the form of Roger Bunco.

While sheepishly peering up at David from below the counter, he muttered, 'Ee, I've got a proposition for you, laddie. I've heard about your split with Johnny. In my opinion, that's a good move, as he's not the sort of person either of us should be associated with.'

In spite of David's previous dealings, he listened intently as Roger suggested he'd like to resurrect his credit account. David couldn't resist and set him up with a Lostalot account. Roger began betting with little money changing hands.

A few weeks later, David answered the telephone to hear, 'Ee, laddie. I want to place three £200 bets and ay up, win or lose, I'll be in tomorrow, come what may.'

The three bets lost, and weeks later a discombobulated David organised an extensive search trying to track the dodger down, but he'd vanished into thin air.

Two months after our split, David asked if I'd like to join him and his partner at the Bookmakers' Ball, courtesy of an invitation from Mr Jenkins. Just listening to this gibberish made me wonder if David understood why our business relationship had failed. In any case, there was no way I was going to join them at such a superficial event. David and his partner were soon to attend the gathering, with David holding a wad of precisely £3,000. This was the total owed to Mr Jenkins, and the perfect opportunity to settle his debt.

He passed the cash over early in the evening, before extensive units of alcohol were consumed. A grateful Mr Jenkins thanked him, and stuffed the banded wedge into his trouser pocket. Conversations deepened, and the night progressed with dinner, followed by tipsy party-goers stumbling around the dance floor. Mr Jenkins downed his fair share, and come the end of the evening he was completely out of it. David was just about coherent, and offered his assistance in carrying him to his awaiting taxi. As he moved in closer to grab one of his legs, he noticed the loosened £3,000 wedge abandoned under Mr Jenkins chair. David paused and furtively glanced around the room, before thrusting the wad back into Mr Jenkins pocket, and began the long haul.

With trade now booming at Winallot, I was facing a new challenge, as trade at the Betting Coup reached an all-time low. I needed to consider the best way forward, and as the months passed, I made a decision to sell Headquarters. This subsequently gave me an opportunity to return to the Betting Coup and concentrate on restoring trade.

During the spring of 1997, I was approached by on-course bookmaker Julian Rimmer, who was going abroad for the summer. He asked if I fancied running his pitches at Warwick and Epsom, as they needed to be manned for a minimum number of days during the calendar year.

There are fifty-nine racecourses throughout England, Scotland, and Wales. UK horseracing is often criticised for a general lack of prize money, which disappoints owners and trainers alike. There are four different racecourse grades, 1 to 4. Money is the main criteria for grading racecourses, based on official Levy Board and British Horseracing Authority general prize figures, which are updated on an annual basis. The greater the prize money offered by the racecourse, the higher it will be graded. Grade 1 courses offer the most prize money, for which the world's top trainers target their best horses. Owners are asked to pay larger entry fees, while punters are more likely to find increased value bets.

It's customary to see top horses appear at various courses, which tend to feature preparation races for horses on their way to major events, such as the Cheltenham Gold Cup. Lower-grade race meetings tend to offer lower entrance fees and remain very popular among racegoers. Some classy horses may appear at these tracks after injury or a long layoff.

Individual racecourse grading, and prize money can vary from season to season. To this day, mixed flat and jump courses receive separate course grades. In the 1970s, course grading was the responsibility of the Horse Betting Levy Board. During this period, there were five grades for National Hunt and four grades for flat racing. These days, there are only four grades, though they are not always readily available to the public, and sometimes held as confidential financial information.

(A full list of racecourse characteristics and estimated grades are detailed in Appendix v.)

Although I had no previous on-course experience, I decided to take Julian's offer and give it a go. I was responsible for my own profit/loss, while assisted by Julian's experienced book clerk, Mick, and floor manager Raymond. I was surprised by Julian's strategy, which was to make a mere £60 profit per day, after expenses. Even in 1997, this represented an abysmal wage for a day's work, and something I had no intention of emulating.

First, I accompanied Julian to Warwick on a Saturday evening, where he showed me the ropes on the quiet side of the course. There were not many punters, and Julian used tic tac (betting sign language) in order to secure me some business from the busier Tattersalls. After each race, someone would appear and settle the cash, which all seemed quite surreal.

Soon after I was let loose at Warwick racecourse, accompanied by Mick and Raymond. It remained pretty quiet without Julian's tic tac expertise, and I ended up even stevens. My biggest obstacle was working out the fractional odds, and calling the punters returns on the spur of the moment. For instance, a £10 win at 13/8 returns £26.25, and £5 each way at 11/2 returns £32.50 for the win, plus one fifth of the odds for a place, a total of £10.50. The old card system gave details of selection, stake and potential pay-out, and was manually recorded in an A2 ledger. Punters were then given a ticket, with a unique number corresponding to the bet details. The clerk would be required to keep a running total of liabilities against the field.

My next port of call was Surrey, on the North Downs, for the Epsom Oaks and Derby. Many punters get excited about gambling, particularly when winning a decent sum or attending one of Europe's most prestigious race meetings such as the Derby. Jack, a regular at Winallot, was renowned for his raucous laugh. In fact, it was so infectious it would instantly transform the shop's atmosphere. He once streaked past the Epsom winning post on Derby day, legging it through incensed picnickers, shortly before being arrested.

The first recorded race meeting at Epsom took place on 7th March 1661, in the presence of Charles II. Race meetings on the downs then became a regular feature, taking place in May and October from 1730, with prizes of cups and plates provided by local nobility. In the summer of 1779, Edward Smith-

Stanley, 12th Earl of Derby, challenged his friends to race their three-year-old fillies. He named it the Oaks, after his nearby estate. The race was a huge success, and the following year a new race was added for three-year-old colts and fillies, the Derby. The inaugural running was won by Diomed.

Twenty-one years later, Diomed's trainer, Mr Cox, on his deathbed, gasped perhaps the most famous last words in turf history: 'Depend on it. Eleanor is a dammed fine mare.'

Eleanor went on to win the Oaks, and the Derby.

In 1784, the u-shaped Grade 1 racecourse was extended to its current distance of one mile and a half, and Tattenham Corner was introduced: the tight bend and camber make it the ultimate test for a racehorse. During the 1913 running of the Derby, suffragette Emily Davison was killed after she threw herself in front of King George V's horse, Amner. The famous course offers significantly fewer racing days than most. However, it hosts a crowd capacity of one hundred and thirty thousand, including all those who view the course from the Downs. The Derby was moved from Wednesdays to the first Saturday in June in 1995, leaving Oaks day to precede it.

I had a disastrous first day, losing a few grand. Therefore I decided to get stuck into the Derby favourite the following day. I was nervous about calling the bets on such a busy day, but at least I had a decent chance to make some money on the big race. Entrepreneur was odds-on favourite, after winning the Newmarket 2,000 Guineas five weeks earlier. The Derby was usually a very competitive race. All the same, the starting odds of 4/6 made Entrepreneur the shortest-priced favourite since Tudor Minstrel was beaten at 4/7 in 1947.

My generous offer of 4/5 about the favourite enticed many punters forward, waving their cash.

This upset my book clerk and floor manager to such a degree that they described my unorthodox approach as reckless. On reflection they were probably right, but I had my mind fixed on regaining Friday's losses, plus interest. Entrepreneur was beaten over eight lengths into fourth place by the John Gosden-trained Benny the Dip. All in all, a great experience, but this was to be my last stand as a racecourse bookmaker, as I preferred the more familiar environment of the betting office.

Chapter 13
Daylight Robbery

On offering Winallot for sale, there was much interest, and I sold out to an independent chain. One of the national companies had been keen to take the shop. I told them their offer was too low, and the buyer advised that was the maximum they would go to. Shortly after, I met with two guys from the independent bookies in a curry house, and sold the shop for a six-figure sum and a chicken jalfrezi. The following week the buyer from the national firm offered me an additional £7,000 above the sale price. I turned him down, as I'd already shaken hands on a deal, and I didn't feel the urge to welsh on this one.

I left Headquarters on a quiet Wednesday, a day filled with mixed emotion. We served up a lavish buffet to show appreciation for our punters' loyal support. Several months later, I bumped into ex-Winallot regular Mike and bought him a pint. To my astonishment, he began boasting that he'd once conned me out of £500. I've run into him a few times since, and each time he shakes my hand, laughs and reminds me of the day he turned me over. It's as if he's proud of it. The saddest thing of all is I don't know when or how he achieved it.

I was soon back in the claustrophobic environment of the Betting Coup, and began rebuilding the business with a skeleton staff. Initially, some of the old faithful from Headquarters were missing me, and made the long drive to continue our association. This didn't last for too long, as they struggled to hide their disappointment over the Coup, and I never saw them again. Also, my old friend Mr Wong telephoned, enquiring if I would take single bets to the tune of £20,000 on Premier League football matches. It turned out that he and some other restaurateurs had formed a betting syndicate, but they were apparently struggling to get their bets on.

While there is always a temptation to make easy money, many small, independent bookmakers are reluctant to risk a big hit on a single event. Having recently sold a business, I had lots of cash to back me up. All the same, I didn't feel this level of risk to be worthwhile. If the syndicate found themselves on a winning streak of, say, four wins in a row at odds of 1/2, I would soon be £40,000 in arrears. In the past I've struggled to place my own £500 bets with national firms, and the prospect of hedging large sums would be difficult. Therefore, I didn't want the hassle of taking them on.

I was right to be wary, because soon after, Asian betting syndicates were infiltrating British sport. In 1997, a Malaysian syndicate received a six-figure pay-out after the floodlights failed seconds after Frank Lampard had equalised for West Ham against Crystal Palace during a Premier League match. The incident resulted in the game being abandoned. Unlike the UK, where bets are void for incomplete matches, illegal betting in Malaysia on games abandoned in the second half were settled on the score at that time. The syndicate got away with the scam a second time, but were caught out on their third attempt in a game between Charlton and Liverpool. A security guard who was bribed to trip the electrics told a colleague about the plan and he in turn alerted the police. Four men were sentenced to between eighteen months and four years in prison.

After his retirement from the factory, Unk announced that he was making a comeback for the works football team. He was an accomplished centre forward back in the day and a renowned goal scorer. I accompanied him to the match, for which he was substitute, though the manager promised to bring him on for the last ten minutes. Before kick-off he was boasting that he would definitely score, even though he wouldn't have much time. He seemed quietly confident taking money off all his teammates, who were betting that he wouldn't score.

Unk's side were winning 3-1 as he proudly ran on for the remaining minutes with his teammates encouraging him. There was a humorous moment as he joined the game, he turned to the referee and said, 'I'll show these buggers.' Within seconds, he received a pass from his goalkeeper and slotted it straight into his own net. Unk pocketed the money, advising teammates that he hadn't stipulated which team he would score for.

Independent bookmakers would sometimes stress over section football coupon bets, where you pick three from each of the five sections. I imposed a maximum pay-out limit of £3,000 in order to avoid hedging bets. David chose not to lower pay-out limits, leaving himself exposed to possible five-figure pay-outs. Each Saturday he'd frantically phone William Hill to hedge these liabilities, just before the deadline. That being said, the task was made impossible when punter's placed wagers at the last minute.

I've always enjoyed betting on Premier League football, and following my fair share of wagers on match odds, I started to realise that there was bigger value to be found on correct scores. As a calculation, I strictly evaluate team selection. I then consider how many goals the home team have scored during their last three home games and divide the number by three. Next, I consider how many goals the away team have scored in their last three away games and again divide the number by three. The two figures act as an indicator of the anticipated score. Where it doesn't appear clear cut, I adjust the scores marginally up or down by considering league table positions.

Rather than bet randomly on televised matches, it might pay to specialise in following one, or just a few teams. I'm particularly keen to bet on calculated low-scoring teams, because it's easier to adjust bets during play. However, bets during play should be limited, otherwise it becomes expensive and the value may be lost.

In 2019, I filed a dispute with the Independent Betting Adjudication Service against a multinational firm, regarding an underpaid return on a football accumulator. The shop manager clearly didn't understand the company rules, and to make matters worse she became rude and abusive.

Shortly after, a senior customer service manager explained, 'Shop staff are no longer fully trained.'

As it turned out, I didn't use the arbitration service as the firm in question agreed to pay up. My colleague Russell also suffered a poor level of service, while trying to place an ante post bet on the famous Doncaster St Leger. Sadly, none of the staff or the manager had ever heard of England's oldest classic horse race.

In 2018, Bet 365 made £2 billion gross profit, with the Chief Executive drawing £265 million. Prior to the 2020 Covid-19 lockdown, some high-ranking betting firms had fallen foul of the Gambling Commission, because of a lack in social responsibility. Betway were fined £11,600,000 for failing to protect addicts and laundering money. The Commission found that one customer deposited £8,000,000 and lost £4,000,000 during a four-year period. Another client lost

£187,000 in two days. There were also findings of £5,800,000, which was likely to have been the proceeds from crime.

In contrast to gambling awareness initiatives, major firms continued to entrap new clientele, with much emphasis on football betting and casino games. In August 2019, the Betting and Gaming Council announced that its members would take a number of voluntarily measures on advertising, including a whistle-to-whistle ban on adverts during live sport. In April 2020, members removed television and radio adverts in exchange for online slots of casino and bingo during lockdown. Previous to this, a ban on credit card betting was introduced. By 2021, no less than eight Premier League teams were sponsored by betting companies, making them an integral part of the English Premier League. Meanwhile, football became the sport with the highest betting turnover.

In the lead up to the 1997 UK General Election, the Provisional IRA made several bomb threats. On 5th April, the Grand National was scheduled to come under starters orders at 3.45 pm. However, a bomb threat was communicated at 2.49 pm. It was claimed that at least one device had been planted at Aintree racecourse, and because the caller used recognised code words, police took the threat seriously. Subsequently, sixty thousand racegoers were evacuated, and police carried out two controlled explosions.

Unk was feeling despondent after his phone stopped ringing. He was spotted sitting by the window, with a black cover draped over the telephone, representing Black Saturday. The race was rescheduled to take place two days later, on Monday. This left some twenty thousand racegoers stranded, before they were generously offered beds by accommodating Liverpudlians. These kind gestures led one newspaper to pen a headline based on Churchill's wartime quote: 'We will fight them on the Beechers.'

The following morning, I placed punters' big race stakes of £7,000 in a briefcase in the boot of my car and set out to view a house that I was considering renting. I parked the car on the street outside and the estate agent showed me around, taking some twenty minutes. On my way out, I looked towards the car, and to my horror, the boot was wide open. I felt physically sick as I crossed the road, fearing the worse. I peered into the boot, and to my astonishment, the briefcase was still there, along with all its contents.

The New Zealand-bred horse Lord Gyllene won the delayed Grand National at odds of 14/1, beating Suny Bay by twenty-five lengths. The postponement cost David an additional £1,000, since Saturday's odds were two points lower. Subsequently, it was announced that a further bomb threat had been made on the Monday, though police treated it as a hoax.

David became aware that the betting office in Badgeport was back on the market. Results had gone against the new owners, who now wanted out, and, as a consequence, the asking price had halved. David approached the bank for a loan and they turned him down. He then turned to his trusted pal, Flatulence Mal, who agreed to loan him the money. He arranged a meeting with the vendors, offering them the asking price of £15,000, and, to demonstrate commitment, he dished out a deposit of £500, sealing the deal with a handshake. The vendors subsequently received a higher offer, but they honoured their original agreement in true bookmaker tradition. On appointing a full-time manager at Lostalot, David set about rebuilding trade at the newly acquired Lostalot, Badgeport.

With or without me, David's business was expanding, and he asked Flatulence Mal to assist with a business plan. The driving force was to secure the bank's support for future acquisition plans, and development. Mal was experienced and keen to utilise his expert accounting skills. The result was a plan that was second to none, leaving David's bank manager extremely impressed. Never had he seen such a detailed five-year financial projection for this size of business.

Shop number three was on the horizon, after David found a site in the city, with significant potential. He organised a meeting with the bank manager, requesting a business loan of £50,000. This was backed up with evidence that both Lostalot shops were performing well. The manager gave David positive vibes, stating that he'd need final approval from his regional manager.

Two days later David received a telephone call, advising that the loan had been turned down. He was perplexed. Even so, the reality is that banks aren't willing to loan bookmakers money without collateral. This was something I had previously put to David, and despite this, he approached the bank again, armed with financial projections on another site. The manager seemed convinced, and put it to the regional manager for ratification. The proposal was again rejected, leaving a dispirited David to describe them as a 'band of thieves'.

David employed one of his old pals, Dai, who'd retired from the Electricity Board a few years earlier. Dai was born in Llanelli and proud of his homeland. A kind and thoughtful man, renowned for his dry sense of humour. His active sporting days had become a thing of the distant past and he was enjoying a good social life, with a quenchless appetite for beer. Both Dai and David were very competitive, and in spite of a twenty-year age gap they once opposed each other on opposite sides during a rugby match. At one stage David was closing in on Dai, playing at fullback, only for Dai to punt the ball far down the field, shouting 'Go and fetch that, Boyo.' Dai the Pencil became a trusted member of staff at both Winallot and Lostalot. He obtained his nickname from punters, after insisting on settling bets by using old long-hand methods and a short stubby pencil. Punters often moaned about him for being too slow.

One such punter was Lostalot faithful Sebastian, an enigmatic, suave individual, with blonde flowing hair. He was very popular with the ladies, a man about town who usually placed wagers of £100. Sebastian once disappeared without trace, after trying to convince his estranged wife about the merits of going on a two-week rugby tour of Australia with the boys. In spite of his efforts she was having none of it, and he secretly packed a suitcase, hiding it under the bed. On the day of departure, his wife was about to leave for work and reminded Sebastian to get some bread. As soon as she left, he was off down under. On his eventual return his wife opened the door and glared at him.

In an attempt to diffuse the situation, he enquired, 'Did you want white or brown?'

Sebastian had a shrewd nose for value, and was known for placing an occasional ante post bet. Hunter chaser Teeton Mill had moved to trainer Venetia William's in early 1998, catching Sebastian's eye after winning the Badger Beer Chase at Wincanton. The horse followed up with wins in the Hennessey Gold Cup at Newbury and the King George at Kempton. He was particularly impressed by the six-length Kempton victory, and placed an ante post bet of £4,000 on Teeton Mill to win the Cheltenham Gold Cup at odds of 5/1.

During January, there were rumours over the horse's wellbeing: nevertheless, the gelding won a Grade 1 Chase at Ascot, in February. A couple of weeks before the Gold Cup, Sebastian heard that the horse had pricked its foot and enquired about the status of his bet. David confirmed that, under ante post rules, he would lose his money should the horse be withdrawn. David had already hedged part of the bet, though he generously offered to give Sebastian half of his stake back, should Teeton Mill be withdrawn. The horse made the starting line up as 7/2 second favourite, behind Irish raider Florida Pearl. Teeton Mill made several mistakes and pulled up lame after the ninth fence, never to race again.

The following morning the door flew open and in charged Sebastian, a man of his word, proclaiming, 'I'm never going to have a bet on a horse ever again.'

He then left as swiftly as he had arrived.

On-course tax-free betting often attracted large stake punters, and Lostalot punter, Vince Gooding, took himself to Ludlow to place a single bet on a sure thing. His selection was travelling well, when the jockey appeared to jump out of the side door. Vince was furious and chased after the jockey, before being rugby tackled by security staff.

Ascot began hosting jump racing in 1965, and I once made the journey to place a £500 wager on one of Sir Anthony McCoy's favourite horses, Deano's Beeno, 9/4 favourite in the Grade 1 Long Walk Hurdle. Unfortunately, the talented colt was beaten fourteen lengths on this occasion by French horse Baracouda. All the same, I'd saved myself £45 in betting duty.

During the 1998 Football World Cup, England were playing Argentina in the last sixteen. David tried to book a taxi to take him and his girlfriend to a local rugby club to watch the game. The taxi companies were extremely busy, so he decided to drive, with a plan to return home in a taxi. England had the upper hand until David Beckham foolishly took a flick at midfielder Simeone, and was sent off, leaving his teammates to lose on penalties.

England were out; another good result for bookies, as we wouldn't have to sweat over the usual big liabilities. Several pints later, David took his partner to the nearby Lostalot office, in order to wait for a taxi. Since there was an Indian takeaway next door, lamb rogan josh and chicken biryani were soon on the table. David then made the mistake of consuming supper while watching the match highlights. This inflamed his partner who'd seen enough football and she stormed out, heading for home some five miles away. The taxi never arrived, so, with concern for her safety, he made the ill-fated decision to jump in his car and drive after her.

One mile or so along the road he spotted her, and tried to coax her into his latest decrepit motor. She ignored his advances and kept walking. He eventually persuaded her into the car, and they headed for home. In the meantime, a police patrol had noticed his antics, which appeared to be a form of harassment. The discordant pair were continuing on their journey when David noticed flashing lights behind and panic set in. The police car overtook, forcing him to brake, as the Cavalier teetered to a grinding halt.

In a moment of madness, David recalled someone telling him to flee the scene, if stopped by police when over the drink drive limit. Impulsively, he clambered out of the vehicle, and legged it in the opposite direction, towards open fields. His misfortune continued, because a police dog handling unit had also pulled over, thus blocking the escape route. Veering off to the left, he ran up a gravel drive and lost his footing, ending up flat on his face, while confronted by an officer of the law and a German Shepherd dog.

During a period of cycling to and fro, David's expansion plans were still at the forefront of affairs, and he made the decision to switch his accountancy business to local accountant Dick Griffiths. He believed that Dick was the man to enhance his business, as he was associated with business growth. Sadly, things didn't go to plan, because Dick was undependable. This became the monumental moment when David instructed one of the UK's leading accountancy firms, a costly affair that would increase his annual fees from £600 to £8,400.

While chatting over a beer, I queried his extravagant decision. He explained that, in spite of a long association with the bank, they remained reluctant to loan him money for expansion. His new theory was straight forward: if the accounts and business projection plan were to be presented by a top firm, the bank would be much more likely to loan the money. There was no changing his mind, as he was determined with this course of action.

Eighteen months later, having forked out some £13,000 in accounting fees, David arranged an appointment with the bank manager to discuss his latest scheme. Banks have often been accused of handing out umbrellas while the sun shines and taking them back when it's raining. In David's case there never was an offer of an umbrella, whatever the climate. However, on this occasion, he was thoroughly prepared, dotting all of the i's, and crossing all of the t's. Things were much different, as his latest presentation offered a set of improved accounts, accompanied by a new business plan, with five-year projections. The icing on the cake was the submission, which had been prepared by a Rolls-Royce firm of accountants.

The meeting appeared to be going well as the manager read through the financial projections. He suggested there was absolutely no reason why the bank would not approve, needing only to run it past the powers that be. David was brimming with confidence, and began formulating an action plan that included shop refurbishment and the acquisition of a new site. With optimism at an all-time high, the bank dropped one final bombshell, blowing both David's plans and posh firm of accountants to smithereens.

Meanwhile, I planned to use the proceeds from the Winallot sale, and move the Betting Coup to a more prominent high-street position. This proved no easy task, because there was no availability on the desired streets, as previously mapped out by Mr Jellops. Eventually, I purchased a freehold some 50 yards away, with a maisonette above. The process had taken fifteen months, and a further three months to carry out general works. The shop fit looked good in the usual shade of blue, with plenty of space for an additional office, kitchen and toilets.

The launch of the new betting site took place in November 1998, on my tenth anniversary as the town's bookmaker. With the Winallot Racing brand advertised proudly above the door, myself and staff, which by now included Graham Cordy, were desperately applying the finishing touches, until the moment the doors opened. I booked a couple of well-known jump jockeys to commemorate the official opening, as a large crowd gathered inside in anticipation. Sadly, the two riders had reportedly run into traffic problems and didn't make it, leaving me to console disappointed punters. Overall, the day went well, with a big turnout and a much-improved cash turnover. Trade increased during the months that followed, proving the new site to be a productive move. During this period, Gordon and Ross took the decision to close Off the Rails, though they continued to trade as high-street bookmakers. Gordon kindly offered to assist me at Winallot whenever I was short staffed.

There was a regular punter who came to the Betting Coup every Saturday, placing bets to the value of £100 and always paying in £5 notes. During one of these visits, a client told me that, all though it was never proved, the punter in question had been sacked by a national bank under suspicion of extorting several thousand pounds from the safe, in £5 notes. Shortly after, it came to light that the same person was now working for David!

In spite of David's regular blackball rebuttals, he remained eager to expand, and was offered the chance of purchasing his third betting office in the small market town of Oldtown, a few miles out of the city. The site was situated next door to a pub and similar in size to the old Betting Coup. Regulars would literally hop in and out of both establishments, thus making the betting office an attractive proposition. The sleepy town allowed many businesses to operate Wednesday as half-day closing. Nevertheless, David decided that the population was sufficient to support a betting office. He asked Phil Jellops to cast his professional eye over the business, and he confirmed the site was viable. David scraped together £10,000, thus avoiding another futile meeting with the bank. Having appointed a new manager at Badgeport, David decided to manage the site in Lostalot, Oldtown. The shop made a modest profit and he soon had its measure. He then offered Dai the Pencil the chance to further his career as relief manager.

Chapter 14
Collision Course

At the start of the 1998/99 football season, David laid a £20 bet at generous odds of 300/1 on Manchester United to win the treble: Premier League, FA Cup and UEFA Champions League. He took the bets with confidence, believing they had no chance. After finishing without any silverware during the previous season, United kicked off with draws against Aston Villa and West Ham in the league.

The FA Cup semi-final replay on 14th March was a Houdini act for United. With the scores level at 1-1, United's Roy Keane, was sent off for a foul on Marc Overmars. Arsenal's Dennis Bergkamp missed an injury time penalty, before Ryan Giggs scored a wonder goal during extra time, sealing a United victory. The second leg of the semi-final of the Champions League recorded another great escape; United had been held at home to a 1-1 draw by Juventus, and were 2-0 down in Turin after 10 minutes. United fought back to win 3-2, booking their place in the final against Bayern Munich. On 16th May, United secured the Premier League title with a 2-1 win over Tottenham hotspur, before winning the FA Cup six days later, with a 2-0 win over Newcastle.

David was a little shaken, as United were now one win away from completing the treble; all the same, they would need to defeat the mighty Bayern Munich in the Champions League Final. He watched the televised match from the shop, which was open for evening racing. Bayern scored within five minutes and dominated for most of the game, missing numerous chances. With only ten minutes remaining, United appeared to have blown their chances, as David wandered up to the rugby club for a couple of pints. On arrival, he heard the stupendous news that injury time goals from Teddy Sheringham and Ole Gunnar Solskjaer had turned the tie in United's favour, recording a historic treble.

With telephone credit betting very much on the increase, David decided to reorganise his business. Answering the phone and jotting down bets during racing was becoming too much of a distraction, affecting service levels. He centralised a telephone betting centre at Badgeport, appointing ex civil servant Tim to manage the new operation. Tim, who resembled Captain Birdseye, was a very efficient administrator. The centralisation improved efficiency and ensured a more professional service to shop clients. With the offices open six nights a week, David introduced a new manager's shift pattern. This comprised three consecutive twelve-hour shifts, followed by three days off. The pattern was well received, giving managers a different three days off each week.

While trade at Winallot was on the increase, there was more interest than usual in golf. The 1999 British Open Golf Championship was held at the famous Carnoustie course on the Angus coast, Scotland, where I stood to lose £3,000 if Justin Leonard should win the tournament. Thirty-three-year-old Jean Van de Velde, a 200/1 shot, was looking to become the first Frenchman to win a major tournament since 1907, having previously only won one European Tour event, the Roma Masters in 1993. Van De Velde approached the eighteenth tee on the final day with a three-shot lead, needing just a double bogey six to win the tournament. Jean seemed like a man possessed, producing a driver and getting away with a wild tee shot. An unlucky second shot hit the grandstand and ricocheted 50 yards backwards. The third shot landed in the burn. Jean then sat on the bank, removed his shoes and socks, rolled up his trouser legs and waded into the water.

BBC commentator Peter Alliss described the scene with the words, 'What on earth are you doing? Attempting to hit a ball out of there is complete madness. He's gone gaga. I've never seen anything like it before.'

Jean has since admitted that he intended to play the ball, as half of it was showing. However the tide was coming in and the ball was soon submerged. He took the sensible option and dropped the ball into the rough, receiving a one-shot penalty. After sinking a six-foot putt, he'd forced a three-way playoff with Justin Leonard and Paul Lawrie. I sat anxiously wondering if Van De Velde had blown his chances, and I began fearing the worse. Fortunately, Paul Lawrie came to my rescue pulling off a memorable victory. Sometimes a tournament is remembered more for the player who let it slip away, rather than the one who came out on top.

I was not so lucky when a regular golf punter put a dent in profits, after placing £200 on a 16/1 shot, at some exotic location in the USA. I watched the last few holes of the final round, as his golfer crept into contention. On the eighteenth tee he held a one-shot lead, and appeared to strike the ball beautifully. As the ball descended from the cloudless sky, the commentator remarked that it was plummeting straight into the stream. This was music to my ears, as he would receive a penalty of one shot, jeopardising his chances of winning. Instead of hitting the water, the ball bounced off a floating coconut back on to the fairway, relieving me of £3,200.

Following my recent shop purchase, I planned to invest the remainder of the Headquarters sale proceeds into additional property. I had my eye on opening an Indian restaurant, though I would need to find the right freehold. I got the idea after driving my two children on a twenty-mile round trip every Saturday evening to collect an Indian curry takeaway. This came about because we didn't like the food in our local restaurant. One night during our weekly excursion, it dawned on me that we were bypassing some fifteen thousand chimneypots and not a curry house in sight. The extra miles seemed worth the drive because this restaurant had an outstanding chef called Abdul. One day, I approached him to come into business with me, and to my astonishment he agreed.

I heard through the grapevine that a hairdresser was about to close her salon and sell the freehold, though it had not yet been advertised. On contacting the owner, she agreed that I might discreetly view the building, which seemed to be ideal. I was keen to pursue this venture, and invited my proposed Bangladeshi business partner to give his views on both the size of unit and the location. The hairdresser warned me that the closure was not common knowledge, and if I should bring him along during opening hours, it would only be to assess the building from outside.

I explained the situation to Abdul, instructing him not to enter, and to avoid drawing any attention to himself. On arrival, I waited in the car, expecting him to take a general look around the parade of shops. I then watched in horror as he entered the busy salon, and started questioning the proprietor on the possibilities of doing a deal. As if that wasn't enough, he stepped outside, produced a prayer mat and went down on his knees, smack bang in front of the window. This ended all prospects of a deal with either Abdul or the hairdresser.

Eventually, I found a one-storey retail unit and applied for planning to turn it into a restaurant. Permission was granted, and I decided to rent it out to the highest bidder. This proved to be the perfect investment, as I retrieved the capital outlay within three years. By coincidence, the curry house was situated close to my dad's house. His second wife had a right go at me when she found out that I was responsible, as she believed it would lower the tone of the area. Having gone to great lengths to establish the restaurant, the kids and I didn't like the food, reverting to curries from Abdul's.

During the 1999 Rugby World Cup, David offered regular punter Cecil, inflated odds, after he took the trouble to drive seventy miles to procure a pair of tickets for England v South Africa. This gave David and Flatulence Mal an opportunity to return to Paris for another boozy weekend. They stayed in Montmartre; a hillside quarter renowned for its rich artistic history. On arrival at Stade Français, the new home of French Rugby, David and Mal were confident of an England victory. Despite being terribly hung over, they managed to locate their seats midway up the stand, adjacent to the halfway line, providing the perfect view. South Africa scored the only try of the first half, through the brilliant Joost van der Westhuizen. In the second half South Africa upped their game, in particular Jannie de Beer, who landed five drop goals in the space of thirty-one minutes, setting a new world record. This was an exceptionally pleasing display for de Beer, who was only playing as second choice after a teammate's injury. South Africa ran out 44-21 winners.

While travelling home on the Eurostar, much to the amusement of Mal, David stumbled into the powerful scrummager South African Os du Randt. David was quick to apologise and promptly moved out of his way.

Soon after, they found themselves chatting with Stefan Terblanche, who acknowledged, 'It was one hell of a test match, but we had Jannie.'

An alternative to fixed odds betting is the pool system, whereby the operator takes a percentage commission of the pool. The remainder is then divided between the winners. Pool betting was introduced in France around 1870 by Pierre Oller, and is known as *pari mutuel*. The Totalisator was invented during the 1920s, a mechanical device used for issuing tickets, and facilitating the winning dividends.

The Tote was founded in the UK by Sir Winston Churchill in 1928, following much government concern over illegal bookmaking activities. Under fixed odds betting, punters know the potential pay-out in advance. However, in pool betting, they're unaware of exact returns until after the race. Sometimes, the pool pays more than the official starting price, though it may frequently pay less. On-course Tote betting was first deployed at Carlisle and Newmarket; the state-owned corporation ploughed all profits back into racing. In 1961, it became known as the Horse Race Totalisator Board (Tote), often referred to as the Nanny in cockney rhyming slang.

The Tote opened its first off-course office in 1972, and pools received a big injection of extra revenue with the creation of Tote Direct in 1992. Tote Direct facilitated other high-street bookmakers, being paid on a commission basis, to contribute to pools. This was a useful tool for independents, giving the option to offer placepot and Jackpot betting without being subject to excessive risk. It became more popular after 1999, when the Tote teamed up with Channel 4 and created the Scoop6, where punters were required to pick the winners of six televised races on Saturdays.

In 2011, the Tote was privatised after being purchased by Fred Done of Betfred. Another operation, Britbet, was originally set up by fifty-five of Britain's racecourses as a rival pool betting operation to the Tote. Nevertheless, an agreement was reached for Britbet and the Tote to work together, rather than have two competing operations. In 2018, a group known as Alizeti bought a 25% share in the Tote, and completed a 100% purchase in 2019 for an estimated figure of £115 million.

Under new owners, the Tote is now known as the UK Tote Group. It's made up of a consortium of over one hundred and sixty individual investors, including many racehorse owners and breeders. These are exciting times, with plans to link the Tote internationally, and the potential to create much bigger pools. Pool betting remains ever present at racecourses and on the high street.

In October 2000, I formed a syndicate in a bid to win the Scoop6. The idea was to create a big fund in order to play with multiple selections. I particularly liked the fact that placed selections offered the chance to scoop a placepot as a consolation. The bet costs a minimum of £2, whereby the stake is split in two: a £1 win accumulator and a £1 place accumulator. Dividends are calculated as £1 unit shares, which are divided equally between winners. During week seven, we scooped a win after six short-priced horses won, generating a total of 432 winning units, which dramatically reduced dividend shares. With the win fund standing at £357,981 dividends were shared out, at £828.60 per unit.

The following Saturday, we played for the bonus fund, whereby all winners from the previous week qualify to select the winner from the Tote's chosen race. On this occasion, it was a three miles four and a half furlongs chase at Haydock Park in heavy going. The bonus fund was standing at £623,507 and would be shared between winners. The selection fell on my shoulders, which should have been made easier, as there were only six runners.

After studying form, I ruled out the first three in the betting, and the outsider of the field, also known as the rag. This left a choice of two likely winners: trainer Tim Easterby's Scotton Green at 11/2, and the 6/1 Nigel Twiston-Davies-trained Lady Gortmerron. I sided with Scotton Green, as I believed the horse would be more suited by the course, and the going. Sadly, our selection fell when tiring at the last, as Lady Gortmerron pulled clear to win by fifteen lengths under jockey Glenn Tormey. Thirty-seven winners shared the bonus fund, receiving £16, 851.50 per unit. We stopped playing towards the end of the National Hunt season, maintaining a marginal overall profit. I was disappointed in my inability to win the bonus prize, though my miscalculation would lead to the design of a new betting system.

One of the unluckiest punters ever to miss out on the Scoop6, was self-employed builder and decorator Joe McGuire from Thatcham, Berkshire. On placing his £8 stake, he successfully backed the winners of the first five races. He nominated two selections for the final leg, one of which was Escape To Glory, in a tricky, fourteen-runner handicap at Thirsk. During the final furlong, Escape To Glory looked the likely winner, trading in running at odds of 1/100. However, the horse was worn down by a 16/1 shot, the Brian Ellison-trained, Llanarmon Lad, who won the race by one and a quarter lengths. The defeat denied Joe a pay-out of £6.87 million.

Sometime after my failure to win the bonus fund, I had a Saturday off, and noticed that the Scoop6 looked particularly winnable. There appeared to be three bankers, while the other races were low on runners. I made a dash to the bookies, where I swiftly marked the Scoop6 card, investing £24 (£1 unit stakes of 1 x 2 x 3 x 1 x 2 x 1), then headed home just in time to watch the first race. After the first four legs won, I checked the betting slip, and, to my horror I'd marked the wrong number in leg five. It was no record-breaking pot; all the same this turned out to be a costly error on my part.

As experienced bookmakers, there can be no excuses for any mistakes made while placing our own bets. During day three of the 2019 Cheltenham Festival, David asked his wife to place him a bet in each of the first three races: Defi Du Seuil, Sire du Berlais and Frodon, in three £10 win singles and a £10 treble. Defi du Seuil won at 3/1, Sire Du Berlais got up late to win at 4/1; and in the Ryanair Chase, Bryony Frost became the first female jockey to win a Grade 1 at the Cheltenham Festival, aboard 9/2 shot Frodon. The accumulative odds were 109/1, although Roxy produced winnings of just £115, having failed to place the winning treble.

During the 2019 Rugby World Cup while betting on France v Wales, David browsed Betfair, and the only player available to back as first try scorer was second row French player, Vahaamahina, at odds of 120. With no knowledge of the player, he wagered a tenner. Within five minutes, Vahaamahina went over for the first try, profiting David £1,190. At half time he decided to invest a further £500, on Wales to win the match. Vahaamahina was sent off after forty-nine minutes, signalling the start of a Welsh comeback. The game ended in a one-point Welsh victory. On checking his Betfair account, David had mistakenly pressed the lay button, instead of the back button, resulting in a £500 loss instead of an £800 gain.

On 18th November 2006, the Sheikh Mohammed-owned Peregrine Falcon trained by Mark Johnson was making a second UK racecourse appearance, after being beaten three and a half lengths over the same course and distance eleven days earlier. Thirteen runners went to post for a Class 5 Maiden Stakes at Wolverhampton, in a race for two-year-olds. Peregrine Falcon headed the market at 15/8, having shortened up from 9/4. Earlier, a Betfair internet exchange player is reported to have hit the wrong button, accidently laying the favourite to lose £237,000, at odds of 999/1. Peregrine Falcon won the race by one and three quarter lengths, with one player reportedly gaining £214,000 from the anonymous punter's misfortune. Peregrine Falcon ran a total of five times on English soil, all in the space of four months, winning on just one occasion.

Spread betting offers a further option, whereby punters win or lose an amount based on their prediction. They sell or buy, depending on whether they predict more or less occurrences than a spread, i.e., the bookmaker's profit. For example, where the spread in England's first innings of cricket is 320 to 330 and a punter predicts England will score more than 330, he can buy at, say, £1 a run. Should England score 432, the punter will win £102, though a total of 100 will result in a loss of £230. This form of betting can prove more volatile, although there are ways in which punters can restrict their exposure, with stop limits.

Dissatisfied with three shops and a centralised credit operation, David invested £10,000 in an internet betting centre. The site began attracting hot money for horses at all-weather tracks: permitting bookmakers to take any amount from bets submitted by punters, though it became very costly. During the Cheltenham Festival, he was expecting large numbers of Cheltenham bets: however, the only transactions were for well fancied horses at Southwell. David persevered with the site for a while, in the hope that the investment might show better returns. All in all, it was a costly affair, rising to the tune of £20,000 before he finally pulled the plug.

David had concerns over multinational companies muscling in on local territory, and contemplated taking his expertise on to the racecourse.

Phil Jellops warned him off, saying, 'On-course bookmakers aren't renowned for making easy money. It's a cut-throat environment.'

That being said, the optimistic entrepreneur blanked his comments and proceeded to sign up for a National Pitch Council training course. This was a bid to understand the rudiments of racecourse bookmaking, where he learnt about building a book, percentages and tic tac.

Prior to securing any pitches, he spent time on course with Silver Ring bookmakers at Ludlow, Southwell, Taunton, Nottingham and Bath. The dead man's shoes seniority system of inherited pitches had changed, as all pitches were now sold at auction, permitting the introduction of new blood. Bookmakers' positions were listed, with Pitch One being obtained at a premium, giving the bookmaker first choice of where to bet from. In contrast, bookmakers betting on the back row would pay considerably less. David was soon to purchase back row pitches at Bath, Cheltenham, Windsor, Leicester, Kempton and Southwell. He paid between £200 and £1,000 per pitch before plunging headfirst into the turf.

The year 2001 heralded many changes to traditional practices. The manual ledger and card system had been replaced by a computer-generated ticket, detailing stake, odds, selection and potential pay-out. Odds were still being displayed on wipe boards, and bookmakers typically had two assistants, one to operate the computer, and a floor man communicating market moves and hedging with on-course bookmakers. Sadly, the retention of hedge money in the betting ring was on the decrease, as on-course bookies began using betting exchanges, most commonly Betdaq, as a tool to monitor price fluctuations and hedge bets online.

Back row bookmakers relied on sizable bets filtering through from the front line, which was crucial to survival. Increasingly, more bookmakers were using betting exchanges for hedging, while David was resisting change. Without access to exchange prices, he was at a considerable disadvantage and consequently picked off by more senior bookies.

Bath is the highest flat racecourse in the country and exposed to the elements. To begin, with David hired a joint, a platform that bookmakers stand on, supporting the display board, and the hod (money bag). Bath offered hire of a flimsy Mark 1 version. During extreme weather, he was often observed with one hand clutching the contraption and the other hand clinging to the umbrella in an attempt to prevent it from becoming airborne.

One day at Bath, bookmaker Gary Wiltshire hurtled towards David resembling a charging rhino. He wanted to bet £200 to win on a 16/1 shot, in a five-furlong handicap. David accepted the wager. He usually obliged fellow bookmakers, particularly those he liked. Gary proceeded to run in the direction of other bookmakers as the odds tumbled. In this type of situation, bookmakers are hopeful of getting a favourable result; when things don't go well, they're left to ponder whether they will oblige the same bookie next time around. At the one-furlong marker Gary's selection still had a lot of ground to make up.

Nevertheless, the horse finished with a late burst to snatch the race close home.

The following Monday, David was wheeling the kit into Windsor racecourse as Gary sidled up, whispering 'I've got another one for you tonight.'

While David was relishing a new challenge on the racecourse, I was questioning my future, after Cuz accused me of fleecing him of inheritance money left to him by his dad. I became increasingly uncomfortable relieving punters of their hard-earned cash, and began fearing I'd missed my true vocation after developing a strong interest in the law. Later that year, my idol, George Harrison, passed away, and I spent time researching his spiritual beliefs. My views on life began to change, and I started contemplating a career change.

The betting ring was full of characters. For example, one prominent racecourse bookmaker can often be heard calling out, 'Money without work.'

The tic tac man stood on a stool, holding court and wearing white gloves. Sign language was used extensively to convey betting information. For example, even money – levels (you devils) – was an extension of the forefingers on each hand, whereby each hand was moved up and down in opposite directions; 5/4 was known as wrist, where the right hand is placed on the left wrist; 9/4 – top of the head – is demonstrated by both hands being placed on top of the head. 10/1 – cockle – is punching both fists.

Cockney rhyming slang and back slang remains popular with some bookmakers. Jolly is favourite, rouf is four and enin is nine. A pony, or macaroni, is twenty-five, and a monkey is five hundred. Sometimes layers would take a wager from other bookmakers via the tic tac man at bigger odds, without the general public being aware. This was a traditional and unique part of the racecourse, which has sadly been replaced by modern technology.

David and his floorman grappled with tic tac and betting parlance in an attempt to communicate prices. A quick-thinking floorman was invaluable, as the communication of fluctuating prices ensured that bookmakers remained competitive, while not being exposed to excessive odds. David was always keen to lay other bookmakers and they'd often ask to take the fractions. This concession was common among bookies – for example, if 12/1 is layed to £100, the fraction is 100/8: this adds an extra £4 to winnings (12 x 8 = £96). Effectively, the odds are 12.5/1 (100 divided by 8). 14/1 as a fraction is 100/7 and 16/1 is 100/6.

Some of David's pitches weren't lucrative, and it was difficult to cover the day's expenses. The amount paid for pitches gave the right to bet on a particular racecourse perpetually. However, daily expenses include a bookmaker's badge, staff entrance fees, wages, joint hire and fuel. On average, daily expenses would amount to £400. Expenses are the same for all bookmakers, whether you're taking £300 a race from the back line or £2,000 from prime positions.

Bookmakers offer an invaluable service to the racecourse, though some feel exploited, often regarding themselves as second-class citizens, while hauling heavy equipment from remote car parking locations. This is an arduous task, posing a security risk. There is also the matter of extortionate entrance fees, where they are charged as much as five times the standard rate.

During an extremely hot day at Royal Ascot, I assisted on-course bookmaker Badger. In spite of my protest, attendants directed me to park approximately one mile from the track. After an uphill trudge to meet Badger, I was sweating most profusely and feeling weak. At this point, I wasn't relishing the thought of trekking the heavy kit a further half mile on to the course, in the midday heat. On arrival, the ordeal had got the better of me, and I was shaking uncontrollably with severe dehydration.

Badger has a theory on each way betting: when the odds are less than 10/1, he believes that you are better off by betting on two selections to win, rather than placing one each way bet.

Chapter 15
Hitching a Ride

In 2001, the Grand National was run in desperate conditions, leaving some critics to describe the ground as unfit to race. Red Marauder won the race by a distance from Smarty. The time of 11 minutes 0.1 second, was the slowest recorded time in over a century. The pair were the only two horses to jump all of the obstacles without incident. During the race, Carl Llewelyn sprinted across the course to catch up with his mount, Beau. He then borrowed a mobile phone from a journalist and called trainer Nigel Twiston-Davies, asking whether he should remount. Nigel, who was watching from the stands, was apparently unsurprised to hear from Carl and left it to the jockey's discretion, though Carl decided against it.

To begin with, bookmakers were rubbing their hands, assuming there were only two finishers. However, after being unseated at the nineteenth fence, Blowing Wind and Papillon, ridden by AP McCoy and Ruby Walsh respectively, remounted to finish in third and fourth place. This spoilt the bookies *ignis fatuus* of a two-place pay-out, leaving punters to collect on the first four places as usual.

The going at a racecourse is assessed by the Clerk of the Course, who inserts a going stick into the ground to determine the amount of moisture. It measures both downward penetration and the force required to pull the stick back to a forty-five-degree angle. The meter has a scale of 0–15 with the higher end denoting firmer ground. Taunton recorded the firmest going on a jumps course on 25th March 2009 (11.7). The heaviest going was at Haydock on 20th February 2016 (2.7). The going stick has been in existence since 2007; prior to this, the going was established by the clerk digging his heal into the ground or by inserting a walking stick into it.

(The various going descriptions are detailed in Appendix vi.)

Throughout history, race meetings have been abandoned for a variety of reasons, such as the outbreak of war, snow, frost, waterlogging, foot and mouth, equine flu and, most recently, the coronavirus. In contrast, bad weather could also be good for betting shop trade, enabling many self-employed workers to seek refuge, and the chance to recover any loss of earnings. David introduced a game called Tossers, in an attempt to entertain punters and keep them betting. Individuals would toss a £1 coin against a wall, with the nearest to the wall scooping all of the coins. David joined in, though he never won, as he wasn't the complete article.

The severe winter of 1947 affected the football season, leaving the First Division to be completed on 14th June. Stoke City needed to beat Sheffield United to win the title on goal difference. However, they lost away from home 2-1 and the title went to Liverpool. In 1963, the football programme was decimated, taking a total of sixty-six days to complete the third round of the FA cup. There were two hundred and sixty-one postponements, and sixteen of the thirty-two ties were called off ten times or more. The competition was completed in May, when Manchester United were crowned FA Cup winners, their first silverware since the Munich air disaster of 1957. The record for the number of postponements occurred in the Stranraer v Airdrie cup game In Scotland, which was postponed thirty-three times. The lack of football created a problem for football pools companies Vernons, Zetters and Littlewoods. In order to predict results of postponed matches, they formed a five-man pools panel, which originally included former footballers Tom Finney, Tommy Lawton, Ted Drake, George Young and ex-referee Arthur Edward Ellis.

In 2002, foreign and virtual racing enabled bookmakers to offer more continuous betting opportunities. The first virtual reality racing was scheduled from the aptly named Portman Park, which may well have been a play on words, Portman Square being the home of Jockey Club headquarters in Newmarket. Original graphics were quite poor, and punters often referred to the spectacle as cartoon racing. In the early days, Dai the Pencil confused a few punters after mischievously posting a notice: 'Today's meeting at Portman Park is abandoned, due to the mouse breaking a fetlock.'

During the early schedules, a regular customer came into Lostalot, after a customary drinking session, placing his usual £50 win on 'the next favourite'. Little did he realise that he'd just bet on a virtual reality race and the bet lost. He insisted on his wager being returned. Even so David was having none of it, and his stake remained in the till. With graphics continually improving, Sprintvalley, Lucksin Downs and others were introduced. Soon punters were betting on virtual racing as just another race.

Virtual racing is a visual representation of a computerised random draw. The odds of the various horses, or dogs, are created by having selections with lower odds having more numbers in the draw than those with higher odds. Sir Winston Churchill once commented, 'Dog racing is animated roulette.' Little did he realise that, in 2003, Millersfield would become the first virtual reality dog track. To some punters, virtual racing represents a viable alternative to the real thing, since there are no non-runners, no stewards' enquiries, no non triers and no human error.

The biggest wager I received on virtual racing came from one of Gordon Bennett's punters, who bet £400 on a 9/2 shot at Portman Park. In order to cover half of the liability, Gordon hedged £200 with me. It was unusual to receive a bet of this size on virtual racing, and it turned out that the punter in question was inebriated. The computer-generated image proceeded to win by two lengths, and the merry punter staggered back to the pub £900 richer.

Gordon's wife won a day out for two at Wincanton races, courtesy of the *Western Daily Press*. She wasn't able to make it and Gordon invited me to accompany him. The day included free entry, a three-course meal and free booze. Out of courtesy I chauffeured Gordon to the course. He has a good eye for value bets and finding big priced winners. Gordon suggests if you fancy two selections in the same race, you should back the one at the biggest odds.

En route he announced that he'd just completed a five-day detox diet, and said: 'Come on, my son, I'm ready for a decent lunch and a drink.'

We were soon in the hospitality suite tucking into roast beef, accompanied by a full-bodied glass of Australian Shiraz. Unfortunately, trouble was on the horizon; Gordon's digestive system was not coping with the alcohol, and he became a complete mess after just half a glass.

Within a matter of minutes, the quiet gentleman disappeared and a noisy, rather vulgar version began stumbling around the room, uttering unprovoked obscenities. He was becoming a real nuisance, as other guests became more irritated, but there was no stopping him. My attempts to calm him down had no effect whatsoever, and I escaped to the betting ring. I was enjoying myself for some forty-five minutes, forgetting all about the earlier mayhem. As I made my way back I was hoping that he'd sobered up.

This wasn't the case, and I was accosted at the entrance by a steward who said, 'If he's with you get him out, before we throw him out.'

We then made our way to the car in single file, with Gordon zigzagging while clinging to my shoulders.

A couple of days later I received a telephone call from Ross, accusing me of getting his business partner plastered. He went on to say Mrs Bennett wasn't best pleased with me either. He soon changed his tune, and we devised a plan where I would write to Gordon pretending to be the editor from the paper. I listed a full account of his bad behaviour, some of which was made up for good measure.

I concluded: 'During thirty years in print, this is the worse behaviour ever recorded by a competition prize winner, thus resulting in your lifetime ban from all *Western Daily Press* competitions and Wincanton racecourse.'

Soon after, Ross called to say Gordon was in a depressed state after reading the letter. I wanted to tell him that it wasn't for real, but Ross was having none of it, and we left him to stew. Ross eventually told Gordon that it was a wind-up and that it was all my idea. I began calling him regularly to explain myself, though my persistent offers of a trip to Wincanton races didn't improve matters. Meanwhile he remained unforgiving and refrained from comment.

I have another business friend called Oscar, who's spent many years researching race form in order to formulate an effective betting system. In his opinion, it's dangerous betting when the going is heavy, because it throws up too many shock results. He's always looked for a winning formula that's non-time consuming, and therefore avoids reading form. Oscar tests each theory by monitoring a minimum of fifty races before considering a wager. From time to time he finds a system with potential, and on one occasion he asked for my assistance in testing it out.

The defined formula was basic: betting on second favourites at a minimum price of 7/2 and stopping at a winner. The accompanying stake plan was to double up on every race until you win. This process was known to me previously as the Martingale system. I was alarmed over the staking; all the same, Oscar convinced me that his trial had proved successful, and I naively agreed to test it out while he was working. With a plan to split the profit fifty-fifty, I loaded up my Betfair deposit account. I started with a fiver and proceeded to lose the first five wagers of £5, £10, £20, £40 and £80, losing £155. My gut was telling me to stop, and I made a decision not to continue. I stayed at the computer and watched a further eight system bets bite the dust. I stopped counting after thirteen races, which would have resulted in a £40,955 loss.

A watershed moment came on 1st January 2002, as the 9% betting duty was abolished. For the first time since 1968 punters were wagering tax free in betting shops. Bookmakers were now taxed on gross profit, favouring outlets with high turnover to the detriment of smaller shops. As a result, David decided to relocate Oldtown to a larger unit and identified a former fruit and veg shop, just a few doors away. He was excited about the prospect of providing a state-of-the-art betting facility for locals; a far cry from the pokey, dated shop they had tolerated for many years.

I invested in another property in Pingford, close to where I'd grown up, one of the minority of England's towns of its size without a betting shop. Having previously spoken with local planners, they advised that they'd most likely permit a turf accountant on to the high street, providing it was positioned to the rear of a retail unit. This was because the visual presence of a bookmaker might lower the tone of the area. They suggested that I look for a sizeable building where I could access via a separate entrance, and they would likely grant permission. It was the responsibility of the council's planning department to allow the change of use from A1, retail, to A2, office use.

In due course, I found an imposing period building that appeared to fit the bill. It had previously been used as a retail unit; therefore I would need to approach planners for a change of use. It was considerable in size, with enough room to fit a side entrance and corridor to a spacious room at the rear. The idea was to signpost the bookmakers on the front door. I met with a senior planner who gave it the thumbs up; nevertheless, it would need to pass a committee vote, with no guarantees. I had the money to pay a 10% deposit and purchased the building for £250,000. The bank agreed to back me with a high-interest loan. However, this was collateralised against my two commercial buildings.

On completion of sale, I approached Phil Jellops in order to apply for a betting licence, and a date was set to appear before the magistrates. It was a bitterly cold morning in Pingford, where Phil, his associate and myself were coincidentally attired in black trench coats and carrying briefcases. As we traipsed the streets en route to court we were seemingly mistaken for the mob, with some people shuffling out of our way, while others took refuge in shop doorways. The magistrates were keen to oblige, granting the licence, and much to my surprise there were no petty objections.

In the meantime, I employed local architect Adam Lane to draw up plans on the shop design, which were submitted for approval. Weeks later we were invited to a meeting, whereby town planners would take a vote on a plausible change of use. At first count, permission appeared to be granted on the strength of one vote. The chairman asked for a recount and proceeded to vote against the change, making the show of hands even stevens. This meant that we had to resubmit the application, and come back for a second time. Before this, Adam and I attended an on-site meeting with town councillors and local objectors. We were shocked by their ill-mannered comments, while making it very clear they had no intention of allowing a betting office into their town.

At the next meeting, Adam, who played it strictly by the book, addressed the planners, explaining our proposal in detail. On this occasion, the new chair recommended not wasting any time, instructing the committee to vote in favour of the change. This was because approval had already passed two of the council's three-point bureaucratic test; this covered all that was required to grant the change. Therefore committee members had no grounds to refuse.

What happened next was mind-boggling. One of the planners appeared to have fallen asleep, and while the majority raised their arms in favour, other members were pulling their colleagues' arms down. At this moment, the chair reiterated the fact that they couldn't refuse to grant the change, because two grounds of approval remained watertight. Members then told the chairman to revamp the rules, in order to reject the proposal. Adam stood up and accused the committee of immoral ethics and manipulating the system. This only fell on deaf ears, as the chair moved swiftly to the next item of agenda.

I was astounded they could just make it up as they went along, though at least I could appeal the decision. I was looking forward to reading the meeting minutes, which would expose how biased the planners had been. The minutes were released, but bureaucrats had doctored all of their underhand comments, and I subsequently lost my appeal. The building remained unoccupied, although I continued to renew the betting office licence. I knew I could easily transfer the licence to another premise, providing it hadn't lapsed. The shop would stay empty for a total of four years, and I adopted the approach of 'don't get mad, get even'. In the interim, I continued to make the heavy interest payments. On the bright side, I was aware that property values were increasing dramatically, and therefore I was still ahead of the game.

During the 2002 FIFA World Cup, a local radio station offered David the opportunity to take part in a penalty-shootout-style quiz, pitting his wits against another bookmaker. This was a golden opportunity for some free advertising, but he was worried about making a fool of himself on air. He identified the ideal replacement, in the form of Dai the Pencil. Dai often ran a quiz at his local rugby club, as well as participating in a weekly pub quiz. As luck would have it, Dai was keen and snapped up the opportunity to broadcast his encyclopaedia of knowledge on live radio.

First question: 'Who played Dave Lister in the hit series *Red Dwarf*?'

Dai's response was not immediate, and after a while he muttered in a strong Welsh accent: 'Oh dear, I can see his face and hear his Liverpudlian accent, I just can't think of his name.'

Zero goals.

Next question: 'Which artist sang 'Like a Prayer'?

Dai's response: 'Oh dear, I have no idea. Music's not my strong point.'

The radio presenter said, 'Have a guess.'

Dai blurted out, 'Phil Collins.'

It was, of course, Madonna. By now, the opposition had racked up three goals, and Dai needed to answer the next question correctly to stay in the game.

'Which TV guide is fifty years old today?'

Dai responded, 'Alan Whicker.'

Not the best result for David, who was left pondering whether all PR is good PR.

For all of our experience, both David and I have fallen foul to many costly errors while operating the exchanges. The mistakes include loading an incorrect stake, betting on the wrong selection, laying instead of backing (or vice versa) and the failure to load value odds. Players can also get suckered in when placing bets behind real time, as they fail to realise that their TV is often running many seconds behind the action. In addition, there have been countless instances where players using advanced technology in order to stay ahead of the game also come a cropper.

During what turned out to be a landmark afternoon at Southwell, on 23rd January 2002. David decided to lay some bets on Betfair while working from his home office. He laid an even £200 on the favourite, Family Business, ridden by champion jockey AP McCoy. The race was underway, and with no live pictures to hand, David viewed the in running betting, noticing the odds of Family Business had drifted to 20/1. Instantly, he pressed the back button and staked £10 to cover his earlier bet. Astonishingly the bet was matched at 345/1, which meant that he stood to win £190 if the horse lost, and a staggering £3,250 if it won.

1.40 Feast of St Raymond Novice Chase (Class E)
(5-year-olds plus) 3 miles 110 yards

Family Business	8/11	6 11-10	AP McCoy	M C Pipe
Joe Luke	6/1	10 11-7	N Hannity	G M Moorc
Oh No Whiskey	66/1	7 11-3	M Bradburne	J G Portman
Red Radish	66/1	7 11-3	B Keniry	B I Case
What A Wonder	7/1	7 10-10	H Ephgrave	Ferdy Murphy
Star Control	66/1	8 10-5	R Hobson	H J Evans
Eaux Les Coeurs	10/3	5 10-0	R Wakley	A M Hales

The seven-runner race was underway, with Family Business setting out as the 8/11 favourite. Oh No Whiskey fell at the first fence, leaving six runners. AP McCoy's mount settled nicely and travelled well. The runners jumped the third, where Star Control fell, leaving Red Radish to dictate terms. The front three cleared the eleventh obstacle ahead of Family Business who jumped the fence and then stumbled. At this moment the odds touched 20/1 on Betfair.

186

However, McCoy was unseated and David's bet was matched at the bigger odds.

The remaining four runners ran to the next, with Eaux Les Coeurs and What A Wonder going clear of Joe Luke and the tailing off Red Radish. At the thirteenth fence, Eaux Les Coeurs fell, and Joe Luke blundered, unseating the rider. This left What A Wonder well clear, but the horse unseated his jockey after jumping the fourteenth. The rider kept hold of the reins, remounted and was still ahead of the only other horse in the race, Red Radish.

Meanwhile, Eaux Les Coeurs' jockey had also remounted, and was trying to catch the leading pair from a distance behind. The sixteenth fence brought more chaos, when What A Wonder fell and both Red Radish and Eaux Les Coeurs refused. The race had come to a standstill, at which point the champion jockey heard the commentator's announcement 'All of the horses have fallen.' The quick-thinking McCoy hitched a lift in a Land Rover and went looking for Family Business, who was back with his handler. On remounting, the pair returned to the fence of departure, this time jumping the obstacle soundly.

Family Business jumped the fences in the straight and proceeded down the far side. With the race at his mercy, Family Business negotiated the final fences to win the race in a time of 10 minutes 30.9 seconds, (four minutes slower than standard). This includes McCoy's horse hunting and vehicle travelling time.

After one of the most extraordinary horse races ever, Jockey Mark Bradburne was taken to hospital for a precautionary check, while the rest of the runners and riders escaped uninjured. AP McCoy is believed to be the first jockey to win a race where all of the horses fell. Thanks to the champ's fast thinking, David was £3,250 richer.

Anthony Peter McCoy, also known as AP or Tony McCoy, was born in Country Antrim, Ireland, in 1974. Standing at 5ft 10, he was taller than most jockeys. At the age of seventeen, he rode his first winner in a flat race for trainer Jim Bolger at Thurles, in Ireland. His first win in England came at Exeter during September 1994, aboard Chickabiddy, trained by Gordon Edwards. He spent his first season riding in Britain as an apprentice to trainer Toby Balding. By the end of the 1994/95 campaign he'd won the Conditional Jump Jockeys title, riding a record-breaking seventy-four winners. He claimed his first Champion Jockey title in '95/96, before joining forces with champion trainer Martin Pipe in 1997, where they'd dominate the world of jump racing for the following seven years. During 2001/02 he rode 289 winners, setting a new landmark for the most wins in a season. The McCoy-Pipe partnership ended when AP sealed a deal to ride for owner JP McManus and trainer Jonjo O'Neill.

AP's fellow jockeys referred to him as Champ. He took losing badly, in an outstanding career that was driven by winning and setting new targets. A unique and brilliant talent who raised the bar in National Hunt racing, he changed the way jockeys approached things. On analysing his achievement, he was punishingly disciplined, a dedicated professional who was a teetotaller and a non-smoker. He survived on four meals a week in order to keep his weight down. He suffered over 1,000 falls, breaking most of the bones in his body. He learned how to shrug off heavy falls by conquering the pain barrier, and was often referred to as the Bionic Man. During 2008 he broke his back in a bad fall at Warwick, and lost the ability to walk. Incredibly he returned to the saddle within seven weeks.

AP has been honoured with twenty Lester awards, more than any other jockey.

Lester Piggott once said, 'He's as good as anyone has ever been.'

He was crowned champion jockey every season throughout his twenty-year career as a professional, a record that might never be challenged. AP won nearly all of the prestigious races, including one King George VI Chase, two Gold Cups, three Champion Hurdles and the Grand National. In 2010, he received a lifetime achievement award, when he became the first jockey to win BBC Sports Personality of the Year. He rode a total of 4,358 winners, which includes ten flat wins. He retired from the saddle in 2015. He was knighted in the 2016 New Year Honours for services to horseracing.

In 2005, up-and-coming Novice chaser Kauto Star, trained by Paul Nicholls, ran in a three-horse race at Exeter. Kauto was twelve lengths clear when he fell at the second last and was remounted by Ruby Walsh, before being deprived by a short head. As a result, the horse sustained a fracture during the race and didn't run again until the following season. This incident led to a review by the British Horseracing Authority, which took a further four years to ban jockeys from remounting their horses. In contrast, jockeys could still remount in Ireland. During a magnificent career, spanning more than seven years in the UK, Kauto Star never finished outside of the first three when completing a race.

Chapter 16
Man or Mouse

Betting exchange companies provide sites where Joe Public are able to match bets between themselves. These companies take a commission from all winning bets, and also provide a service for clients to cash out during play. Players have the option to lay bets, but some novice punters struggle to comprehend the difference between laying and backing. Laying is where you act as the bookmaker, and backing is where you take the odds and bet as a punter. For example, if you lay the home team to win a football match, you are taking money in the hope that the home side loses or draws. All the same, this type of gambling exposes the layer to risk more than they can win, when the odds are greater than evens.

Whether you back or lay, you need to establish a cutting edge to make it pay. On Betfair, bets available to lay appear in pink, while odds in blue represent backing opportunities. When the odds of a required selection are not available, they may be submitted and subsequently matched. Many people consider that more value is obtained on the exchanges by backing. This is true in comparison to bookmakers' prices, but the value is partially eroded when the exchange's commission is factored in. Traditional bookmakers suffer additional operating costs, which layers on the exchange do not endure. That said, backing on the exchanges offer marginal percentage advantages over laying.

Following his windfall at Southwell, David attempted to lay a substantial bet on French rugby side, Stade Français, one hour before kick-off on Betfair. In those days and unbeknown to David, Betfair didn't suspend all bets at the start of a match and the bet remained on the system at excessive odds, until it was picked off late in the game. This was an avoidable loss costing him in excess of £2,000.

Fixed odds betting terminals (FOBTs) were first introduced into betting offices in 2001. The terminals allow players to bet on the outcome of various games and events that have fixed odds. Among the most popular games are roulette, poker and blackjack. When David first introduced the machines, regular blackjack player Bert commented on the odds being stacked too high in the bookies' favour. This resulted in David asking the machine suppliers to adapt them, in order to give punters a better chance.

A few days later, self-employed punters Patrick and Glyn entered Lostalot a little earlier than usual after being rained off. Patrick asked Glyn for his thoughts on the afternoon race card. However, an uninspired Patrick opted to play poker on the newly modified FOBT. Patrick was soon accumulating winnings, and within half an hour he'd banked over £1,000. Dai the Pencil phoned David to advise him of the situation.

'Patrick's playing small stakes, boyo, but he can't stop winning, and he's up to £2,000.'

A panic-stricken Dai made a further call to David, by which time Patrick had amassed £3,000. Patrick's winning streak continued, as intrigued punters congregated around the machine. Dai relayed the pattern of bets to David, who was now convinced that something was amiss. He was facing a real dilemma: should he order Dai to switch the machine off, or sit it out until closing time? Patrick had recently been on a losing streak, and David chose to leave the machine running. Patrick continued to play small stakes, and the bank soon reached £5,000. By closing time, he'd won over £6,000. Had Patrick decided to increase stakes, the sum may well have been much higher. At least David saved face by leaving the machine running. His decision was vindicated when the suppliers admitted that the machine had not been sufficiently tested, refunding all losses.

Before the 2005 Gambling Act, *sponsiones ludicrae* applied. This meant that the courts considered promises relating to gambling were too trivial to be considered by the legal system. In 2007, UK laws changed, permitting the enforcement of gambling debts. The Gambling Commission also has the power to void a bet, if it was deemed to be substantially unfair. Prior to any court action, disgruntled punters can take disputes to arbitration.

Before 2007, there was something regarded as a collateral contract. For instance, if two people agreed to split their winnings at bingo, this could be enforced by a court of law, providing that the agreement was established. Verbal agreements are binding if all of the relevant terms are clear and independently verified. There is, however, a defence – *non est factum* – whereby one party was so drunk that they didn't know what they were doing, and the other party should have realised this was the case.

In the Republic of Ireland, gambling debts remain unenforceable. Judge Francis Comerford relied on the 1956 Gaming and Lotteries Act, in Sayed Mirwais v Automatic Amusements Ltd (2017). Mr Mirwais could not collect winnings of €11,713, after playing an automated roulette machine, at a club in Dublin. Mirwais said he won approximately €7,500, but was only given €2,500, and the remainder in chips. He was then assured that he'd be able to cash in at the end of the evening. He continued playing, winning an extra €6,713 and was told to come back the following day, the reason being that the casino did not have enough cash, and also required an engineer to check the machine.

The next day, the casino refused to pay on the basis that the machine was paying out a suspiciously high amount of money. The casino claimed that he'd taken advantage of a software problem, permitting him to bet after the roulette ball had stopped. Mr Mirwais said the machine was operating correctly on the previous evening, when he lost €9,000.

The judge commented, 'Gambling operators can simply say, no, you are not entitled to the money. That is simply the law in Ireland.'

Mr Mirwais went on to appeal the decision. However, a compromise settlement was achieved before reaching the High Court.

In the autumn of 2002, David and Badger decided to head to Dubai to watch the Dubai Sevens. In addition, it gave an opportunity to visit Flatulence Mal, who was now residing in Abu Dhabi. Their old poker mate Bunny was also on the flight, in the form of his ashes, as he'd recently passed away. They challenged Mal to a reunion game of poker, and adopted Bunny's ashes as an additional memory for the prevailing poker champion. This was a bid to emulate the Australia v England cricket matches, which are played for the ashes of a burnt cricket bail. Badger affectionately retains Bunny's ashes to this day.

At Badgeport, turnover was going through the roof, while the other Lostalot shops were also making healthy profit. David decided to invest £1,000 each for Stratford, Chepstow, Leicester and Worcester pitches, plus £5,000 for Chester. He particularly enjoyed the three-day May meeting at Chester, where he was accompanied by Captain Birdseye and floorman Tom, an old rugby pal. David and Tom enjoyed the Chester nightlife, though much to the disapproval of Captain Birdseye.

Chester can be a tricky place for bookmakers, as the tight course often favours the inside draw numbers (1-5), which, in turn, assists punters to predict winners more frequently. Chester is the oldest operating racecourse in England. It has the tightest race circuit, measuring approximately one mile and one furlong, with a very short straight of 239 yards. It's known as the Roodee, taken from Roodeye, meaning the island of the cross, which is situated in the middle of the course. Legend has it that the cross is the statue of the Virgin Mary. The first race was reportedly held in 1540, and consented to by Mayor Henry Gee, from whom the term 'gee-gee' originated.

On day two, Captain Birdseye called the prices, as a hungover David priced up the first race. He marked one horse at 9/2, and, almost immediately, a front row bookmaker jumped off his stool, placing £200 to win. After processing the bet, the captain pointed out that the correct price should be half the odds, at 9/4. The horse drifted to 11/4, giving David hope that his error may go unpunished. The horse won and he paid the unscrupulous bookie with a smile, although the rules stated otherwise: If a price is given in error the correct odds should still apply. While some racecourse bookmakers would shut shop if they were sufficiently ahead, David was of the opinion that he wanted to avail himself of all betting opportunities, especially with the high costs of operating on the racecourse. This mentality suggests that the last race of the day should be approached in the same manner as the first, thereby measuring profit over a period of time.

The measure was put to the test during a quiet afternoon at Stratford. David was not the most technical of bookmakers, relying on Captain Birdseye to operate the racecourse computer system. The first race was notoriously trappy for bookmakers and punters alike. Hoping for a turn-up, he got stuck into the first and second favourites, the unexpected occurred making a tidy £3,000 profit. The next five races appeared to be competitive, and he took a similar aggressive approach. He began thinking about the possibilities of a very lucrative pay day. However, five winning favourites later, the end of day balance revealed a £500 loss, plus expenses.

On 28th July 2001, I took a frantic drive to Stratford racecourse, making it just in time to bet in the opening race, on the Philip Hobbs-trained Invictress, a 5/1 shot in a Class 4 Hurdle. I'd been so wrapped up in getting there on time, I hadn't given any consideration to the possibility that the horse might not win. As I ran from the car park, I bumped into one of my clients who advised that he'd just won £2,000 off me on a credit bet. All the same, I was chuffed with myself for making it on time, and I placed the £50 wager before taking my viewing position in the stand. Invictress was never a factor in the race and was eventually beaten by forty-two and a half lengths.

David liked to lay large bets, and wanted punters to believe he was fearless. Picking up the phone to hedge may be construed as a sign of weakness. Through the years, like many bookmakers, he'd paid out lots of losing hedge money, and in 2003 he devised a new strategy to increase profit. The unorthodox plan was to take his chance at the more competitive festivals, in particular Cheltenham and Royal Ascot. This latest inspiration had been fuelled back in 1996, when only one favourite won during the whole of the three-day Cheltenham Festival.

Since the opening of Cheltenham's Princess Royal Grandstand in 2015, the annual March Festival draws an average crowd of 70,000 on Gold Cup day. In 2018, Cheltenham racecourse was reunited with the original 1924 Gold Cup, which has become the perpetual trophy since 2019. It's regarded as the blue riband of jump racing, offering the largest UK prize money for a non-handicap chase. The race has been cancelled five times: in 1931 (frost), 1937 (flooding), 1943/44 (Second World War) and 2001 (foot and mouth disease).

As Cheltenham approached, David rolled up his sleeves in anticipation of taking the punters on with his new strategy: standing all bets to the full. At Oldtown, a regular known as Edward invested £400, taking ante post odds for favourites in graded races: placing a series of permed accumulators over three days. Things began to go wrong for the pragmatic bookie on day one, with two favourites obliging; Back in Front won the Supreme Novice hurdle and Azertyuiop took the Arkle Challenge Trophy. Moscow Flyer continued the sequence on day two, winning the Queen Mother Champion Chase, followed by Liberman claiming the Champion Bumper. Despite liabilities of £20,000, David remained averse to hedging and stuck to his guns.

Things were hotting up nicely on day three, after favourites Barracuda won the Stayers Hurdle and Best Mate cruised to a ten-length victory, making it two blue ribands in a row. David was left in the mire, with only two favourites left to run, Kingscliff in the Foxhunters and La Landiere in the Cathcart Challenge Cup Chase. While the grey-faced bookie sat pondering his gung-ho approach, Kingscliff proceeded to win. His only hope now was to pray for divine intervention.

La Landiere was a big, rangy mare, trained by Richard Phillips, and not easy to keep straight. That said, she'd already run up a sequence of six very impressive chase wins. La Landiere was royally connected through the Queen's granddaughter Zara Phillips, who was riding out for the Adlestrop stables and doing lots of physio work with the mare. The race got underway, with David pinning his hopes on second favourite, Tarxien, who fell at the sixth. La Landiere didn't appear to be at her best, as she took a narrow lead two out ahead of 14/1 shot, Irish Hussar. Nevertheless, Richard Johnson coaxed La Landiere up the hill to win by one and a half lengths, thus completing a magnificent seven.

Royal Ascot presented an opportunity to turn things around. Ascot held its first race, Her Majesty's Plate, in 1711, after Queen Anne founded the course in the same year. The Queen Anne Stakes, the first race of the annual Royal meeting, was named in her honour. Ascot is situated six miles from Windsor Castle, and the monarchy's great passion remains to this day. Thousands of racegoers line the racecourse to view the daily parade of royal carriages during the five-day June festival.

In 1901, Lord Churchill had the responsibility of vetting the letters for attendance in the royal enclosure, and would stack them into piles of three: certainly, perhaps and certainly not. Until 1945, Ascot's only event was the royal meeting, which traditionally boasts some of the world's greatest racing. The oldest Royal Ascot race is the Gold Cup, which dates back to 1807, and is traditionally run on day three, Ladies Day. It's reported that an anonymous poet described the day in 1823 as, 'Ladies Day – when the women, like angels, look so divine.'

Results were kind to David during the first four days, but in spite of his Cheltenham warning, there was another dark cloud on the horizon. One of the Lostalot regulars invested £35 in a £5 win Patent. The bet consisted of *Racing Post* tipster (Pricewise) selections, at early odds of 5/1, 16/1 and 33/1.

Pricewise tips were always popular, and therefore prices would usually shorten. After the first selection won, most orthodox bookmakers would hedge the double. David's contemporaneous non-hedging strategy was a cause for concern, as he pondered a potential £22,000 pay-out. The next selection also won, offering him one last chance to reconsider and place a single bet.

The final selection was a chestnut colt called Attache, top weight in the ultra-competitive Buckingham Palace Stakes Handicap. The price had shortened to 10/1, but nevertheless a wager of £2,000 would cover 91% of the liability. Unfortunately, he was not thinking like a bookmaker or a businessman, he was walking a tightrope. The thrill of the gamble and adrenalin rush had consumed him. He needed to stop and consider the consequences, and the fact that his paltry bank balance would not support such a big loss.

A member of staff pointed out that Attache was reportedly drawn on the wrong side of the course. David's fate may have been sealed when the same person uttered the immortal words 'Are you a man or a mouse?' This question ended all possibility of the perilous bookie hedging the bet. The twenty-seven-runner field set off and Attache raced among a small group on the far side. Meanwhile, most of the runners chose to race up the nearside. At the two-furlong pole Attache led his group, and by the furlong pole he was the overall leader. The nearside runners were edging closer with every stride, and as they flashed past the post a photograph was called. David's spirits were low, and his worse fears were confirmed when Attache was announced the half-length victor. David was left licking his wounds, as he came to the realisation that he'd taken the bait, and succumbed to a self-inflicted mouse trap.

The days that followed were dark and his mood was sombre. Outwardly he tried to project a positive persona, but the losses were gnawing at his insides. Holding a conversation was difficult, as he would drift away and picture the outstretched head of Attache crossing the line in first place. He was constantly thinking about the bet and how he was going to raise so much money. He also wondered if he would ever be able to expunge his gambling demon.

Both Cheltenham and Ascot losses stretched David's finances and he was lucky to have loyal friends who were often there to bail him out. On the positive side, David's honest nature commands that he always finds a way to settle his dues. In spite of a strong belief that the new site at Oldtown was a winner, expansion plans had been dealt a serious blow, and he sold out for the same price he'd paid three years earlier.

Many punters pursue betting for fun, with no expectation of making a profit. While others take a more serious approach. I have spent numerous years relishing the challenge of beating the bookies. Some gamblers are inhibited by confirmation bias, where they are influenced by preconceptions, and ignore information which may contradict. The ability to apply the lessons learnt from previous betting experiences should always be considered.

In January 2003, I devised a jump race tick box betting strategy known as the 14 Pointer, whereby the likely winner can only be established with a full set of ticks. Ticks are gained by matching favourable factors for today's race and previous races. I decided to place single wagers of £200 on each selection. During a three-month period of February–April, 16 horses gained maximum ticks and all sixteen won. The prices ranged between 10/11 and 2/13, totalling winnings of £2,020, with odds averaging close to 8/13, and a profit of £126.25 per wager. I continued the tick box testing throughout the spring and summer. Disappointingly, it wasn't throwing up any selections, and I decided to park the system up.

14 Pointer

1. *Racing Post* favourite
2. Top jockey
3. Top trainer
4. Good weight (max 7lb rise since latest race)
5. Going
6. Maximum seven runs a year
7. Maximum thirty days since last run
8. Suitable distance (within one furlong of latest run)
9. Suitable track (similar to previous good runs)
10. Suitable grade race (same or lower than latest)
11. Previous race type, chase or hurdle (same as latest)
12. Won or beaten a maximum of one length in latest run
13. Favourite or second favourite latest run
14. Moderate opposition

Finding value is a crucial part of making profit, though it's not always easy to decide where the line should be drawn. Some gamblers argue there is no value in any bet that pays less than 3/1, while others suggest there is no value in backing odds-on favourites. This is backed up by the fact that bookmakers are usually eager to lay odds-on shots. I know a professional gambler who goes by the name of Noah Gamble. He places a moderate number of bets during the year and has used various systems and staking plans to increase the win rate and profit margin. He now relies on one method that picks fewer selections but most bets are odds-on favourites.

Noah uses the philosophy, bet one a day and go away.

'You need a win rate of 80% at odds averaging 1/4 to break even, or any price that's bigger to make a profit. I usually use 1/3 as my guideline, as four winners are needed at odds of 2/7 or greater from every five bets to make a minimum profit of £14 on £100 level stakes.' Since adopting this method he's had winning runs of up to 17 and the occasional but rare losing run of 3. He bets singly to a percentage of his bank, and can wait days for the one horse that ticks all the boxes.

Seasoned gamblers can only be measured by the profit in their betting bank. Every betting system should run hand-in-hand with a good stake plan, since one without the other is likely to fail. For this reason it's best to bet with an exact stake plan, or a maximum 5% of the bank, on any one event. Individuals have varying levels of financial comfort, and the introduction of cash into betting banks should be considered accordingly. Where a betting system allows you to bet more than one horse in a race, divide the maximum 5% stake into equal proportions.

Ideally, gamblers should try to identify where bookmakers' odds appear to be too high. For this purpose, after studying form for an event you could create your own prices, and only place bets when you feel the market is in your favour. Whatever the price, it's only value if it's greater than the perceived chances of a selection winning, and boils down to personal judgement.

In 2020, David and I teamed up, betting a succession of winners at the Cheltenham Festival, netting a profit of £2,972. After much research, we designed our ultimate betting system (the Cert System). We planned to hit the bookies for six, by betting seven racing certainties on the trot, utilising these winnings.

On July 28th, we placed the first of these wagers, £2,972 on the John Gosden-trained Stradivarius taking early odds of 8/13, in the two-mile Group 1 Goodwood Cup. Frankie Dettori drove Stradivarius up behind the leaders at the two-furlong pole, where for a few strides they found themselves short of room. Fortunately, the horse found an impressive turn of foot, as Frankie steered the six-year-old through a gap between Santiago and Eagles By Day. Stradivarius powered clear to beat Nayef Road by one length, winning the Goodwood Cup for a record-breaking fourth time in a row. We were up and running, returning the initial stake to our betting bank, the profit of £1,829 would soon be invested on race number two.

Chapter 17
The Jinx

A regular rugby punter once bitterly complained, 'You're unlucky for me, Johnny. I've never ever won a single rugby bet with you. You're a curse.'

He then uncharacteristically placed a £2,000 wager on England to beat Australia in the final of the 2003 World Cup in normal time. The match was played in Sydney, and as history records, England were on the verge of winning, when Elton Flatley landed a penalty goal in the dying seconds to level the score at 14-14. The draw was the perfect result for me, and as the game entered extra time, I could now fully root for England. Flatley and England's Jonny Wilkinson exchanged penalties to level the score once again at 17-17. With only 26 seconds remaining, Wilkinson kicked a right-footed drop goal, giving England a 17-20 victory. The Rugby World Cup was first played in 1987, and only one other final, South Africa v New Zealand in 1995, has gone to extra time. In contrast to my good fortune, having laid some hefty ante post bets on England to win the tournament, a subdued David Watts watched the final with his euphoric mates in a local rugby club.

David invested in three further racecourse pitches: a Silver Ring at Royal Ascot, Newmarket - the July and the Rowley Mile. He enjoyed the trips to Newmarket. They also offered a stayover and an opportunity to visit his favourite Cambridge restaurant, enjoying exquisite Algerian cuisine with new girlfriend Roxy.

During the 17th century, King James I discovered a unique sector of land in the Suffolk countryside that was ideal for racing and began sponsoring race meetings. The area is now known as Newmarket. The first recorded race took place in 1622, a match between Lord Salisbury and the Marquess of Buckingham, for a prize of £100. Newmarket's historical course was founded in 1636. The vast area incorporates the highest number of training yards and various racing organisations, and also regarded as flat racing's headquarters. Charles II, who reigned from 1660 to 1685, is regarded as the Father of the English Turf. He inaugurated the Town Plate, after passing a law stating that the race must be run forever.

Keepers recorded the agreements of all horse matches, while King Charles established the early racing rules, before the Jockey Club came into existence. In 1773, James Weatherby created the Racing Calendar. The Jockey Club owns fifteen racecourses, the National Stud, Racing Welfare and Jockey Club Estates. Since 2006, the Jockey Club has had no role in the governance of horseracing, which now rests with the British Horseracing Authority.

Newmarket comprises two individual racetracks, the Rowley Mile and the July Course. The Rowley Mile operates throughout the spring and autumn and is named after Old Rowley, King Charles II favourite racehorse. The course has a one mile two furlong straight with a dip in the final furlong. During summertime, racing switches to the nearby July Course, inaugurated in 1765. The straight is known as the Bunbury Mile.

The Rowley hosts two classic races: the 2,000 Guineas, first run in 1809, a race for three-year-old colts and fillies, over a distance of one mile; and the 1,000 Guineas, which came into being in 1814, for three-year-old fillies, also run over one mile. The races are named after the original prize money; a guinea was equal to one pound and one shilling, or £1.05 as it would be today.

The 2,000 Guineas remains part of the Group 1 Triple Crown, which comprises two other classics for colts and fillies: the Epsom Derby, run over a distance of one mile and a half in June; and the one and three quarter miles St Leger Stakes, founded in 1776 by Colonel Anthony St Leger, which is held at Doncaster during September. The term Triple Crown originates from Western Australia's three famous victories in 1853. It is considered the greatest accomplishment in thoroughbred racing. Allowing for disruptions during the First World War, a total of twelve three-year-olds have accomplished this feat, the most recent being Nijinsky in 1970. Since then, three horses have won both the 2,000 Guineas and the Derby: Nashwan in 1989; See the Stars in 2009; and Camelot, in 2012. Camelot is the only horse to attempt the treble, gallantly failing to win the St Leger by three quarters of a length behind Encke. These days, stud value is more reliant on speed. The fifth classic is the Oaks Stakes for fillies, which is also run at Epsom in June, over one and a half miles.

(A list of horse race grades is detailed in Appendix vii.)

In 1985, Lester Piggott rode the Michael Stoute-trained Shadeed, to win the 2,000 Guineas. Mr Piggott, who'd gained a ruthless reputation for riding winners at all costs, was due to ride Bairn for trainer Luca Cumani. After a change of mind, he opted to ride Shadeed, who was currently the highest-rated horse in Europe. Shadeed hit the front two furlongs out, and was strongly challenged by Bairn, as Piggott rousted his mount to win by a head. He retired at the end of the season, and artist Jacquie Jones painted *Maestro –The Final Classic*. The limited-edition print featured the famous jockey on Shadeed winning the 2,000 Guineas; the unfashionable print has since found space on my snug wall.

Having set himself up as a trainer, Lester's new career was cut short when he was stripped of his OBE and jailed for tax fraud. He returned to the saddle in 1990, winning the 1992 2,000 Guineas aboard the Peter Chapple-Hyam-trained Rodrigo de Triano, a horse bred and owned by Robert Sangster. This proved to be the maestro's thirtieth and final winning classic. His record-breaking career includes nine Derby wins, eight St Leger's, six Oaks, five 2,000 Guineas and two 1,000 Guineas. In 1990, the annual jockey awards known as The Lesters were launched and named in his honour, recognising the achievements of jockeys from both flat and jump racing. Lester rode his final winner on British soil in October 1994, aged 58. He is affectionately remembered as one of the greatest flat jockeys of all time.

Among the array of Lostalot punters was a character nicknamed Get Paid. The Geordie could be described as kind and thoughtful, though a little obnoxious after visiting the pub. He had a few teeth missing, which he'd reportedly extracted himself, after one too many shots of whisky. He was a notorious favourite backer, and would sound off and curse whenever his horse fell, or lost. In contrast, he would shout, 'Get paid,' when his selection was assured of winning. Most of the punters found his language amusing, and David tolerated Get Paid's behaviour, until the day Roxy witnessed him in full flow.

David was issued with an ultimatum: 'Either he goes, or I go.'

He pondered for somewhile and made a decision to ban Get Paid, who was effectively banished to the pub next door.

David was soon to drive Roxy to Kempton Park, where she was assisting for the day. In spite of Frankie Dettori winning three races, he was showing a healthy profit. Frankie was riding a 9/2 shot in the last, and everyone wanted a piece of the action. This included the representatives of major bookmakers looking to reduce betting office liabilities, causing the price to shorten to 7/2. David viewed this as an opportunity to make easy money, believing the odds were reduced because Frankie was on a four-timer. He got stuck in, laying all of the bets available from punters and bookies alike, including a £2,250 to £500. Frankie's mount, Little Eye, won by half a length, completing a 675/1 accumulator. The narked bookie was left to pay a long queue of punters stretching halfway down the betting ring. As the last of the punters disappeared, one remaining payment of £22.50 was that of Roxy, who'd also muscled in on the act.

One of the most obvious betting systems is to back the favourite, the shortest price and, in theory, the most likely winner. Get Paid got paid 32% of the time, which is the average for UK winning horse race favourites, combining flat, all-weather and National Hunt. On average, 25% of handicap favourites win, along with 40% non-handicap favourites. When the market is tight, there might be joint favourites, or co-favourites of three or more. Sometimes prices fluctuate, and the starting favourite may not be known at the time of the off.

I've backed my fair share of odds-on favourites, and in July 2004 I took a steady drive to Newton Abbot Races for an afternoon's entertainment in the sunshine. I particularly liked the look of Westender, a gelding trained by Martin Pipe, in the Beginners' Chase. Westender had cost me a few quid after finishing second a couple of weeks earlier on his chasing debut, and I was out to recoup my losses. As race time approached, I bet £500 on the nose at skinny odds of 1/2. The race was soon off, and the five runners set out on the two-mile trip. Westender was leading as they hurtled towards the first flight, but suddenly slammed on the brakes, and in the process unseated jockey Timmy Murphy.

On 31st July 2020, three days after the success of Stradivarius, we placed our second racing certainty wager on the Charlie Hills-trained Battash. After being quoted as the 'World's fastest thoroughbred', Battash was running in the King George Qatar Stakes, over five furlongs at Glorious Goodwood. We were feeling quietly confident as we bet our £1,829 at odds of 1/3. Battash never looked like being defeated, keeping on to win by two and a quarter lengths under jockey Jim Crowley. This took our running profit to £2,439.

The annual bread-rolling race takes place every Spring Bank Holiday on Reaney Hill. The event may have origins dating back to the Phoenicians, who inhabited south-western parts of Britain prior to the Roman invasion of 54BC. Another theory is that it stems from a pagan custom of rolling items down the one-in-three hill. Bundles of burning brushwood were also rolled down, to mark the birth of a New Year after winter. The Master of Ceremonies would scatter buns, biscuits and sweets at the top of the hill to encourage the fruits of harvest.

Lots of spectators gather from far and wide to watch this crazy tradition, which attracts competitors from all around the globe. A loaf of bread, usually a giant cob, is rolled down the hill by the Master of Ceremonies, and a few seconds later the competitors hurl themselves in pursuit of the loaf. The first runner to reach the bottom wins the prize of the large cob. Physicians are on hand, as many get injured, and local rugby players act as catchers at the bottom of the hill. A great deal of people consider it to be the most dangerous foot race in the world, as competitors customarily lose foothold, tumbling head over heels. Some entrants are assisted with Dutch courage, having frequented local hostelries en route to the slaughter.

Lostalot regular Thomas was landlord at the nearby Bread Rollers public house. Thomas wasn't the biggest fan of the event, mainly because of the large crowd, bringing disruption to his usual steady trade. On the morning of the 2004 race, David telephoned a resentful Thomas, asking the time of the first race.

'Don't know, and don't care.'

On the other hand, David was keen to know because he'd laid one of the contestants, Stephan, to win all three men's races, during a drinking session at the rugby club. David was renowned for giving generous odds at the bar, having once given Dai the Pencil 1,000/1 on Wales to beat England in a Six Nations game at Twickenham, all be it for a mere £2 stake. David failed to realise that Stephan had previously won all three races and generously offered him odds of 10/1 to repeat the feat: the correct odds should have been close to 3/1. The contrite bookie had been caught off guard, as Stephan staked £200 on himself to win.

The event almost didn't take place, as a few days earlier, none other than David had driven his latest jalopy up to the car park at Reaney Hill to go mountain biking with his daughter. As the car came to a halt under a canopy of trees, smoke began appearing from under the bonnet and the engine caught fire. David ran to a nearby house, where the homeowner dialled 999. The fire soon engulfed the trees, and the whole side of the hill was ablaze. He was concerned that he might be accused of sabotage, in order to avoid paying out. Coincidentally, an unsuspecting Stephan happened to be driving past and noticed the hill on fire. The Fire Brigade arrived in the nick of time, and soon had the blaze under control.

The damage to the hillside was superficial, and the event was given the go ahead. Another contestant, Martin, bet £10 on himself to win any one race. It was a glorious sunny day, as David made his way to a good viewing point at the bottom of the hill. A large crowd assembled and extreme excitement filled the air. Sweating most profusely, David gazed upwards into the sunlight, and the first men's race was underway. As the contestants came into view, a Gurkha soldier was leading the field, with Stephan nowhere to be seen. Meanwhile, Martin summersaulted through the air, resembling a ragdoll, having knocked himself unconscious. The Gurkha held on to win the first race, and David made his way back to the shop. Shortly afterwards, a few punters came in announcing that Martin was again conscious, thanks to the medic's smelling salts.

It was bad news for Stephan, as he was seriously injured. Rumour has it that his main rival and former multiple race winner Mickie Pride cunningly tripped him up. He required the attentions of the Air Ambulance, and it was subsequently revealed that he'd broken his leg in several places. David felt guilty over pocketing Stephan's losing wager, especially as he hadn't made the effort to visit him in hospital.

David's ill-judged involvement with greyhound racing was some twelve years behind him when another opportunity presented itself.

This time, a couple of experienced course bookmakers persuaded him to part with £8,000 for the privilege of going into partnership at a newly established dog track. David believed the diversity would complement his portfolio of racecourse pitches, in the evolving world of bookmaking.

To begin with signs were positive, as a fair share of results favoured the bookmakers, although this was not always the case at new tracks. David was led to believe that he'd made a shrewd business move. However, the honeymoon period only lasted for a few months before results took a turn for the worse. He began taking Roxy along for a night out. Roxy was naive when it came to betting, and commented on the fact that greyhound trainers would huddle together in conference between races.

Much to the exclusion of others, certain dogs were heavily supported, frequently winning as odds-on favourites. A one-dog book is not good business for bookmakers, while many punters found the betting patterns unattractive, and attendance greatly diminished. David's investment was no longer the lucrative business opportunity he had hoped for, and the association with his new colleagues was short lived, removing a further £8,000 from his enfeebled bank account.

Chapter 18
The Last Straw

The Tote Trifecta often yields big returns from small stakes. The bet is available in most high-street bookmakers and is similar to a tricast, where you need to predict which horses will finish first, second and third. I find the bet to be most productive in handicap chases. One of the selection's needs to be odds of at least 8/1 to have any chance of a decent pay-out. On completion of form study, the short list needs to throw up three contenders, or a maximum of four, in order to keep the cost of combination stakes down. To calculate the number of combinations, multiply the number of selections by the next two numbers down: three selections = 3 x 2 x 1 = six bets: four selections = 4 x 3 x 2 = twenty-four bets. Five selections combined equates to sixty bets, which becomes expensive.

In the back office at Badgeport, David was contemplating recent favourable results at both offices. However, trade was slow, with just a couple of punters betting on Portman Park. Virtual racing usually provided Lostalot with a good percentage profit. Suddenly the manager burst in, presenting David with a winning betting slip that belonged to Baz, who ran the local kebab shop. Baz enjoyed betting £10 forecasts and tricasts on virtual racing. On this occasion he hit the jackpot, with a pay-out totalling £8,355, leaving a speechless David to sink deep into his new, leather executive chair. After a moment he gathered his composure, walked into the shop and congratulated the kebab man on his win. He asked Baz to return for his winnings the following day, which he somehow managed to scrape together. This type of bet is often presented just before the off and gives little opportunity to cover liabilities, demonstrating the volatility of small independent bookmakers.

A few weeks later, two smartly dressed individuals presented themselves at the Lostalot counter. It turned out they were bookmakers from Wales, showing interest in purchasing the good will of the business. David had not considered selling, but that being said, he remained open minded and promised to consider any proposal they might put his way.

Within a couple of weeks, an offer arrived for £150,000, which he forwarded to Phil Jellops. Phil considered it was a good opportunity, given the level of business, leaving David to ponder the possibilities of selling up. At least it would enable him to pay off the debts, consolidate the business at Badgeport and free up more time to increase course attendance. Three weeks later, with only one shop left to stress over, he joined Roxy for a holiday in South Africa.

Boxing day found David a little dejected, after taking a hammering at Kempton Park. Just to make matters worse, during the drive home, Tom and Captain Birdseye were discussing the Thailand Tsunami disaster. David had concerns for Dai the Pencil, who was holidaying in Koh Samui. The following day the trio made their way back to Kempton, and David received good news from Dai, to say he'd survived. On arrival, they realised that the meeting was in jeopardy after overnight frost. This resulted in a succession of ground inspections, as they were hoping the meeting would go ahead. David instructed none other than Captain Birdseye to test the frozen ground with his foot, which was standard course practice at this time. He attempted to sink his heel in, only for it to part company with the main body of his shoe. Subsequently the meeting was abandoned, forcing the topsy-turvy trio to return home empty handed.

On the eve of the 2005 Grand National, two strangers appeared at the Badgeport office, just as David's colleague Mark was about to leave. The till was brimming with cash after a couple of winning days. Suddenly, one of the men jumped over the counter, landing on a startled David, as the pair began grappling. Meanwhile, his ginger-haired accomplice ensured that Mark was kept at arm's length. The assailant pulled a kitchen knife and pushed David towards the till, before helping himself to its contents. He then held the knife to his throat screaming, 'Safe!', as David knelt down to open the empty safe.

In total, the robbers helped themselves to nearly £3,000, though, they were not overly observant and failed to notice his bulging pocket, which contained a further £1,000. Within a few seconds they'd scarpered, no doubt satisfied with the afternoon's results. Police were soon at the scene taking statements, as well as David's shirt for forensics. Having relinquished £3,000 and his shirt, the half-clad, bookie departed for home. One of the assailant's was subsequently arrested for a crime in London, and confessed to the Lostalot robbery. Bookmakers are unable to obtain any insurance cover for cash, and the police were unable to recover any of the money.

The ill-prepared robbers may have waited twenty-four hours, as they struck on the eve of the bookie's most active cash handling day. David was taking no chances on Grand National day, and called on brother Jeff to stash the float in a secret hideaway. Jeff was perhaps a little too conspicuous; attired in shades, black leather jacket, and black and white winklepickers. Resembling a hitman from *The*

Godfather, he sauntered out of the shop with the day's take compressed inside a Primark carrier bag.

David was now questioning his future as a high-street bookie, and started viewing the racecourse as a less volatile proposition. After a consultation with Phil Jellops, he made a decision to sell the last of the Lostalot branches, placing all of his eggs in one basket. It was a good time to sell, as Coral was acquiring further units as part of an expansion scheme, and paying top dollar. Phil wasted no time in negotiating a big sum, and Badgeport was sold.

With the intention of using the proceeds to purchase some more racecourse pitches, he became eager to upgrade the pitch on the Newmarket Rowley Mile, and I agreed to loan him £4,000. This enabled him to secure the purchase ahead of the completion of sale. David also obtained pitches at Cheltenham Festival, Newbury, Wolverhampton and Tattersalls at Royal Ascot, costing a total of £53,000 for the five venues.

When it comes to business, I have my own views on car status, as I don't need to appear too successful, but equally, I didn't want to look like an underachiever. David maintained that the reason for driving old bangers was that he didn't want punters to get the wrong impression, as a decent car would suggest he was earning too much. Clearly, he'd taken this thought well beyond a healthy balance of reason. On one occasion, he drove a rusty Ford Mondeo to Royal Ascot, with the bumper held together by gaffer tape. He wangled himself into the owners' car park, which saved trekking the equipment on the usual long haul to the course. His trusted staff were a tad embarrassed to say the least, as he edged the fumy vehicle between a Bentley and a Jag. Meanwhile, some very well-dressed picnickers looked on in dismay, quickly coming to a conclusion: there is such a thing as a poor bookie.

One afternoon, Hank came into Winallot Racing, placing a system bet on a virtual reality race at Portman Park.

As his horse took the lead, he was shouting, 'Go on, my son.'

Soon after, he was cursing his luck, when his selection faded out of contention. He then turned his attentions to the jockey for not trying, and accused him of throwing the race. I was quite shocked at this latest outburst, even by Hank's standards. In fact, it shook me to such an extent that I knew that my bookmaking days were numbered.

A couple of weeks later, Hank returned to test out his new system, backing second favourites in novice chases. During a quiet moment of evening racing, he overheard a lady saying that she had a tip.

'I've come in to bet a couple of pounds on Dicky Johnson's mount at Uttoxeter.'

Hank was a man with his ear to the ground, constantly alert to the word 'tip', and homed in on the conversation. The lady went on to say that she was a friend of the jockey's family, and that the horse was strongly fancied. Seconds later, a very confident Hank stood before me, beaming from head to toe, slamming his £40 on the counter, taking 7/4 on the evening's whisper.

During the race, Johnson's horse travelled with ease, and on jumping the penultimate fence the pair were looking sure to win.

Approaching the final obstacle, this sweet lady shouted, 'Come on, Dicky!'

In a split-second horse and jockey parted company, leaving Dicky stretched out on the turf. Hank was fuming, and began shouting obscenities.

'You put him off, you silly cow. You shouted, "Come on, Dicky." That's what made him fall.'

This was the last straw, and I decided to quit the bookmaking industry for good. It wasn't just because of this incident. It had been a slow build-up, in an ever-changing industry under threat from internet betting exchanges. There were also other issues, such as long hours, noisy inhouse gaming machines, fictitious reality racing and increased lucky number draws. The traditional betting office was but a shadow of its former self, and I was no longer enjoying it.

During the weeks that followed, I was seriously contemplating my prospects of going to university to study law. By chance, I happened to be listening to the radio, when Johnnie Walker was interviewing a clairvoyant on the legitimacy of her work. She mentioned that people often seek her assistance when they're about to make life-changing decisions, such as emigrating or a career change.

She went on to add, 'It's best to use someone who's recommended, as the industry has its fair share of fakes.'

A few days later, a friend suggested a suitable lady in this field, and set me up with an appointment. In a nutshell, she suggested that I would likely succeed in whatever I turned my hand to. During the session, she kept asking who Francis was, as he was desperate to get a message to me from the other side. The name didn't ring any bells at first, and I didn't take any notice. Francis remained persistent, and I realised that my old friend, Frank Black, was also known as Francis.

He wanted me to convey a message to his first wife, Rose, (whom I had never met): 'She was the only woman I ever loved. And I'm sorry things didn't work out between us.'

217

I still had Frank's daughter's telephone number, and after a few days of pondering, I plucked up courage and made the call. I feared she might think I was stark raving bonkers. Nevertheless, a man's gotta do what a man's gotta do.

On delivering the message, Lisa replied, 'Oh Johnny,' and put the phone down on me.

We haven't spoken since, but, as uncomfortable as it was, I believe I did the right thing by Frank.

My next stop was a year of college studies, on the Access to University course. However, I would need to pass a maths and English test in order to become eligible. The English test was a breeze, though much to my embarrassment I scored less than 33%, and flunked the maths test.

This confused the college principal, who said, 'You're a bookmaker. Aren't you supposed to be good at maths?'

She accepted me on to the course, with a proviso that I worked an extra weekly session in mathematics.

Graham Cordy agreed to manage Winallot, leaving me to man the shop at weekends. In the intervening period, I was spending all of my time reading up on English law, as I had serious concerns that my lack of academic talent would come back to haunt me at university.

In 2006, David paid £16,000 for Cheltenham pitch number 33, which was situated in Tattersalls. This enabled him to operate at both the four-day March festival and the three-day November meeting. The thirty-third pick usually allowed him to stand fourth in the third row, close to the action. Attracting larger bets wasn't easy, because he still had to offer slightly bigger odds, which in turn lowered the profit margin.

With the festival looming, ex bookie George Wily, an old mate of the illusive Roger Bunco, advised David to stand every Cheltenham favourite for a grand. David ignored his advice in the opener, the Supreme Novices Hurdle, laying the second favourite Noland, to lose a grand. The Paul Nicholls-trained Noland stormed through under Ruby Walsh, to get up in the dying strides. He then made the decision to go with the Wily theory, and by the end of the day he was £3,000 out of pocket.

During days two and three, he made no inroads. Nevertheless, he persevered with the system through to the final day, laying the winner of the Triumph Hurdle Detroit City, 7/2 favourite, followed by even money Black Jack Ketchum, which also won. The third race was the Gold Cup. David threw caution to the wind, adopting an all-or-nothing approach. He proceeded to lay six of the twenty-two runner field, with liabilities of £3,500 apiece. As the bunched runners came down the hill for the final time, he was contemplating the worse and the prospects of another festival loss, to the tune of £8,000. The result fell in his favour after War of Attrition prevailed, and by the end of play the despairing bookie had recouped the week's losses.

David came to the conclusion that it was difficult to make a profit from his position in Cheltenham's Tattersalls, because layers were strong, standing most of their own liabilities. He sold the Tattersalls pitch, and bought shares with Captain Birdseye and Tom in the Best Mate enclosure. This area was formerly known as the Cabbage Patch, because of the odd weed sprouting up from the ground and the thin sprinkling of bookmakers.

Unfortunately, he was about to be dealt a body blow. The Gambling Act of 2005 had made no provision for bookmakers' positions, which were originally intended to be owned by the bookmaker in perpetuity. The new laws would be enforced in 2007, while the Racecourse Association decided that, as of

2012, it would not acknowledge a bookmaker's list position. The consequence of this was an instant and devastating effect on pitch values, which was outside the spirit of the Act. The Association's intention was to dispense with bookmaker's existing agreements and negotiate new contracts. In the interim, small bookmakers feared being pushed out by bigger off-course operators.

Post 1998, some bookmakers had invested huge sums, including one who had reputedly spent £1.25 million. The Racecourse Association's intention would render these assets worthless. Bookmakers were up in arms and lobbied MPs, highlighting a grave travesty of justice. During the years that followed, many meetings took place, leading to a debate in Parliament. The dispute would go on for years, and was eventually resolved in 2014, whereby bookmakers were granted a tenure until 2054.

David married Roxy in 2006, though celebrations were cut short, as he faced the dilemma of depreciating racecourse investments. By now, the pitches were only worth a fraction of the purchase price. The portfolio was insufficient to support general living costs, particularly during the winter jumps season, when shrewd punters and quick-thinking experienced bookmakers would often get the edge. In order to stay afloat, he offloaded various pitches at a considerable loss. Sadly, enough was enough, and David made the decision to leave the industry.

In the wake of much sufferance, I sold the building at Pingford, and, whilst it had remained dormant for a long period, the venture produced a considerable profit. Unbeknown to the council, I continued to renew the betting licence on the sold building, as I was on the lookout for a site on the same street with current office use. I was desperate to put one over on both the town council and the planners. Deep down, I knew my day of retribution would come; it was just a matter of time.

Having completed one year at college, I found myself at university on a three-year course studying for a law degree, and carrying a whole new level of anguish. Being one of the oldest students on the entire campus, I was also one of the slowest when it came to retaining information. The first year's studies included contract law, public law, legal method, and criminal law. Clearly, I'd underestimated what I was letting myself in for, and drove full throttle into one of the most stressful periods of my life.

Lawrence's son Clive started frequenting Winallot armed with shedloads of cash, and looking like a man on a mission. Having known him as a little boy, when I used to ask his dad to make him wait outside, I began wondering if he'd plotted a vendetta against me, for not allowing him in. He was now a striking six feet tall, with the same old blonde curly locks, and a polite, almost studious manner. One day, Clive unexpectedly bet £3,000 on Arsenal to win the second leg of a 2006 European Champions League semi-final, away to Villarreal. Ironically, I was on holiday in Spain with my son, and we are both Arsenal fans. While we were on our way to watch the televised game in a local bar, Graham Cordy phoned, advising me of his bet. Unfortunately for Clive, the game ended in a 0-0 draw, after Arsenal goalkeeper Jens Lehmann saved a penalty in the ninetieth minute, sending Arsenal into the final.

The young man soon became our biggest punter. This didn't last for too long, because he wasn't very lucky. Clive had quickly shifted from £10 to £3,000 wagers, and it crossed my mind as to where he'd got the money. I liked him, he was a nice young man, though I had concerns that he might be ruining his life. Around this time, the Gambling Commission provided bookmakers with a DVD on problem gambling. The idea was to offer it to gamblers who bookmakers believed had an addiction. I considered discussing the situation with both Lawrence and Clive. After much consideration, I opted not to, as it felt too uncomfortable.

On 5th August 2020, even money favourite Soldier Of Love, trained by champion trainer Paul Nicholls and ridden by Harry Cobden, became our third racing certainty. The horse was running in a Class 3 handicap chase at Newton Abbot. Despite four decades of gambling, and a well thought-out plan of attack, the thrill of the gamble still set my nerves jangling as I wagered our £2,439 stake. Soldier Of Love tracked the leaders and struck the front at the second last fence. He pulled clear to win by seven and a half lengths, taking our profit to £4,878.

While contemplating a return to Human Resources, David set himself up with a couple of interviews, and became disillusioned with ever increasing legislation. Desperate to survive, he decided to take up his ex-brother-in-law's offer, labouring on a building site. For the first time in his life he was grafting, losing four stone in weight. A few months later, I made the decision to put Winallot up for sale. I approached David to see if he was interested in running the shop, with a view to building up trade, before putting it on the market. Meanwhile, he would take on the profit and risk, while I would reward him, by paying him a bonus at the point of sale.

David snapped up my offer, swapping his high-vis, safety footwear and hard hat for a baggy shirt, trousers and a pair of brogues. I explained that I wanted him to succeed and that this was a chance to get back on his feet. We targeted his comeback ahead of the Cheltenham Festival. I had concerns that he might take needless risks and blow it. His response sounded all too familiar: 'Don't worry about it, pal.'

During the first week, he paid Lawrence £1,800 on a full house Lucky 15. David was popular among customers, who warmed to his friendly personality. Some former clients were also returning, and the early signs were encouraging. David ran the shop more or less single handed during the first few months. This was not ideal, especially during busy Saturday's, as he continued to take hits on both horse and greyhound racing. Eddie was another bugbear, regularly clocking up in excess of £1,000 on the roulette machine. However, his 'easy come, easy go' approach meant that the cash would eventually find its way back into the till. In June, David laid a sizeable golf bet on Angel Cabrera to win the US Open, costing him a further £3,200. On 1st July 2007, the UK smoking ban came into force, good news for all non-smokers, though a little too late for David and me, after decades of inhaling other people's smoke.

David started using Dai the Pencil to cover days off, though Dai's slow settling began annoying some patrons, particularly Hank, who would often lambast Dai. On one occasion, Hank began cursing his luck over another losing system bet. In fact, he was so wound up that he backed £2 to win on all twenty-seven runners in a handicap race. This was merely an attempt to change his fortune, as he would be certain to bet the winner. After cramming all of the numbers on to a betting slip, he proceeded to slam the £54 wager on to the counter. Sadly, the winner returned at odds of 5/1, leaving Hank with a £42 deficit.

Whilst David was striving to get back on an even keel, a Saturday punter backed four horses in a £2 win Lucky 15. The bookie was aware of the first two horses going in, but the third and fourth runners were closely timed, leaving his hedging strategy flawed. The final two selections won, costing him £8,500. With closely timed bets such as this, David might have hedged a £5 four-horse accumulator, eliminating most of the risk from the outset. Soon after, he introduced the cool and calculating Captain Birdseye, who assisted in manning the business until it was sold.

Back in Pingford, I found a vacant building with office use on the high street, and I needed to approach the magistrates to ask for permission to transfer the licence. The court date fell during a week of law studies, where I was shadowing leading specialist barrister Adrian Maxwell, who kindly offered to address the magistrates on my behalf. This was a cakewalk for Adrian, and the magistrates readily obliged the transfer.

Frankly, I had lost all interest in operating as a turf accountant at Pingford. In the meantime, I'd approached another bookmaker who was in attendance at court, and we shook hands on a deal immediately. Two weeks later, the bookies opened their doors in the enhanced position, directly next door to the town mayor's office. Shortly afterwards, David negotiated a deal with the same bookmaker to take the lease at Winallot. David for his part had worked extremely hard, though he finished out of pocket.

Towards the end of my first year at university, I failed two exams, and had to endure anxious resits. Fortunately, I stumbled across mediation, a process whereby a neutral third party assists disputants in finding solutions to conflict, hence avoiding court. After speaking with a couple of university lecturers, I came to understand that I didn't need a law degree to work as a mediator. They also believed I would never be taken seriously without one, and therefore I'd be unable to obtain work. Ignoring their advice, I wasted no time and made the decision to work as a self-employed commercial/civil mediator.

Chapter 19
No Time for Losers

After quitting my studies, I wasted no time in qualifying as a commercial mediator. I soon came to realise that the best mediators aren't usually lawyers, because they don't need to specialise in law, they merely need to think on their feet, and apply common sense while remaining impartial. Bizarrely, there I was in my late forties, sensing that my parents were disappointed in me for quitting school. On the bright side, I had at least obtained my financial goal, being in a position to retire before the age of fifty.

Mediation is a speedy process that is less stressful than litigation and saves on costs. I have been fortunate enough to obtain plenty of work, and I now operate as a Senior Mediator.

On celebrating my newfound career, Gordon Bennett accompanied me on a sodden winter's day to Sandown Park. Having caught the train to nearby Esher station. We'd backed the same horse in the final race, which jumped the last hurdle well clear of the field. On the run to the winning post, we were so busy high fiving, we didn't notice our horse faltering in the heavy going, and getting chinned on the line.

Gordon suggested we drown our sorrows with a glass of red. As we walked into town, the rain continued to fall, and we took shelter in a friendly Italian restaurant. Gordon was soon a little worse for wear and needed to board the last train home. Back at the racecourse car park, we found my solitary car with its back wheels sunk into the wet turf. Ironically, I recently watched former jump jockey Mick Fitzgerald on *ITV Racing*, talking about horses running at Sandown.

He'd said, 'Some get stuck in the mud, and simply can't travel.'

Gordon offered to give me a push from behind, though I suggested it wasn't such a good idea, since it was a rear-wheel drive. He wasn't having any of it, sprawling himself over the rear end, bellowing 'Full throttle!'

In a flash the car jerked to the side, and the wheels spun round, splattering him from head to toe.

Gordon decided to leg it to the station and fell over, cutting his hand. I sat waiting patiently in the Sandown car park for a bigger tow truck, after the first truck failed to tug the Mercedes out of its deepening position. I finally emerged back on the road, at way past midnight. Gordon arrived home much earlier, covered in mud with his hand wrapped in a blooded bandage and feeling a little sorry for himself.

He was greeted by his startled wife, and the words, 'Gordon Bennett.'

With very limited funds available, David was looking to make a few quid towards general living costs and pay off some household bills. He turned his attention to betting on rugby, a sport that had served him well in the past. Bath were in good form in the Guinness Premier League and a confident Mr Watts was predicting them as a certainty to beat Harlequins, away from home.

He explained to Mrs Watts, 'The best team usually prevails in rugby.'

After reviewing what she'd signed up for, Roxy gave the thumbs up, and David placed £500 on Bath, at odds of 4/6. Cruelly, Bath lost by six points.

The following day, the deflated apprentice went back to labouring, while training as an electrician.

He's not one to worry about hard graft, and embraced the work as a stepping-stone to a new career. His labouring tasks varied from loading out materials and sweeping the floor to installing festoons of temporary lighting. He persevered with the training, and soon completed a City & Guilds qualification. On setting up his own limited company, he embarked on a new career. He coped well with the academic side, though it took a while to pick up the practical aspects, along with squeezing through narrow loft hatches and crawling around in the dark.

Soon after, David came up with the design of a new horse race laying system, based around jump racing. At 10.30 am, he'd browse Oddschecker, in order to identify drifting favourites. He'd then lay these horses, on the exchanges where the odds were no greater than 3.5 (5/2). David convinced me that his system was infallible, and I joined forces to test it out. We laid our first horse, which romped home in first position. Our second and third lays also won. Suddenly we were struggling to pick a loser!

I was invited to a wine tasting where I first met the irresolute Mr Stevens, a well-dressed Moroccan gentleman, in his mid-forties. He clearly lived for the moment, and knew how to enjoy life to the full. Mr Stevens drank a lot of red wine, and ran his own wine import business, describing himself as a 'partially Muslim' wine connoisseur. He was infatuated by my old bookmaking business, and asked me lots of questions about gambling. It turned out that he enjoyed a visit to the casino, and invited me along as his guest. He said he was an experienced roulette player. I spent most of the evening watching him on the table, where he proceeded to lose a couple of thousand pounds.

He seemed to have enjoyed himself and was keen to go again, though I suggested that wasn't such a good idea, advising him to find a new hobby. I managed to talk him into staying away for several months, though he was quite persistent, and we returned for a second bite of the cherry. On arrival, management greeted him like a long-lost friend, and commented on how good it was to see him again. They insisted on a drink on the house, and we followed them to the bar. The manager served Mr Stevens with a large glass of the house merlot, while I was completely ignored.

A few sips later, the experienced connoisseur turned his nose up and we made our way to the roulette table, where he exchanged £500 for casino chips. He met an acquaintance at the table called Mr Hing. Mr Hing had reportedly gambled his entire restaurant empire away in this very casino, and was frequently in attendance as a voyeur. Astonishingly, Mr Stevens passed all of his chips to Mr Hing, asking him to play on his behalf. After a couple of spins, Mr Hing apologised most profusely for the casual loss, and a bemused Mr Stevens decided to call it a night.

My cousin Pete Ponting rode pointers as a lad and showed much desire to become a professional jockey. However, in spite of an offer of a place at racing school, things never materialised. He remained with a keen interest in horseracing, and dreamed of one day owning a racehorse. In 1998 that dream came true, when he purchased a broodmare that went into training, finishing second under rules at Exeter. Sadly, this was the mare's last run before breaking down. Ginger, as she was affectionately known, went on to produce six foals. In the interim, I introduced Pete to Robin Butterworth, a local point-to-point rider, who also had an interest in training pointers. In turn, he introduced Pete to trainer Jo Davis. Having raised the foals, Pete turned his hand to training, assisted by Robin. With an instinctive flare, they soon developed a knack for producing winners.

Pete introduced his eleven-year-old son Joe to pony racing. Joe developed a natural talent for riding, which led to lots of memorable family days out. The young jockeys would race on the same card as professionals at major racecourses. Hope was Joe's star pony, winning his fair share of races at various tracks, including Goodwood and Newmarket. Joe began riding pointers for both his dad and Robin; he rode his first winner at the age of sixteen.

In 2008, Pete combined with a couple of drinking buddies, entrepreneurs Kevin and Harry, to purchase a racehorse. The German bred Passato cost the trio £6,000, after it failed to make the frame on all seven previous UK runs. Passato went into training under Jo Davis. Remarkably, Jo trained the horse to win by ten lengths on his debut run at Exeter, over hurdles under jockey Danny Burton. I would often collect Pete's winnings when accompanying him to the races. He maintains that his favourite moment is my beaming smile as I relieve the bookies of cash. Pete and Kevin were both well versed in betting, while astute businessman Harry appeared to be clueless. During a four-month period, the gutsy Passato ran seven times, winning twice and being placed four times. Given that Harry was a novice punter, Pete and Kevin were greatly surprised at the sheer amount of money he was staking. In the interim, Harry was assuming the game was easy, regularly filling his boots.

In May 2009, Passato was running at Stratford, and Pete invited me to make up a party of twelve. Passato was in good form, and the group were sweet on his winning chances. Having studied the form of the opposing horses, I wasn't convinced, and warned them not to get carried away. As we approached the betting ring, Pete, Kevin and most of the others moved in for the kill. I assumed Harry was going to place a modest sum, but to my surprise he staked £500 each way at 6/1. Jockey Seamus Durack coaxed Passato to win by a head, and it was champagne all around. Over in the winner's enclosure, Kevin and Harry were cock-a-hoop, spinning each other around. This was followed by Harry, dancing gracefully in his snakeskin shoes. The whole party's pockets were now bulging with cash, apart from mine. I had to concede to being the party pooper, the only one who hadn't backed Passato. Back in the champagne bar, I was also the only one without a glass of house champers. The consensus of opinion was that I didn't deserve it, as I'd bet against the star of the show.

Come November, Pete had a runner at Chepstow and kindly invited me along. To my surprise Kevin and Harry were present, as they had shares in another horse called Lady Jinks, who was running that afternoon. Lady Jinks had behavioural issues and a fierce reputation at home, after slicing a stable girl's ear with a double-barrelled kick that required stiches. The mare was also refusing to behave on the gallops. I was with Kevin and Harry when Jo Davis advised them on the horse's deficiencies and warned them off betting.

This fell on deaf ears, as Kevin and Harry approached the betting ring, lumping on each way at odds of 250/1. I took notice of the trainer's warning, placing a wager on the Paul Nicholls-trained favourite Tito Bustillo. Lady Jinks and Tito Bustillo pulled clear of the field and fought out the finish, with the favourite prevailing by two and a half lengths. Kevin and Harry were delighted, as they had effectively bet a 50/1 winner. Whilst the speculative duo stuffed their wallets, I collected a paltry £50.

The biggest priced National Hunt winner was recorded at Kelso during 1990, in a novice handicap hurdle. Equinoctial won for Durham-based trainer Norman Miller, at odds of 250/1.

On the flat, Theodore was the biggest priced winner, winning the St Leger under trainer James Croft in 1822, at odds of 200/1. Mr Croft came under great suspicion for race fixing, though no allegations were ever proved. In July 2016, trainer Jose Santos saddled Dandy Flame to win at Wolverhampton, equalling the 200/1 record odds. In June 2020, another 200/1 shot, Intercessor, won a novice stakes race by a head at Newbury, for trainer John Gallagher and rider, Cieren Fallon Jr. Incredibly, two months later, a three-year-old called He Knows No Fear won over a mile at Leopardstown, at odds of 300/1, under trainer Luke Comer and jockey Chris Hayes.

Passato was entered in a Listed Class 1 Handicap Chase at Newton Abbot. This was to be Harry's biggest bet, after Jo Davis advised that the horse was in peak condition and expected to win. Harry emptied his pockets, wading in with £1,420 on the nose at 16/1. Passato took up the running three out, and kept on gamely to win by half a length from the Paul Nicholls-trained joint favourite Classic Swain. A jubilant Harry made a profit of £22,720. Racehorse trainers who wish to attract owners, generally understand that they're in a gambling environment, and some owners want to know when the time is right for a gamble. Any gambler worth his salt knows the risks attached, and won't blame the trainer when things don't go to plan. Jo Davis did an exceptional job, transforming Passato to win nine times, including once over hurdles, six chases and two wins on the flat, netting the owners over £100,000 in prize money.

After the good run at Chepstow, Lady Jinks disappointed in her next couple of runs. It was decided to send her to Gary Witheford, much respected among elite trainers, for his profound understanding and psychological analysis of problem horses. Gary worked with Lady Jinks, and advised that as a foal, she'd probably been taken away from her mother too early. He went on to say that she was very strong, and predicted that she'd win next time out, while also proclaiming that she would not win again afterwards!

Unfortunately, I wasn't privy to this information, as Kevin, Harry and the rest of the syndicate set out on a daytrip to Wincanton. At the racecourse, Kevin lumped on and Harry bet £500 each way. As predicted, Lady Jinks won her race, rewarding Harry with a £9,600 profit, having backed the horse at 16/1. In the interim, Kevin's account was closed down by one of the national bookmakers. The owners ignored both Jo Davis' and Gary's advice, running the horse twice more without success, before selling her on. Gary Witheford's assessment proved correct, as Lady Jinks never won again under rules.

Joe Ponting won a scholarship to attend the Newmarket Racing School, after excelling in pony racing. He's since become a very proficient jockey, riding under rules in amateur flat races, bumpers, hurdles and hunter chases. Often complimented for his soft hands on the rein, he stylishly rode Passato to a seven-length victory in an Amateur Riders flat race at Warwick. Professional flat jockeys are currently paid a fee of £148.44 per ride, plus 7.5% of the prize money for a win and 5% of prize money for a place. In comparison, jump jockeys are paid £201.24 per ride, plus 10% of prize money for a win and 5% for a place. Amateur flat jockeys and conditional Jump jockeys earn the same fee as their fellow professionals.

Despite spending much time in the sauna, Joe struggled to keep his weight down and has since joined the trainers' ranks, taking over from his dad. Joe trained his first point winner at the age of fifteen, showing significant ability at training both flat and jump horses. In the summer of 2019, as a twenty-three-year-old, he pre-trained Baywatch to within two weeks of a run, under rules. The horse had not previously won under trainers, Andrew Balding, or Tim Reed and went on to win three times in eleven days, at Bath, Salisbury and Lingfield.

During the spring of 2021, he completed the British Horseracing Authority training course, where he obtained a combined, jump and flat trainer's licence. Joe's first winner arrived under the new licence during November, when 33/1 shot, Gavin, pulled off a shock result, easily winning a class 5, two-mile handicap hurdle at Uttoxeter, under Danny Burton.

In order to obtain a licence, trainers need to demonstrate at least five years' experience in training yards or stables, and at least two years in a senior position. They also need an NVQ Level 3 in Racehorse Care and Management. In addition, they must pass three one-week courses at the British Racing School, Newmarket, or at the National Racing College, Doncaster, as well as attending a one-day seminar at Weatherbys. There are further requirements and checks, which include knowledge in such areas as horse anatomy, feeding and the rules of racing. It takes, on average, three to four months to complete the course.

York has a splendid racecourse, which is sometimes referred to as the Knavesmire, historically remembered as the scene of the hanging of Dick Turpin. In 2009, I accompanied Mr Stevens, who was now favouring the racecourse over the casino. He was planning a four-figure wager on odds-on favourite Sea The Stars in the Group 1 Juddmonte International Stakes. Mr Stevens, not renowned as the shrewdest of punters, had been impressed by the horse, after it won the 2,000 Guineas, the Derby and the Eclipse Stakes at Sandown, all in the space of nine weeks. This was the first horse to accomplish the treble since Nashwan in 1989. Close to the off, Mr Stevens had a change of mind, and talked himself into betting the Aidan O'Brien-trained Mastercraftsman. Sea The Stars won the race, and a very disgruntled Mr Stevens blew the remainder of his cash on a series of losers. The John Oxx-trained colt remained unbeaten as a three-year-old, partnered on each occasion by jockey Michael Kinane. Sea The Stars retired to stud after winning the Prix de l'Arc de Triomphe, and is remembered as one of the best.

Racing thoroughbreds can be traced back, in tail male line, to three foundation sires: Byerley Turk, Darley Arabian and Godolphin Barb. Tail male line is the continuous, unbroken line of sires. Nowadays, the breeding of racehorses commands extortionate fees in order to produce the next superstar. Some owners retire horses to stud early, to maximise stud value.

The mighty Frankel, sired by Derby winner Galileo and owned by Prince Khalid Abdullah, was trained by ten-time champion trainer Sir Henry Cecil. In 2005, Sir Henry's stable had shrunk to approximately fifty horses, leaving him to saddle just twelve winners. The famous Warren Place stable remained supported by Prince Khalid Abdullah, who sent Frankel to Sir Henry in January 2010.

Frankel made his racing debut at Newmarket on 13th August 2010. I was fortunate to be in attendance, on an extremely wet Friday evening. All the same, the mood on the July Course was about to change. Having got drenched, I made a dash for the car and changed my clothes. Luckily, I was back in time to bet on Frankel, who warmed punters' hearts with an eye-catching performance, at odds of 7/4, the highest of his career.

Partnered each time by jockey Tom Queally, Frankel remained unbeaten, winning all fourteen starts, including ten Group 1 races, incorporating the 2,000 Guineas, where he won unchallenged. He won on various types of ground, and over distances ranging between seven furlongs and one mile two and a half furlongs. He was a sight to behold, a racehorse with gears and a visible turn of foot. He went off favourite for each of his races, the shortest price being 1/20. His race career earnings totalled £2,998,302, before going to stud on 14th February 2013. The cover fee started at £125,000, rising to £175,000 by 2017.

Sir Henry described Frankel as, 'The best I've ever had, the best I've ever seen, and I'd be very surprised if there's ever been a better.'

I was most privileged to meet Sir Henry one afternoon at Glorious Goodwood. Having been described as a genius trainer of racehorses, he was also a much-loved gentleman. My short conversation with this exceptional man, along with witnessing Frankel's race debut eleven days later, has left an indelible memory. Horseracing's most impassioned pairing will be remembered as one of the greatest of all time.

On 20th August 2020, another flat horse became our fourth racing certainty: the Aidan O'Brien-trained Love, partnered by Ryan Moore in the Group 1 Darley Yorkshire Oaks at York. On this occasion, David admitted that he was suffering from the jitters. He had concerns about the Knavesmire course, where the going was being described as soft in places. We monitored further going reports, and by the start of racing we were convinced that there was sufficient good ground. We took the plunge, placing £4,878 in a succession of bets at odds of 1/2. We decided to spread the wager among various betting shops, in order to avoid too much attention. Love settled in second position tracking the leader. As the field entered the straight, Moore steered the filly off the rails to mount a challenge. Love, who was described by Aidan O'Brien as the finest filly he has trained, pulled clear to win by an unextended five lengths, netting us a profit of £2,439 and a running total of £7,317.

Soon after, Mr Stevens and I travelled to Paris for a weekend of wine tasting, and a visit to Longchamp for the Prix de l'Arc de Triomphe, where the Sir Michael Stoute-trained Workforce was bidding to win the race, after winning the English Derby. We took a train from the city and completed the nine-kilometre journey by bus, as there is no direct train to the racecourse. On arrival we were surprised by the casual dress code. The midday heatwave found us perched at a picnic table, feeling extremely uncomfortable in jacket, collar and tie.

I left Mr Stevens sipping a glass of old Beaujolais, as I crossed the lawn to join the long queue and grab us some lunch. On my way back, I suddenly remembered that he was a 'partial Muslim'. All the same, I placed the disguised *chien chaud* in front of him.

With a distinct look of repulsion written all over his face, he asked, 'What is this?' and proceeded to hurl the pork sausage across the lawn, straight into a party of outraged Parisian racegoers.

Longchamp racecourse, also known as Hippodrome de Longchamp, is a flat course, sitting in fifty-seven hectares within the picturesque surroundings of the Bois de Boulogne, on the river Seine. The course is famed for its forty-six starting posts and various interlaced tracks, along with a famous hill that provides a strong test for

237

thoroughbreds. Longchamp hosts over 50% of the French Group 1 races, and holds a capacity crowd of fifty thousand. The first race was run in 1857, where Napoleon III and his wife were both present after sailing down the Seine. Racegoers continued sailing to the course, often on steamboats, until approximately 1930.

The Group 1 Prix de l'Arc de Triomphe takes place annually on the first Sunday of October. The race was named after a famous monument that had been the scene of a victory parade by the Allies in 1919. The inaugural running took place in 1920 and was won by a three-year-old colt named Comrade, whose owner received the winning prize of 150,000 francs. The Arc, as it is universally referred to, is open to thoroughbreds aged three or older, running over a distance of one and a half miles. While attracting the best horses from all around the globe, it's Europe's most prestigious all-aged horse race. The Arc is currently the world's second richest turf race, behind The Everest, which takes place at the Randwick Racecourse in Sydney, Australia.

In 2003, a promotional poster described the Arc as, 'Ce n'est pas une course, c'est un monument.' (It's not a race, it's a monument.)

We spent much time discussing the form, and Mr Stevens, who was still inclined to bet large sums, became very sweet on the chances of Workforce. I bet £100 on the horse at fixed odds of 8/1, while Mr Stevens suffered another last-minute change of mind, backing Aidan O'Brien's Fame And Glory. Jockey Ryan Moore weaved a path through a big field of runners, encouraging Workforce to win by a head. I proceeded to get a little over excited by cheering and punching my fist into the air. Suddenly, I became aware of an extremely dejected Mr Stevens, and a mass of hostile French supporters looking down their Gallic noses.

In April 2011, I accompanied Pete, Joe and Harry to Aintree, where Passato was due to run in the Topham Chase, on the Grand National course. Curiously, we took a brisk walk in the spring sunshine around the sixteen-fence circuit, with jockey David Crosse. David was excited, as he would be riding over the big fences for the first time, and like most jockeys he felt privileged. Passato was racing at the rear when falling at the eighth, though thankfully, horse and jockey returned uninjured. Many course modifications took place between 1990 and 2010, including the lowering of fences and the narrowing of ditches, in an attempt to improve safety. Even so, some notable Grand National achievers have raised the 'speed kills' argument, suggesting that the alterations have an adverse effect by encouraging horses to run faster.

In 1829, pub landlord William Lynn created a racetrack close to his pub in Aintree. In 1836 he opened a new grandstand, before organising a four-mile steeplechase, which was won by Captain Beecher on Duke. Some historians consider this race as the first true Grand National. The Jockey Club lists Lottery as the first winner of the Grand Liverpool Steeplechase in 1839, a race that would become famous as the Grand National. Edward William Topham, a respected handicapper, was responsible for turning the Grand National into a handicap in 1843. To date, Red Rum is the only horse to win the race three times.

British horses have their official ratings reviewed and published each week by the British Horseracing Authority. A horse will gain a rating after it has won a race, or been placed once in the top six during any of its first three runs. If it does not achieve this, it continues racing until it does. The rating will determine how much weight a horse will carry and what class of handicaps it can enter. Flat horses are rated between 0 and 140 and jump horses between 0 and 170. *Racing Post* has its own ratings, which take into account the conditions of the next race the horse is due to run in.

Chapter 20
On the Cusp

During the spring of 2011, Dai the Pencil and a group of pals were due to go on their annual rugby trip. As they were waiting for the coach, Dai slipped off to the bookies to place a bet on a horse he'd received a tip for. The coach arrived and the party began boarding. Dai had not returned, and a mate went to find him. The front door of the bookies was locked, though he could see a paramedic tending to someone on the floor. It transpired that Dai was standing at the counter when he collapsed, suffering a fatal heart attack.

While carrying out some electrical work at a local church a couple of days later, David received a bizarre text. He was talking with the church warden regarding Dai, and the protocol for a cathedral funeral, when his phone bleeped. David was both embarrassed and surprised, since he would not usually be able to get a signal within the church walls. It was a message containing two square boxes, and the sender was D. Later, he tried to show Roxy the text, but it had disappeared. David believed that Dai was either trying to tell him that he didn't want a cathedral funeral or merely wanting to know the fate of his tipped horse. David still holds Dai in great esteem, and his dry wit is sadly missed.

Towards the end of July, I joined Mr Stevens at Glorious Goodwood, for the second day of the festival. We arrived in anticipation of betting Frankel, who was taking on the highly regarded, Canford Cliffs, in the Group 1 Sussex Stakes. I placed £200 to win at 4/5, meanwhile, Mr Stevens was holding a wad of cash, and planned to bet £3,000 on the wonder horse. As usual, he changed the game plan, and lumped on trainer Richard Hannon Senior's Canford Cliffs. Needless to say, Frankel quickened clear, to beat his main opponent by five lengths.

Soon after I was to attend the August Bank Holiday meeting at Cartmel, accompanied by Terry, who was now adamant that he'd never play pool again. This visit would complete my journeys to each and every UK racecourse. The small National Hunt venue is situated in the charming village of Cartmel in Cumbria. It's well worth a visit, boasting the third highest average jumps attendance, behind Aintree and Cheltenham. Locals suggest that the meeting originally began with mule races, organised by Medieval monks from the nearby Cartmel Priory. My other favourable small National Hunt course is Fakenham, in Norfolk.

It took some thirty-five years to attend all of the racecourses, a genuinely wonderful experience, offering the opportunity to visit some amazing towns and rural areas of England, Scotland and Wales. Goodwood has to be the most spectacular, set in twelve thousand acres of glorious Sussex countryside. The Rowley Mile course at Newmarket remains etched in my mind as the most atmospheric, while both Ascot and Cheltenham are my favourite bigger courses. For betting purposes, I find jump racing at Kempton Park the most reliable for holding up form, along with jumping at Newbury.

Having been on both sides of the fence, as punter and bookmaker, the fundamental difference reveals that the odds are stacked in the bookie's favour. One Sunday in May 2014, I received a call out of the blue from ex Passato owner, Harry. The trio had sold the out-of-form Passato, who was nearing two years without a victory. Harry had obviously kept his ear to the ground, and fancied the horse to make a winning comeback that same afternoon, at Stratford. He explained that he couldn't get to the bookies, and asked if I would place a bet of £500 to win for him, assuring me he was good for the money. I was happy to oblige, and headed off to the bookies. On arrival I noticed the horse had drifted to 8/1, and my old bookmaking instincts kicked in. Rather than place the bet over the counter, I decided to lay it myself and make an easy £500 in the process.

The race was a close-run affair, with Passato and 6/1 shot Deciding Moment trained by Ben De Haan, well clear of the field. Richard Johnson had Passato out in front, while Jack Doyle's mount closed with every stride nearing the finish. The pair flashed past the post in a tight finish, and a photo was called. I then had to suffer a further agonising three minutes, awaiting the outcome. The appropriately named Deciding Moment was eventually announced as the winner, officially winning by a nose, and saving me from a £4,000 pay-out.

Throughout our bookmaking careers, both David and I identified the punters with recurring luck, while others seem to have no luck at all. Small-stake punters winning large sums caused issues, because their wagers were too small to recover losses. On closer examination, we recognised that successful punters are often using in-depth or simplistic betting systems, or they're simply in the know.

Small wagers, such as £5, and £10, were often referred to as the 'turf accountant's bread and butter'. Bookies generally don't like taking bets on short price, each way, doubles and trebles, because there's not much profit margin, particularly when disciplined punters are involved. Another pet hate, is when a stranger rolls up and pulls off a big win, never to be seen again. Most high-street bookies welcome race-to-race, three-figured, single wagers, because punters who bet in this fashion are usually ill prepared, and often end up chasing losses.

During May 2015, I went to Newbury on Lockinge day for an afternoon of flat racing. Surprisingly, it turned into a day that would lead to a change in my betting strategy. On studying the card, I'd drawn up a short list of three for each race. The eye-catching jockey was Ryan Moore, and I decided to back his six mounts, taking the early odds in a 15p each way Lucky 63. It's imperative when betting a single jockey accumulator that you take fixed odds. His first ride came on the Richard Fahey-trained Birchwood, a 12/1 outsider who won by one and a half lengths. The next three selections won, at odds of 4/6, 5/1, and 7/2.

The fifth race was the Group 1 Al Shaqab Lockinge Stakes. The 11/4 favourite, Night of Thunder, won the race, with Ryan Moore on Integral finishing one and a quarter lengths behind, in fourth place. Moore capped a very successful afternoon, by steering 7/2 shot Crystal Zvezda to victory, a good day's work for the ex-champion, netting me a Lucky 63 return (including Betfred bonus) of £1,340. I felt inspired while driving home, and began thinking that small stakes for big returns might be the way forward.

I also won a few hundred pounds on the placepot. This highlighted the fact that placepots often pay well, when at least one favourite finishes out of the frame. The starting price of the first, second and third in the opening Newbury race were 11/1, 12/1 and 8/1. Considering the favourites were placed in the other five races, the return of £134.40 for a £1 stake was favourably high.

The Placepot is a Tote bet available at all UK racecourses and most high-street bookmakers.

Punters have to select a placed horse in races one to six at their chosen meeting. Individuals are allowed as many selections as they desire; however, combined selections equal bigger stakes. At least one selection has to finish placed in all six races, or the bet is classed as a loser. The pot is distributed between winners and divided into £1 unit shares.

The festival meetings are well worth targeting, because the pay-outs tend to be sizeable. I believe it's important to include bankers, with ideally only one selection, in at least two races. It's often one or two races that puts the majority of players out; therefore I need to try and predict which races this may happen in. The aim is to remain in when the majority of players go out, thus sharing larger dividends. Having decided on the bankers, I need to identify the race or races where I need multiple selections, in anticipation of a shock result, for example; a £1 unit stake of 1 x 1 x 2 x 1 x 4 x 1 = £8.

Quadpots are also of interest, whereby you bet on four races, i.e. races three, four, five and six. The bet works on the same principle as the placepot. It's always advisable to consider non-runners, and, for this reason, place bets as late as possible. This can be to the advantage of players in the first leg, particularly where the favourite is withdrawn as there is still time to adjust your thinking or place a further bet.

Within a couple of weeks, I was to suffer my most humiliating experience on a racecourse. The venue was in the seaside town of Tramore, County Waterford, on another rain-sodden evening. I arrived early with my girlfriend Mat, and the night got off to a perfect start, with Arsenal beating Aston Villa 4-0 in the FA Cup Final. I braved the elements and made my way to the betting ring, which was a scene of high activity, staking €40 on the Mullins-trained 5/4 favourite, Avant Tout. I then headed to the bar for a tot of Jameson whiskey and a warmup.

Ruby Walsh steered Avant Tout to victory, and during a mad dash back to the bookies, I remembered tossing a betting slip into a trash can. Back in the ring I realised that I'd thrown the wrong slip away. At first I thought I'd sweet talk the bookie by explaining my dilemma; however, there were so many bookies, I had no idea which one I had placed my bet with. I retraced my steps and began rummaging through the garbage. The bin was full to the brim with scores of discarded betting tickets, obscured beneath chip cartons covered in tomato sauce and half-empty coffee cups.

After emptying the bin in search of the elusive slip, I found myself blocking a mainstream path. As the torrential rain continued to fall, I was knelt over sifting through the slips, getting soaked to the skin. By now dozens of punters were squeezing past, taking great pleasure in my beggarly dilemma, offering me money to get a sandwich and a hot drink. In the interim, Mat came over to see what the commotion was all about and pretended not to know me. Nevertheless I stuck at it, eventually unravelling my winning ticket. Embarrassingly, I spent the rest of the evening at the mercy of native racegoers taking the mick.

I find my brain is most alert first thing in the morning. After an hour and a half of studying form I need to take a break, as I lose focus. It's important to remain with a clear thought process, in the zone. I use gut instinct whenever it feels appropriate, and I accept that luck will always play a part. I'm not swayed by superstition, as this may influence views negatively.

During the 2017 Cheltenham Festival, Ireland's record-breaking champion National Hunt trainer Willie Mullins had surprisingly drawn a blank on the first two days. Reading the form bright and early on day three, I noticed that five of the Mullins runners had Cheltenham specialist Ruby Walsh on board. Three of these horses appeared to be the day's bankers, York Hill, Un De Sceaux and Let's Dance. I took early odds of 7/4, 5/2 and 5/2 respectively. On consideration of Ruby's other two rides, Isleofhopendreams, 14/1, and Nichols Canyon, 12/1, I backed all five, in a £1 win Lucky 31. Both my gut and the form were telling me that it was going to be a good afternoon for the talented team. In fact, I was so confident that I began contacting my betting associates, advising them to bet on all of Ruby's mounts. This included my good friend Josh, who'd offered me a free ticket to watch the action live.

York Hill won the opening Grade 1 JLT Novice Chase by one length. This was followed by a disappointing run from Isleofhopendreams, who trailed home in fourteenth position. The very consistent Un De Sceaux won the Ryanair Chase, before Nichols Canyon won the Stayers Hurdle, making it three Grade 1 wins for Mullins on the day. At this point I met Josh for a beer. Josh is a shrewd punter with some very inspiring views, and regularly tips me winners; however, he hadn't jumped on the Walsh bandwagon. I advised him to bet Let's Dance in the next, and, interestingly, he was of the opinion that Ruby was unlikely to ride another winner during the same afternoon. Josh was making an erroneous assumption, another example of the gambler's fallacy, whereby the frequency of Ruby's lucky streak was unlikely to continue.

Walsh gave Let's Dance a superb hold up ride in the Grade 2 Mares Novices Hurdle, making headway between the last two flights, before quickening up and drawing clear on the run in to win by two and three quarter lengths. A good afternoon all round for the Mullins team, and punters alike. I also made a good profit, which included returns of £1,062 for the Lucky 31.

Psychologists Roney and Trick suggest that the gambler's fallacy can be overcome by getting gamblers to think their bet is part of a sequence of future events and not related to previous occurrences. This way of thinking would help gamblers adopt a more objective outlook. Often, while on a losing streak, they begin chasing losses, in the belief that their luck is bound to change.

During the months that followed, it dawned on me that the year's profit might be measured by a handful of big wins, providing I bet with more discipline and consistency. In other words, the avoidance of significant losses 'in between' is vital to making annual profit. My luck continued, as I pursued the small stakes for big returns strategy.

I arranged another day out with Gordon, this time a trip to Worcester Races. The racecourse is situated on the banks of the River Severn, and Gordon, who is a keen sailor, commented that he'd previously sailed past the racecourse.

We placed a few bets, though it wasn't the best of days, leaving one regular bookmaker to comment, 'There's always the river.'

Later, we made our way to a nearby bar for a couple of Belgian beers, and then on to an Indian restaurant for a curry, and a bottle of the house red. I should have been fearing the worse, after Gordon fell into a passing curry trolley. As if this wasn't enough, we tottered into another bar and sank a late nightcap. By now we were both well under the influence, in particular Gordon, who was wide-eyed and legless.

Later we found ourselves stumbling along the riverbank, where Gordon announced he needed to relieve himself and couldn't wait. I wandered on, and, as I glanced back I could just make out his silhouette.

Moments later he vanished, and all I could hear was a muted groan. He'd fallen into the undergrowth among thistles and stinging nettles, and although I couldn't see him, I knew he was teetering on the river's edge.

Being a non-swimmer, I was panicking, when I heard him say, 'I'm slipping.'

I came up with a plan to lie flat on my back, feet first in the nettles. After some ten minutes he grabbed hold of my feet, enabling me to haul him out, and the rescue was complete.

He limped tamely towards a lamp post, which illuminated a muddy, torn, shirt and tattered trousers, along with scratches and stings to his hands and face. He also had a leg injury. The following day, I went back to assess the scene, and realised that he'd been frightfully close to sliding into the river. We said our goodbyes, as Gordon hobbled towards the train wearing a pair of my trousers, which, quite frankly, looked hideous on him. For Gordon, the worst was yet to come, as he was still to endure the wrath of Mrs Bennett's tongue.

Glyn worked as a builder, and organised his work around the National Hunt fixture list. He once sauntered in unusually early, explaining that a crow perched on the scaffolding was a bad omen, and therefore he was unable to work. He proceeded to place a string of losing bets, and became concerned that the crow was still cursing his luck. Glyn was an astute follower of the betting market, and spent several summers removing the coffers from David's till. He was a notorious flat favourite backer, a bet slammer, keen to make a statement. He had the ability to determine periods of winning favourites, and raised the stakes accordingly. This was particularly noticeable in July and August, when the weather was holding up for long periods and producing good going. Glorious Goodwood was usually a big target and he'd move in for the kill.

On 21st August 2020, we identified Battash as a racing certainty for the second time. Battash was running at York in the Group 1 Coolmore Nunthorpe Stakes. We placed bet number five in various shops, totalling £7,317 at odds of 1/2. The classy thoroughbred, under usual pilot Jim Crowley, took up the running inside the final furlong and found himself in a battle with Que Amoro. Battash prevailed by a heart-stopping one length. This gave us a running profit of £10,975.

During August, I chauffeured Mr Stevens on a return visit to Glorious Goodwood for the opening day of the festival. We paid for tickets in advance and en route he insisted on stopping for a leisurely breakfast. While studying the card, I shortlisted five rides out of six for jockey Andrea Atzeni. The stylish flat jockey looked set for a good pay day, and I advised Mr Stevens to back all six, in an each way Lucky 63. On arrival, we found ourselves queuing with many other disgruntled prepaid racegoers. The unexplained chaos lasted for twenty-five minutes, leaving me pushed for time, and unable to place the Atzeni Lucky 63.

Atzeni's mount was placed fourth in the first race at 6/1, and I considered backing his further five runners in a Lucky 31.

I also reminded Mr Stevens, to do the same, who replied, 'I'm not interested.'

Meanwhile, I went to the racecourse office to complain about the earlier delay, where I gave my details and was assured that someone would write to me with an explanation. All the same, I only received advertising blurb. Back in the betting ring, I forgot all about the Lucky 31. Neither did I bet on his second mount, 7/4 favourite, Expert Eye, because I couldn't see the value of a single, though the favourite duly obliged. Atzeni also won the third race, pulling off a shock result aboard 50/1 shot Bretton Rock.

I was now kicking myself and fearing the inevitable. At least I had a decent bet on his next mount, Stradivarius, who won the Goodwood Cup at 6/1. As the afternoon progressed, I was trying not to think about Atzeni, and I was chuffed when his fifth mount, 9/2 favourite Atletico, finished out of the frame. In the last, trainer Roger Varian's Shenanigans gained a one and a quarter length victory at odds of 15/2, giving Atzeni an 8,345/1 four-timer.

Chapter 21
Clever Cookie Syndrome

Between March and August, my personal bets were showing a profit of several thousand pounds. I wanted to continue the challenge of finding new ways to beat the odds. I considered a statistician's supposition: it's too difficult to predict winners of horse races accurately, because there are too many equations. This quote led me to design a new jump race formula called The Buffer System. The design involved ring-fencing the prospective winner, by betting on two or three selections per race in permed trebles and accumulators. While testing out the new system, I went through the card (backing all the winners) at Warwick, Worcester and Kempton Park National Hunt.

(The buffer system is detailed in Appendix viii.)

October marks the beginning of Kempton's National Hunt season. This has become one of my most lucrative betting days, where I'm often accompanied by Gordon. Other meetings I find particularly lucrative are the Kempton Christmas meeting, the Cheltenham Festival and the Grand National meeting at Aintree.

During October, I formed a twenty-two-member betting syndicate, made up of betting associates and friends. I allocated shares of £100 per unit, and a couple of members took multiple shares, giving us a starting bank of £2,600. I was particularly excited about the Buffer System, utilised with standout jockey bets, placepots and quadpots. We agreed to run the syndicate for twelve months, and suggested £10,000 as our initial goal.

The plan would involve texting members the day's selections before the start of racing, followed by an update of our financial position the next day. Alas, things didn't go to plan; we experienced twelve months of treading water, along with all of the usual hard luck stories. I believe everyone enjoyed the thrill of the gamble, while I have to admit to feeling pressurised while betting with other people's cash. David pointed out that I was over cautious, having refrained from placing several winning wagers. Regrettably, we ended up all square.

Come June, I accompanied Mr Stevens to Royal Ascot for Ladies Day, with my eyes firmly focused on the Irish contingent. Legendary trainer Aidan Patrick O'Brien was born in County Wexford, Ireland, in 1969. He became champion Irish National Hunt trainer at the tender age of twenty-four, during 1993/1994, a feat he would maintain for a total of five successive seasons. Since moving to Ballydoyle in 1996, he's been crowned Irish champion flat trainer twenty-four times. In 2001, he was crowned England's champion trainer, the first Irish trainer to achieve the honour since Vincent O'Brien, in 1971; despite the two trainers having much in common they were not related.

In 2012, Aidan and his son, nineteen-year-old jockey Joseph, became the first father and son combination to win the English Derby with Camelot. Aidan set a new world record in 2017 by training twenty-six Group/Grade 1 winners in one calendar year. Having already trained well over three hundred Group 1 winners, he became the most successful English Derby trainer of all time, saddling his eighth winner in 2020. Other English Classic winners include nine Oaks wins, ten 2,000 Guineas, seven

1,000 Guineas and six St Legers. Irish Classic winners include fourteen Derbys, six Oaks, eleven 2,000 Guineas, ten 1,000 Guineas and five St Legers.

After studying form for the last race of the day, my short list threw up four contenders. The horses were all trained by Aidan O'Brien, and my gut was telling me to back all four in a combination Trifecta or tricast. Mr Stevens, who'd been losing heavily, was down to his last £80. He asked me for an opinion, so I led him to the Tote counter, and told him to invest the last of his cash on the o'Brien combination Trifecta. All the same, he was having none of it. The competitive, sixteen-runner handicap was also offering Ascot specialist Frankie Dettori an opportunity to ride his fifth winner of the day, on the well-backed 7/2 favourite, Questionnaire. I changed my bet, and instead of placing twenty-four £1 combination perms on the four O'Brien horses, I played it safe, by adding Dettori's mount, perming sixty 25p combination Trifectas.

Remarkably, Aidan O'Brien pulled off the one, two, three – South Pacific 22/1, Constantinople 11/2, Eminence 25/1 – with Dettori's mount finishing well back in fourteenth place. In the interim, Mr Stevens became extremely irritated for not placing the Trifecta. Nevertheless, he split his investment into two £40 win singles, which included the winner at fixed odds of 28/1. I hadn't given too much thought on whether to place a Tote Trifecta, or a tricast, and opted to bet at the Tote, simply because it was closest. The Trifecta paid odds of 1269/1, giving me a profit of £302.25 for my 25p unit stake. The tricast, on the other hand, paid a whopping £3,149 to a £1 stake. Hindsight is a wonderful thing, and, if I'd invested £24 in a £1 combination tricast I would have shown a profit of £3,125. Betting involves some element of risk, and this was another example of betting with too much caution, something that ex-bookmakers are renowned for.

The difference in pay-outs can vary immensely from Trifecta to tricast, and you can never be sure which one will offer the biggest dividend. The most straightforward option is to place a Tote Trifecta, because you can bet Trifectas on every horse race, down to a minimum of three runners. High-street bookmakers are less accommodating when offering bets on tricasts, particularly in small fields, where rules vary from a minimum of six to eight runners, and are only available on handicap races plus some listed and graded races.

Come October, I went to Kempton Park for the opening National Hunt meeting, accompanied by Gordon. We shared a winning £1 tricast on a nine-runner handicap chase, with the one, two, three paying odds of 8/1, 7/1 and 14/1 respectively. I placed the bet with William Hill, which paid 778/1. We were lucky on this occasion; had I placed the bet with the Tote, who were positioned on the opposite side of the room, the return would have been processed at 473/1.

Having bagged five racing certainties, our concerns were growing over the wagering of five-figure sums. On 5th September 2020, Enable looked unbeatable in the Group 3 Unibet September Stakes on the all-weather track at Kempton Park. We placed our £10,975 wager at different outlets taking skinny odds of 1/10. We questioned whether there was any value, as we stood to win a penny pinching £1,097, while we risked losing all of our winnings. We concluded it was a sound investment and better than the prevailing interest rate. The race was a warm up for the Prix de l'Arc de Triomphe the following month. Enable dwelt in the stalls, before accelerating into the lead, and winning the race unchallenged. With an all or nothing approach and a profit standing at £12,072, we were about to take aim at winner number seven.

In a bid to emulate my early career in show business, David dabbled in the entertainment industry as a DJ, supporting his singer guitarist brother Jeff. David's crowning glory came at a lavish wedding held in an ancient castle. Jeff was known to the couple, who booked him to play. What they hadn't bargained for was David's disco, and during the evening the groom asked David to play 'Nights in White Satin' for the first dance. The party was in full swing as the newlyweds made their way on to the dance floor, while wedding guests moved closer with their cameras.

Track 23 on disc two - *Ready Steady Go! The Number One Sixties Album* - was supposedly loaded, as the groom gave a signal and David pressed play. To everyone's embarrassment, Lesley Gore's *It's My Party* started blasting out. David became flustered, and accidently pressed play for a second time as the famous lyric continued echoing around the castle. By now the bride was in tears, and a very antagonised Jeff made a beeline for David, demanding professionalism. At the third time of asking, the happy couple smooched to 'Nights in White Satin'. Jeff was appalled by his brother's antics, firing him on the spot.

When it comes to beating the bookies, it's no easy task, therefore you need to create a strategy that shows an overall profit. I salute any punter who doesn't lose at this game. If you bet for entertainment, you'll be doing well to break even. When betting more seriously, you need to be either in the know or very knowledgeable, with good preparation and discipline. You might approach each gamble by considering the value of your bet, something I have often failed to achieve. When it comes to the reliability of betting on flat or jump races, the consensus of opinion suggests it's a close call.

I reunited with the evergreen David Watts in an attempt to give the bookies a bashing, under the dangerous assumption that two heads are better than one! We planned to combine our many years of experience, and produce the ultimate winning formula, based on three underlying principles:

1. Discipline: wait for the right opportunity and avoid chasing losses.

2. Preparation: failure to prepare is preparing to fail. The entire history of every racehorse is fully documented on the internet. Good preparation leads to confidence and success.

3. Identification: it's important to establish the best betting opportunities. We find the higher-grade races more reliable. Finding winners is an elimination process, which often draws up a shortlist. Wise gamblers suggest, 'Anyone can draw up a short list, but the real skill lies in determining the winner.' Assessing races with less than ten runners, assists in narrowing down the equations. Where a race appears too complicated, it might be a race to avoid.

We established the most significant factor in assessing race form as pattern: designing a tick box check list, whereby the likely winner is identified as the horse that gains the most ticks. We do this by comparing latest form against previous patterns and considering the conditions of today's race. Our top-rated horse needs to be clear of its closest rival. The bigger the gap, the more likely the most ticked horse is to win.

(Details of our test is available in Appendix ix and a summary of our findings is contained in Appendix x.)

Armed with our new pattern system, we were ready for some action at the Cheltenham Festival. After initially looking at placing a permed accumulator over four days, we refrained because it looked too competitive. Day one offered us no standout win bets and we opted to wager a £3 combination placepot, staking a total of £12 (1 x 1 x 2 x 2 x 1 x 1). All eight selections were placed, paying us a total dividend of £384. It's worth noting that the only favourite not to reach the frame was in race one.

On day two, the Gordon Elliot-trained Envoi Allen gained a full set of ticks, while the evidence suggested that the opposition were well held in the Grade 1 Ballymore Novices' Hurdle, making it a racing certainty. We bet an even £500 in advance of the race and enjoyed watching the unbeaten Irish-trained gelding win in impressive fashion.

Later, 8/11 favourite Tiger Roll, fell well short of ticks in the Glenfarclas Cross Country Chase. After applying the system, the favourite scored three points less than 3/1 second favourite Easysland. Instead of betting Easysland, we laid Tiger Roll to win £500. Easysland cruised to a seventeen-length victory, making us a profit of £1,000 on the day.

Day three offered the value bet of the week, Gordon Elliot's Samcro, in the Grade 1 Marsh Novices' Chase. At this point, in spite of the painstaking amount of time and effort we had invested in the pattern system, David began questioning our strategy. This came as somewhat of a surprise, as he was jointly responsible for its inception.

Samcro was taking on the classy Willie Mullins pair, 3/1 favourite Faugheen (the machine), who'd already won his seasonal target race after a hard-fought battle the previous month, and Melon (14/1) who usually finds his best form at Cheltenham in March. I also believed that the Cheltenham Festival had been mapped out by Elliot as Samcro's main target, while second favourite Itchy Feet (7/2) appeared not good enough on all known form. On completion of the test, Samcro scored two points more than Faugheen and Melon, while Itchy Feet fell way short. Davy Russell drove Samcro up the famous hill to beat Melon by a nose in a photo finish, with Faugheen a length back in third. Having bet £200 on Samcro at 9/2 we made £900 on the day. Unfortunately, we failed to spot an opportunity of betting all three in a combination Trifecta.

Friday 13th March brought the Gold Cup into play, which we identified as the best betting race of the day. With a good depth of knowledge of the participants, we were determined to make it four winning days in a row, as I set about testing the runners. Willie Mullins, who would soon be crowned Champion Irish Trainer for a sensational thirteenth time in succession, trained our highest rated horse, Al Boum Photo, scoring two points more than his closest rival.

Unfortunately, David was keen to bet another of the Mullins runners, Kemboy, who was one of his old favourites, and began challenging the system selection, despite Kemboy scoring less ticks than several of the other runners. Fortunately, I ignored his protestations and invested £200 to win on Al Boum Photo at 7/2. Jockey Paul Townend steered the horse to a neck victory, giving us a full house on the week and an overall profit of £2,972. On analysing the week's performance, aside from David's hinderance, there were several contributing factors: identifying the best races to bet in, knowledge of the horses and their performance patterns, and the presence of high-calibre horses engaging in graded races.

Chapter 22
Seven

On accompanying my son and daughter to London for a few days, we found ourselves having too much to drink in a Chelsea wine bar. Continuing our jaunt in the late afternoon sunshine, we walked across Westminster Bridge, where some Romanian people were enticing a gamble on three upturned cups, a familiar game, where you have to guess which cup has the small ball hidden under it, after they're swiftly swapped around. I once watched, a similar game outside Windsor racecourse, and I believed I knew their strategy of swapping the cups, just as the unsuspecting player passes the cash over. I told Sarah and Rodney that it was a con, but I would keep my eyes fixed rigidly on the correct cup and take their money.

We watched half a dozen games, and I clocked a couple of ladies winning. Brimming with confidence, I moved forward, placing an even £40. Much to everyone's amusement, the cup was raised with no ball underneath. At this moment, a well-dressed businessman presented himself. He was articulate, and carried a copy of the *Financial Times*. He advised that I was distracted on passing the money over, and that I should play again. This time, he'd keep his foot on the cup, thus avoiding any monkey business. I moved in for the kill with my eyes riveted on the fixed cup, placing a further £80 wager. Meanwhile, the obliging businessman positioned his foot firmly on top of it.

Seconds later the cup was raised, revealing the absent ball, providing the best laugh of our mini-break.

On 17th March 2020, UK horseracing came to a standstill, six days before the enforced Covid-19 lockdown. By the end of March, many National Hunt horses were put out to graze, after a high percentage of owners removed them in a bid to save fees. Some of the top yards were reportedly left with a skeleton number of horses. Throughout this period, horses maintained a general need for care. In the meantime, flat trainers did their best to train during a time of social distancing, in hope that racing would return as forecast on 1st June. Some jump jockeys who were otherwise redundant assisted flat trainers by riding out. It was also an opportunity for them to keep their own fitness levels up.

MPs were soon urging government to impose stricter curbs on gambling, with concerns that long Isolation periods would fuel more addiction. In the interim, David turned his attention to betting on Belarusian Premier League football. Despite our collective thoughts on betting strategies, we were both guilty of placing increased numbers of individual wagers.

While calling for a suspension in gambling, MPs accused the betting industries own proposals as very weak. They also requested government to assist in adopting new measures during lockdown. This included the suspension of advertising bonus offers and an end to controversial VIP schemes, which reward heavy losses.

The government were soon to launch a review of the gambling laws. The plan was to gather evidence that would explore the possibilities of maximising online stakes and spend limits, while also looking into the protection of young adults, promotional offers and advertising. Betting patterns had changed with smartphones singled out as the main culprit, creating new opportunities for people to gamble 24/7.

The Gambling Commission held the power to enforce new licensing conditions, such as affordability checks and maximum monthly deposits. They also raised the possibility that online gambling losses might be capped at £100, unless the customer could prove they could afford to lose more. While the issue of affordability was under close scrutiny, there was also concern that, if betting companies start asking customers for their tax return, they will only succeed in driving them full circle to a black market.

Following ten weeks of sports fans being penned in, they'd become desperate for some live action. During the end of May, I tuned into TalkSport Radio, where much to my surprise they were covering chicken racing from the Peak District. The 11.54 was won by Goldie, after the disappointing favourite, Mrs McFeathers, failed to make any impact from an inside draw. A national interest in pigeon racing was also gaining momentum, following publicity on the BBC TV sports news. Months later, a three-year old-female Belgian pigeon named New Kim made headlines when it was sold at auction for over £1.4 million, setting a new world record.

It was confirmed that UK flat racing would be the first major sport to return on 1st June. However, for an extended period of time racing and all other sports would take place behind closed doors. This left on-course bookmakers out in the cold and without income. Meanwhile national Hunt racing would return on Ist July.

The Guineas meeting took place at Newmarket one month behind schedule, while the Derby was pushed back to July. Royal Ascot went ahead as usual in mid-June, where Stradivarius won the Gold Cup for John

Gosden and Frankie Dettori for the third time in succession. In late July, the pair were also triumphant with Enable, who made history after winning the King George VI and Queen Elizabeth Stakes for a record third time.

The English Premier Football League returned on 17th June. The title was eventually won by Liverpool with seven games to spare. The season came to a close on 26th July, the longest in its history. The FA Cup was won by Arsenal, who beat Chelsea 2-1 on 1st August. History records the game as the first FA Cup final to be played behind closed doors.

Lockdown offered an opportunity for David and I to reflect on the pattern system, and the 14 Pointer test which served me so well back in 2003. These two systems would formulate a combined jump and flat racing betting formula known as the Cert System. The strategy behind the thinking was that we were unable to find a reliable accumulator during one day. Therefore, we would place a seven-horse accumulator over multiple days. The icing on the cake is the stake plan, which will reduce the risk of losing any money to one race only. In order to qualify as a cert, all fourteen categories need to be satisfied:

The Cert System
1. *Racing Post* favourite
2. Weak opposition: not evidently good enough to oppose
3. Going: compare today's going to previous wins on similar going
4. Maximum seven runs during last twelve-months
5. Running within thirty days of latest run or running to pattern
6. Suitable grade: same as latest or lower
7. Suitable distance: running within one furlong of latest run

8. Course: similar course to previous wins
9. Previous race type: same
10. Won latest start, or finished within one length of winner
11. Favourite or second favourite, latest race
12. Weight, maximum 7lb rise from latest race
13. Top jockey
14. Top trainer

Stake plan
a. Place an affordable first bet
b. Remove initial stake after first winner
c. Bet all of the profit from race one on race two
d. Place all accumulative winnings on races three, four, five, six and seven
e. Stop after seven consecutive winners

The Cert System offers a disciplined form of betting that bookmakers may not relish, particularly as there is no risk for the punter after race one. We waited several weeks in order to get a flavour of the form. Armed with £2,972, we would bet the lot on the first horse that ticked all of the boxes. We'd continue by gambling all of the accumulative winnings on the next six races, having returned the initial stake safely to our betting bank. However, with bookmakers still absent from the racecourse, we had concerns that placing large bets at early odds would prove no easy task.

Little did we realise, we would have to wait until the summer of 2021 before normal attendances of racegoers and bookmakers would return to the course.

While the increase in online betting continues, more high-street betting shops are closing down. Companies offer more incentives if you bet online, banishing traditional culture into the past. Today's staff frequently encourage punters to use shop terminals in order to discourage them from bothering cashiers at the counter. Bookmakers are still renowned for restricting or limiting large-staking punters who think things through, particularly when they're taking early odds. In comparison, no-thought gambling of chance such as bingo or casino games is always welcomed without restriction. It's worth noting that virtual racing and numbers games have fixed parameters; therefore you're more likely to lose on them, compared to traditional racing.

During the summer of 2021, ITV hosted the first ever UK Sunday evening racing, from Edinburgh, Haydock and Sandown. The industry now offers an onslaught of betting attractions, fuelled by an outrageous campaign of TV, radio and press advertising. On the high street, city-centre bookmakers operate for approximately fourteen hours a day. In addition to the number of fixed odds betting terminals offering casino games, you can bet on a different event almost every minute of the day. This includes lucky number draws, bingo, virtual horseracing, virtual greyhound racing, UK horseracing, UK greyhound racing and a whole host of foreign racing. In contrast to the early 1990s when there were approximately one hundred daily betting events, betting shops now offer up to one thousand betting opportunities every day.

Our day of reckoning arrived on 9th November 2020, when the Cert System offered the chance to complete seven winning bets. The Nicki Henderson-trained Vegas Blue was running in a five-runner Class 4, two-mile five-furlong, novice hurdle at Kempton. David was now questioning the rationale of betting in a Class 4 novice hurdle, after all, we'd already identified that higher grade races were more reliable. Vegas Blue had already won a Class 1 National Hunt flat race, as well as easily beating a previous Class 3 hurdle winner in his penultimate start. On this occasion he appeared to be taking on inferior horses at level weights.

We came to the conclusion that it was another solid bet and placed a total of £12,072 to win at odds averaging 2/7. We confess to being both tense and apprehensive as we tuned in to Racing UK. Vegas Blue was soon into stride, tracking the leaders for the first two miles. Four flights from home jockey Nico de Boinville started sending out distress signals, as he began pushing the struggling horse. Three out, the writing was on the wall, and we'd done our dough. Vegas Blue struggled home in third place, five and three quarter lengths behind the Paul Nicholls-trained Switch Hitter.

Anyone for bingo?

The Gambler's Epilogue
More or Less

Identification leads to preparation

More preparation leads to finding value

Finding value leads to discipline

More discipline leads to less wagers

Less wagers lead to more profit

Less is more

Johnny Winall
14th February 2022

Appendix i

Race card descriptions/abbreviations

Weight
Weight is measured in stones and pounds. Each horse has to carry an exact weight, which is a combination of the jockey, saddle and any additional weights in the saddle bags. Weights are determined by race conditions: for example, if the race is a handicap or if a horse attracts a penalty for a previous win.

Jockey
Top jockeys will always attract attention; some punters will take notice if a top jockey only has one ride. The number in brackets after the jockey's name denotes a weight allowance for more inexperienced riders.

Draw flat only
The position in the starting stalls may be an advantage on some courses because of the layout and varying going conditions.

Letters after horse's name
BF: beaten favourite last time out
C: course winner
D: distance winner (within 55 yards flat, one furlong jumps)
CD: previous course and distance winner

Letters under horse's name
B: blinkers
V: visor
e/s: eye shield
e/c: eye cover
h: hood

t: tongue strap
p: cheekpieces

Key to form letters
B: brought down
CO: carried out
D: disqualified
F: fell
P: pulled up
R: refused
RO: ran out
S: slipped up
U: unseated rider
V: void race

Appendix ii

Popular bets

£1 win single (one selection) stake £1

£1 each way single, £1 win + £1 place, stake £2

£1 win double (two selections), stake £1

£1 each way double, stake £2

£1 win treble (three selections), stake £1

£1 each way treble, stake £2

£1 win accumulator, also known as four-fold, five-fold, six-fold, seven-fold, eight-fold, etc, stake £1

£1 each way accumulator, stake £2

£1 win Trixie (three selections, comprising of three doubles and one treble), stake £4

£1 each way Trixie, stake £8

£1 win Patent (three selections, comprising of three singles, three doubles and one treble), stake £7

£1 each way Patent, stake £14

£1 win Yankee (four selections, comprising of six doubles, four trebles and one four-fold), stake £11

£1 each way Yankee, stake £22

£1 win Lucky 15 (four selections, comprising of four singles, six doubles, four trebles and four-fold), stake £15

£1 each way Lucky 15, stake £30

£1 win Super Yankee, also known as a Canadian (five selections, comprising of ten doubles, ten trebles, five four-folds and one five-fold), stake £26

£1 each way Super Yankee/Canadian, stake £52

£1 win Lucky 31 (five selections, comprising of five singles, ten doubles, ten trebles, five four-folds and one five-fold), stake £31

£1 each way Lucky 31, stake £62

£1 win Heinz (six selections comprising of fifteen doubles, twenty trebles, fifteen four-folds, six five-folds and one six-fold), stake £57

£1 each way Heinz, stake £114

£1 win Lucky 63 (six selections, comprising of six singles, fifteen doubles, twenty trebles, fifteen four-folds, six five-folds and one six-fold), stake £63

£1 each way Lucky 63, stake £126

£1 win Super Heinz (seven selections comprising of twenty-one doubles, thirty-five trebles, thirty-five four-folds, twenty-one five-folds, seven six-folds and one seven-fold), stake £120

£1 each way Super Heinz, stake £240

£1 each way Goliath, stake £494

£1 win Goliath (eight selections comprising of twenty-eight doubles, fifty-six trebles, seventy four-folds, fifty-six five-folds, twenty-eight six-folds, eight seven-folds and one eight-fold), stake £247

£1 straight forecast, also available with the Tote and referred to as a Straight Exacta (two selections to finish first and second in nominated order), stake £1

£1 reverse forecast, also available with the Tote and referred to as a Reverse Exacta (two selections to finish first and second in any order), stake £2

£1 straight tricast, also available with the Tote and referred to as a straight tricast (three selections to finish first, second and third in nominated order), stake £1

£1 combination tricast, also available with the Tote and referred to as a combination trifecta (three selections to finish first, second and third in any order), stake £6

Appendix iii

Arena Racing Company Racecourses

Bath
Brighton
Chepstow
Doncaster
Ffos Las
Fontwell Park
Great Yarmouth
Hereford
Lingfield Park
Newcastle
Royal Windsor
Sedgefield
Southwell
Uttoxeter
Wolverhampton
Worcester

Appendix iv

Place terms

All races 1-4 runners all to win
All races 5-7 runners two places 1/4
All races 8-11 runners three places 1/5
Non-handicaps 12 runners or more three places 1/5
Handicaps 12 runners or more three places 1/4
Handicaps 16 runners or more four places 1/4

Appendix v

Racecourse information

UK National Hunt Courses

24 National Hunt and 17 mixed courses compiled from previous Levy Board information.

The grades for all National Hunt courses in this list have been estimated to the best of our knowledge.

Tight tracks 8–10 furlongs (approximate)

Track	Grade	Right/Left-handed	Circuit
Cartmel	4	L/H sharp	8 furlongs
Catterick	3	L/H sharp	9 furlongs
Fakenham	4	L/H sharp and squarish	8 furlongs
Fontwell	3	L/H sharp hurdle/figure-of-eight chase	8 furlongs
Kelso	4	L/H sharp/undulating	9 furlongs
Market Rasen	3	R/H sharp	10 furlongs
Musselburgh	3	R/H	10 furlongs
Perth	4	R/H tight bends	10 furlongs

Plumpton	3	L/H sharp/undulating	9 furlongs
Newton Abbot	3	L/H sharp	10 furlongs
Sedgefield	4	L/H sharp/undulating	10 furlongs
Southwell	4	L/H	10 furlongs
Stratford	4	L/H sharp	10 furlongs
Taunton	4	R/H sharp	10 furlongs

Circuits beyond 10 furlongs

Track	Grade	Right/Left-handed	Circuit
Aintree	1	L/H Grand National Circuit	18 furlongs
Aintree	1	L/H Mildmay Course	11 furlongs
Bangor-on-Dee	4	L/H sharp	12 furlongs
Chepstow	2	L/H undulating	15 furlongs
Kempton	2	R/H triangular	13 furlongs
Hereford	4	R/H sharp/squarish	12 furlongs

Lingfield	2	L/H undulating/triangular	12 furlongs
Ludlow	4	R/H sharp	12 furlongs
Newcastle	1	L/H uphill	14 furlongs
Sandown	1	R/H uphill run in	13 furlongs
Uttoxeter	3	L/H undulated	11 furlongs
Warwick	3	L/H sharp	14 furlongs
Wetherby	2	L/H	12 furlongs
Wincanton	4	R/H	11 furlongs
Worcester	4	L/H	13 furlongs

Galloping tracks: 12 furlongs plus

Track	Grade	Right/Left-handed	Circuit
Ascot	1	R/H	14 furlongs
Ayr	1	L/H	12 furlongs
Doncaster	1	L/H pear-	16

		shaped (wide)	furlongs
Ffos Las	4	L/H	12 furlongs
Haydock	1	L/H	12 furlongs
Huntingdon	4	R/H	12 furlongs
Newbury	1	L/H (wide)	15 furlongs

Stiff tracks uphill finish

Track	Grade	Right/Left-handed	Circuit
Carlisle	4	R/H pear-shaped	12 furlongs
Cheltenham	1	L/H undulating	12 furlongs
Exeter	4	R/H undulating	16 furlongs
Hexham	4	L/H undulating	12 furlongs
Leicester	3	R/H undulating	14 furlongs

Flat Track Grades (2019)

Information obtained from FLATSTATS.co.uk

Ascot 1
Ayr 2
Bath 4
Beverley 3
Brighton 4
Carlisle 4
Catterick 4
Chelmsford 3
Chepstow 4
Chester 2
Doncaster 2
Epsom 1
Ffos Las 4
Goodwood 1
Hamilton 4
Haydock 2
Kempton 3
Leicester 3

Lingfield 3
Musselburgh 3
Newbury 2
Newcastle 4
Newmarket 1
Nottingham 3
Pontefract 3
Redcar 4
Ripon 3
Salisbury 3
Sandown 2
Southwell 4
Thirsk 3
Wetherby 4
Windsor 3
Wolverhampton 4
Yarmouth 3
York 1

Appendix vi

Going descriptions for turf courses

FIRM, very dry ground, usually found in summer during the flat season

GOOD to FIRM, on the slower side of firm, but still quick

GOOD, a little give and easy to run on (ground that courses strive to achieve to attract more entries and will very often water)

GOOD to SOFT, mostly good ground holding a degree more water

SOFT, holding more water and horses go in deeper, usually found during the winter jumps season

HEAVY, very wet and few horses relish this going, sometimes referred to as a bog

YIELDING, good to soft (description in Ireland)

Sometimes ground conditions can be a mixture of two goings, for example, good to soft, good in places

All-weather tracks

FAST, quick and dry with minimum moisture

STANDARD, optimal conditions, not too dry or containing much moisture

SLOW, surface has moisture, similar to soft going on the turf

Appendix vii

Grading of races

Group races (flat) also known as pattern races are the highest level of races Group 1, 2, and 3 (Group 1 being the highest).

Grade 1 (jumps) and Group 1 are of the same status. Grade 1, 2, and 3 is the term used in jump racing (Grade 1 being the highest.)

Listed races are a step down from group races/graded races. All of these races are Class 1.

In flat racing there are further classes of 2-7 (Class 2 being the highest).

In jump racing there are further classes of 2-6 (Class 2 being the highest).

Appendix viii

The buffer system

Comprising seven overriding principles in a tick box system to evaluate contenders, a staking plan of 2.5% of the bank, a maximum of ten runners and the discipline not to bet if there were more than three potential winners. As a check the worst-case-scenario of winnings should not exceed the stake.

i. Identification: maximum field size nine runners
ii. Discipline: where a race throws up more than three potential winners, don't bet
iii. Consistency: relies on a safety net of multiple selections
iv. Stake plan: introduce a betting bank
v. System: design a tick box system
vi. Stakes: bet a maximum 2.5 % of the betting bank
vii. Returns: minimum forecast returns must exceed the stake.

Buffer system example bet

Warwick 26th September 2017

3 x 3 x 3 = 27 x 50p win permed trebles at fixed odds

2.25

Pretty Reckless won 4/1

Dotties Dilemma lost

Drumlang lost

282

2.55

Guerrilla Tactics won 10/1

Shantou Tiger lost

Premier Rose lost

3.30

Belmount won 3/1

Fortworth lost

Buachaill Alainn lost

Stake £13.50 – returns £110

The example relates to early fixed odds, revealing the shortest price on each of the three races at 5/2, evens and 3/1. Had these three selections all won, my returns would have been reduced to £14. There is no hard and fast rule on taking fixed priced odds. Before using the system, you'll need to design an effective tick box system.

Appendix ix

Pattern tick box system

i.   Current form
ii.   Going
iii.   Suitable grade: same as latest or lower
iv.   Course: similar course to previous wins
v.   Distance: running over same distance as previous win or within one furlong of latest run
vi.   Weight: allow a maximum 7lb rise since the latest run
vii.   Top trainer
viii.   Top jockey
ix.   Time of year
x.   Intervals between previous races and victories
xi.   Horse with the highest-grade wins
xii.   Horse with highest number of wins going left or right-handed

Stake plan

i.   Introduce a betting bank
ii.   Where a selection emerges clear on points – maximum 5% stake

Appendix x

Summary of findings

Daily form reading makes form study easier.

Look out for horses that are withdrawn from races, as connections are usually waiting for the best winning opportunities.

Note trainers' patterns/courses with high strike rates.

Calculated percentages leaving your betting bank matter more than the amount you might potentially win.

Don't bet too many selections in any one race.

When your system reveals a good value bet, back it to its full potential regardless of the price.

Get the edge by identifying races with vulnerable short-priced favourites: for example, too much weight, too many days since last run or no recent form.

Identify value bets.

Small fields of four or fewer runners can be particularly tactical, often running at a false pace. These races may produce value bets.

Identify the most reliable courses for betting.

Remain disciplined during losing streaks.

When it looks too complicated, don't bet.

Trust your gut instinct.

Use your eyes and note when a horse has a turn of foot or jumps particularly well at speed.

Note if a horse wins easily, hard held or forges clear, as it will often win next time out.

High-grade horses/races tend to be more predictable.

Look for familiar winning patterns in previous runs.

Horses often run well after leaving a trainer and are having their first run for a new trainer, (identified by 1 next to trainer's name in *Racing Post*); new surroundings frequently bring improved form.

Source acknowledgements

Horseracebase.com
BBC Sports Intercessor
BBC Sport
Talk Sport Radio
The Guardian
The Telegraph
The Sun
The Daily Mirror
The Coventry Telegraph
The Evening Standard
The Daily Mail
Western Daily Press
Racing Post
Sporting Life
RTE Sport
Google
Wikipedia
Flatstats grades
Racecourses of Great Britain (James Gill)
Racing UK
ITV Racing
Sky Sports Racing
At The Races
British Horseracing Authority
Weatherbys
UK Tote Group
SIS
Brittanica.com
The Jockey Club